Coming Full Circle

Essays in World History
William H. McNeill and Ross Dunn, *Series Editors*

COMING FULL CIRCLE

An Economic History of the Pacific Rim

Eric Jones,
Lionel Frost,
& Colin White
La Trobe University

Westview Press
Boulder • San Francisco • Oxford

Essays in World History

Copyright © 1993 by Westview Press, Inc.

Published in 1993 in the United States of America by Westview Press, Inc., 5500 Central Avenue, Boulder, Colorado 80301-2877, and in the United Kingdom by Westview Press, 36 Lonsdale Road, Summertown, Oxford OX2 7EW

Library of Congress Cataloging-in-Publication Data
Jones, Eric L. (Eric Lionel)
    Coming full circle : an economic history of the Pacific Rim / Eric Jones, Lionel Frost & Colin White.
      p.   cm. — (Essays in world history)
    Includes bibliographical references and index.
    ISBN 0-8133-1240X. — ISBN 0-8133-1241-8 (pbk.)
    1. Pacific Area—Economic conditions.   2. East Asia—Economic conditions.   I. Frost, Lionel.   II. White, Colin, 1943–
III. Title.   IV. Series.
HC681.J66   1993
330.9182'3—dc20
                                                                        93-4130
                                                                        CIP

Printed and bound in the United States of America

∞   The paper used in this publication meets the requirements
     of the American National Standard for Permanence of Paper
     for Printed Library Materials Z39.48-1984.

10   9   8   7   6   5   4   3

To Our Children

Contents

Maps and Tables

Preface

The "Coming Full Circle" of the title of this book refers to the fact that the center of gravity of world economic life was once on the edge of the Pacific, shifted away as Europe and the Atlantic economy rose, and is now returning in force. One thousand years ago the center was the China of the Song (or Sung) dynasty. This civilization, which lasted from the tenth through the thirteenth centuries A.D., had inherited a range of remarkable technologies from even earlier periods of Chinese history. The tool kit of Song China anticipated—on a large scale—much of what was to appear in the Europe of the Middle Ages. It has even been suggested that much of the commercialization that took place elsewhere in Asia and as far away as Europe resulted from the westward spread of Song Chinese ideas. The diffusion continued after the dynasty had fallen to invaders from the steppes. Chinese notions went on spreading, like light reaching earth from a dead star.

Today the largest group of fast-growing economies in the world is once again on the Pacific Rim. It is composed of the East Asian countries—Japan, South Korea, Taiwan, Hong Kong—and the coastal provinces of China (some of which have larger populations than France or Germany). Stretch a geographical point and the more successful of the Southeast Asian economies—Singapore, Thailand, and Malaysia—might be included.

The rise of the Asia Pacific economy is the dominating fact of modern economic geography, the most striking event in the economic history of the late twentieth century. On the face of things, this is a virtual break in the trends of history—the first achievement of sustained growth by a major cultural area outside Europe or regions of European settlement.

What explains this massive shift, and where is it taking us? Despite its recency and unprecedented scale, the change was not totally divorced from the historical past. Certainly it cannot be understood without a look at its historical setting, just as the process of growth cannot be fully grasped without consideration of long stretches of past experience. Economic history offers the best hope of understanding the recurrent range of possibilities and removing the "noise" of short-term trends and fluctuations so we can glimpse the likely tendencies of the future.

Where the shift is as marked as it has been with the new importance of the Pacific, its origins and the problems it provokes become matters of everyday concern for thinking people. The centerpiece of the change was the unexpected postwar recovery and continued outstanding performance of Japan, marked above all by the astounding increase in U.S.-Japanese trade. Other parts of East Asia shared in this growth.

Westerners had not expected the phenomenon of East Asian growth. They were agreeably surprised by the recovery of Europe after the Second World War, but few of them thought (or knew enough Japanese history to understand) that Western achievements could be matched by Asians. "The Jap has no business savvy," Rudyard Kipling observed—or thought he observed. As late as the 1960s some writers were still pooh-poohing any suggestion that the initial recovery of Japan would continue into faster and faster industrial growth. But it did continue. The process spread out to embroil and transform more and more of the East Asian region, including, astonishingly, the southern part of Communist China, which at the moment has the highest growth rates of all.

Many people in the United States and Europe find this novelty frightening. The high-quality manufactured exports from East Asia, especially Japan, represent severe competition. The alarm is greatest in the United States, where disquiet often takes the form of "Japan bashing." The alarm is stronger because Japan has not only built up a big trade balance in its own favor but has also invested heavily in the United States and elsewhere, as if it were taking over by purchase what it had failed to capture militarily during the Second World War.

During the long cold war between the West and the USSR, the United States deemed it wise to keep Japan in the anticommunist camp by helping to build up the Japanese economy. The United States transferred advanced industrial methods to Japan and paid much of the cost of defending parts of East Asia and the Pacific against communism. Hence many U.S. commentators now look on a prosperous, competitive Japan as a "cuckoo in the nest" that once looked like any other little nestling but is now a hulking brute, threatening to tip U.S. industries over the side. Why U.S. (and other Western) responses have been so angry and not produced a more vigorous adjustment to meet the competition is an interesting puzzle.

The English-speaking countries of the Pacific Rim as a whole have done nothing so well as East Asia. Elsewhere around the Rim—for instance, down the west coast of Latin America, in the Philippines, or in Papua New Guinea—economic performance has continued to be very weak. Nevertheless, the success of just the East Asian part of the Rim and its "frontier" of high-performance economies in Southeast Asia has been sufficient to reshape the economic geography not only of the Pacific but of the world. A third great zone has come into being alongside the older developed areas of Western Europe and North America.

The implications for the well-being of everybody in the world are profound, and not only in the economic sense: Already Japan and Taiwan, rich for a generation past, are starting to demand greater diplomatic and even military roles. For the elderly who remember the Second World War or the Depression of the 1930s, and for those who were brought up on the twofold division of the world into communist and Western cold war blocs, the idea of an East Asia that is rich and powerful is unsettling. This world, in which the Pacific Rim takes a prominent place, is, however, current reality. Where did it come from, and, to repeat, where may it be taking us?

The key changes have been absolute and relative. In other words, the Pacific Rim has grown much richer over the past thirty years, both in absolute terms and relative to the older developed parts of the world. The English-speaking countries around the Pacific have not been the ones to lead the Pacific's surge. We have to turn back to East Asia for the true source of the Rim's energy.

In about 1960 U.S. trade with Asia, across the Pacific, was worth only half the value of U.S. trade with Europe, across the Atlantic. By 1980 the trade was of equal value, and after a mere seven further years its Pacific trade was half as big again as its Atlantic trade. It was as though the United States were turning around, faster with each passing year, to acknowledge the new importance of East Asia.

An alternative way of looking at the about-face is that in 1960 the sum of the gross national products of the Pacific Rim economies, excluding poor China and Latin America, was less than 30 percent of that of the North Atlantic Basin (the countries of the European Community and the eighteen Atlantic states). By 1980 the figure had reached 50 percent, and this relative growth has gone on. Yet another indicator: Asia (again excluding China but this time including Australia) saw its share of world output rise from 8 percent in 1967 to 20 percent in 1987.

The Japanese economy, which was the initial pacesetter, maintained a remarkable average annual growth rate of virtually 6 percent from 1960 to 1984, two-thirds higher than that of the United States and double the rate in the leading Western European economies.

Why East Asia? Why was Japan first? At the end of the Second World War in 1945, some other parts of the world, such as India or even Africa, were thought to be more promising. Why has the performance of the "old rich," English-speaking countries around the Pacific Rim tailed off? After all, they had the advantage at first. What was there about the less-developed shores of the Pacific that rendered them less willing or less able to grow than the East Asian core?

There are plenty of questions. Will the whole world "East Asianize"? Will the success of Japan and "Little Dragons" such as Taiwan and Hong Kong—a success that has already spread to parts of Southeast Asia and southern China—continue until the entire Rim or even the whole world is developed? If not, what will stand in the way? Can China sustain rapid economic growth in its coastal regions given the cruel unrepresentativeness of its politics and the backwardness of its vast interior? These are urgent matters, and given the poverty still found in so much of the world, we would applaud if peaceful growth were indeed to succeed. Growth brings its problems, but they are fewer, even for the environment, than those of mass poverty (and an endless increase in population), especially as economic growth alone can provide the resources to cope.

Long-run history gives us clues about the processes involved in growth. Despite the difficulties of looking at a few astonishing recent years and the delusions always possible when forecasting the future, the historical background does help to explain how the English-speaking countries around the Pacific grew rich in the first place, what may have checked growth in some other areas, and why East Asia was the site of the true "Pacific miracle." History can indicate which processes have in a general sense occurred before, how economic leadership has moved around, and why leadership may be expected to stay on the move in the longer term. We have interspersed a lot of general ideas about how economic processes take place throughout our narrative; these could be read together as a kind of commentary on economic history.

The least-developed parts of the Rim are diverse. Some are tropical, others polar. The more populous countries do share certain attributes—cheap labor may attract capital and technology from the developed world, but fear of political unrest may deter it. The political and institutional stability of the poorer countries is largely an internal matter, but otherwise their fate, and the progress of "East Asianization," depends heavily on investment from, and access to markets in, more advanced economies. The prospects for the East Asian and English-speaking groups of Pacific economies are therefore of primary concern.

The export-oriented countries of East and Southeast Asia include one established giant, Japan; one awakening giant, China (potentially a real goliath); and several economies in between. In the early 1990s, China's growth has been astounding. Although the need to clamp down on inflation may check growth for a time, China should pick up again, political upsets apart. Conversely, Japan has a maturing economy and the most rapidly aging population in the world. The enterprise of Japanese corporations remains without equal, but there are early signs that the population would like to work a little less, save less, consume more, and see more government spending on public works and cleaning up the environment. Similar signs have already appeared in South Korea and Taiwan; politicians may start to take notice; the relentless chase after growth may suffer, unless more and more advanced technology manages to compensate for changing attitudes.

These problems, minor though they still are, may be inherent in the very prosperity that growth brings. Western history certainly suggests as much. East Asian economies are, however, more given to the political steering of economic life than are the Western democracies. Although they will soften, no East Asian success looks likely to fade away gracefully. In any case, there is plenty of scope for rapid growth to go on spreading in the region. The torch may pass to the "fifth dragon" of Guangdong province in China and to the looser networks of overseas Chinese businessmen who connect up so many East and Southeast Asian economies.

Graciousness soon leaves any fading economy. The English-speaking countries of the Rim show this effect, from Canada and California to Australia and New Zealand. The troubles of the developed world are evident in them. They have large debts and low savings rates, and high welfare expenditures yet low spending on technical education. Their railways, sewers, bridges, and docks tend to decay; their rates of inflation have been high, though inflation is being suppressed for the moment at the expense of very serious youth unemployment.

The English-speaking economies of the Pacific display the social problems apparent throughout the West, including the emergence of an underclass. These difficulties are among those that seem to reduce educational and work motivation. Furthermore, the traditional art of compromise has broken down. Intransigent single-interest groups threaten to distort the process of economic, political, and social decisionmaking.

The societies in question are all attempting the mass experiment of becoming "multicultural," which is a generous and humane idea. The mixing (history suggests) may also promote bursts of creativity. But cultural mixing is not easy to manage without the frictions of real or imagined racism and high costs for socializing and educating immigrants with low skills and many different languages. Whereas Japan, though now slowly relaxing its xenophobia, is a homogeneous society that does not welcome permanent settlement by its immigrant workers, Australia and Canada, which were once almost as homogeneous, have become two of the most mixed societies in the world.

Above all, the English-speaking countries are democracies that, in contrast to the "dominant party" states of East and Southeast Asia, find it hard to respond consistently and with one voice to the imperatives of change. Closing unproductive industries is hard where voters in the constituencies affected can at the next election throw out politicians who will not protect the failing factories. The ability of East Asia to abandon blue-collar industries is almost as outstanding as its achievement of growth, though even there change is not automatic. Japan itself has difficulty in closing unprofitable coal mines. Yet East Asia has generally managed much better in such respects than the Western democracies, whose overall capacity to confront economic and social problems is hardly getting better. The historical nature and emergence of these divergent types of economy are set out in the chapters that follow.

Eric Jones
Lionel Frost
Colin White

Acknowledgments

The Department of Economic History at La Trobe University has been a pleasant and stimulating place to work. It strove, as early as or earlier than similar departments, to adjust both teaching and research to the reality of growth in the Asia-Pacific region. Operating mainly as a service department in the School of Economics and Commerce, its focus has been long-term, comparative, institutional, and environmental. Events in the world at large have not shown that this is a bad way to go about educating students of history, economics, or business.

This is the seventh new book to be published by members of the department in six years, and our secretary, Lorraine Chai, has shouldered the load wonderfully. We appreciate Lorraine's patience and competence. Our colleague John Anderson has always been a sounding board for the ideas presented here. Greg O'Brien, dean of the School of Economics and Commerce, has been very supportive of our work. The collection at the Borchardt Library has been invaluable, and the staff has been helpful; we are grateful to the Interlibrary Loans staff, too.

For information, ideas, and advice, we are indebted to our colleagues Tom Fisher (History), Warwick Frost (Economic History), Harry Clarke, Sisira Jayasuriya, Rod Maddock, and Glenn Withers (Economics); a number of our former students at La Trobe—Vincent Lim (now of Linacre College, Oxford), Gary Magee (now of Nuffield College, Oxford), Zhou Linong (now of Deakin University), Deng Gang (now of Victoria University, Wellington, New Zealand), Ian Watt (currently "minister economic" in Australia's Washington embassy), and Geoff Raby (now head of the East Asia Analytical Unit, Department of Foreign Affairs and Trade, Canberra); as well as to David Christian (Macquarie University) and Gary Hamilton (University of California, Davis).

For excellent research assistance, we are indebted to another of our former students, Lee Poh Onn (now of the Institute of Southeast Asian Studies, Singapore), and to Meredith Sherlock, Julie Rowe, and Sylvia Jones.

Lionel Frost is grateful to many friends and colleagues who have provided support and encouragement. He would like to thank the following in particular for their friendship and the example of their scholarship: Martin Daunton, Tony Denholm, Philippa Mein Smith, Donald Olsen, and Anthony Sutcliffe. Thanks once again to Carol, Mark, Robert, and Monica Frost.

Eric Jones would like to thank for their attention his students in the honors class in economic history at La Trobe, in the international business environment class in the Graduate School of Management at the University of Melbourne, and in the graduate seminar on social theory and comparative history at the University of California, Davis. He is, as always, grateful to his wife, Sylvia, and to Deborah and Christopher.

Colin White would like to thank friends and colleagues on the Rim—in particular within Australian, New Zealand, and U.S. universities and at the East China Normal University and the Academy of Social Sciences in Shanghai. He would also like to thank colleagues at the Center for Soviet and East European Studies at the University of Melbourne who are conducting a major research project on "Pacific" Russia. He is ever thankful for the continuing support of Sandra, Julia, Anna, Frances, and Daniel and for enthusiastic discussions with many past students and conference participants.

E. J.
L. F.
C. W.

1

Introduction:
Geography and Meaning

The high noon of European and American industrial supremacy has passed,
bringing to an end the brief period of a few hundred years in which Asia, es-
pecially the eastern part of Asia, did not dominate the world.

R. Hofheinz and K. E. Calder, *The Eastasia Edge* **(1982)**

The second part of the title of this book, "An economic history of the Pacific
Rim," is intriguingly difficult to interpret. This particular area of the world has
had a growing number of alternative titles applied to it: Pacific Rim, Pacific Basin,
Pacific Edge, Asia Pacific, even Euro-American Pacific, are the most prominent.
The exact specification of the regions included under these broad headings varies
greatly. There is considerable ambiguity.

Pacific Geography

Geographically the Pacific area covers as much as one-third of the earth's surface,
stretching variously from the Bering Strait to Antarctica, from California to Korea, from Alaska to Tasmania, and from Kamchatka to Chile. Even here there is
room for disagreement in delineating exact boundaries. How far into the connected seas and surrounding lands of Southeast Asia does the Pacific penetrate?
Often Thailand is included in the area, not because geography clearly demands it
but because it seems to be following East Asia on the upward path of development. The thousands of islands located on the continental shelf of the western Pacific constitute a region strikingly different from any elsewhere on the Pacific
Rim. The well-defined coastline of the Pacific disappears in this region.

The Pacific Ocean is vast (see Map 1.1). It is the largest ocean, more than twice as big as the runner-up, the Atlantic. Pacific waters cover more area than all of the world's land. The Pacific's greatest width—between the Philippines and Panama—is 10,600 miles, slightly farther than the air distance from London to Sydney. A flight from Sydney to San Francisco (via Honolulu) covers the same distance as one from Los Angeles to Moscow (via London). A person who jets from Sydney to Tokyo travels almost as far as one who flies from Johannesburg to Rome.

Despite the size of the Pacific Ocean, the amount of land from which water drains into it is relatively small. The Atlantic Ocean has a land surface four times greater draining into it. Much of the Rim is encircled by narrow stretches of land bounded by mountains. These mountains, and the incidence of earthquakes and volcanoes, have given rise to the name "Rim of Fire." The Andes tower over the coast of South America, rising a mere 30 to 150 miles inland. A further chain of volcanic mountains, interspersed with small areas of plains, plateaus, jungle, and forest, runs through Central America. North America's Pacific Rim is a slope of land draining the Rocky Mountains and Sierra Nevada. Here lie hundreds of river valleys, plateaus, and grasslands, and a series of lower mountains (the Coastal and Cascade ranges) hugging the Pacific.

On the other side of the Pacific, the walls of the ocean basin rise steeply before forming a flattened shelf that leads to the coast of the Asian and Australasian continents. This continental shelf has a number of shallow seas, such as the Sea of Japan, the China Sea, and the Tasman Sea, and tens of thousands of islands stretching from New Zealand to the Kamchatka Peninsula. There are three major archipelagoes: Indonesia (with over 3,000 islands), the Philippines (over 7,000 islands), and Japan (over 3,000 islands). The larger islands are of considerable extent: Borneo, for instance, covers a greater area than Texas or Alberta.

From the Bering Strait, a wall of mountains hugs the Asian side of the Pacific. Then, at the Sea of Okhotsk, the mountain wall starts to curve inland, encircling the Mongolian Plateau and Gobi Desert. The wall climbs until it reaches the Tibetan Plateau and the Himalayas. Great rivers drain from these mountains like spokes from the hub of a wheel: the Indus, Ganges, Brahmaputra, and Irrawaddy rivers drain to the Indian Ocean, and the Mekong, Yangtze, Huangho (Yellow), and Amur rivers to the Pacific.

The fertile floodplains of the Yangtze and Huangho became the heartland of Chinese civilization. The area that is now the People's Republic of China, slightly larger than that of the United States, is the one big land mass that drains into the Pacific. However, about 60 percent of China is made up of mountains and plateaus; some 94 percent of the population lives in the densely settled eastern regions that are suitable for agriculture. Here farming is small-scale because monsoon agriculture creates an enormous demand for labor during the ploughing, planting, and harvesting seasons, and there is a limit to the amount of land a fam-

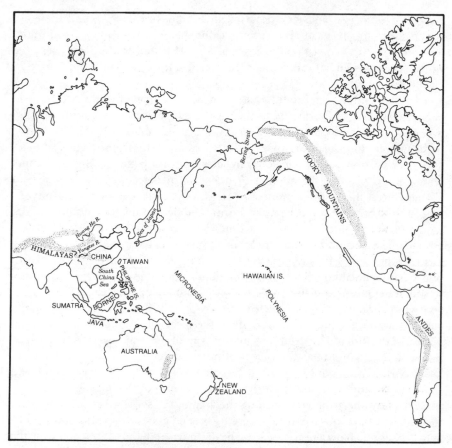

MAP 1.1 *Physical Geography of the Pacific Rim*

ily can farm using labor-intensive technology. In China's agricultural regions, which account for about 2.5 percent of the world's land mass, live 20 percent of the world's people. The immense fertility of the river deltas helps explain the high population density, but every scrap of land needs to be cultivated in order to support such large numbers.

The physical geography of the Pacific is the result of intense folding of the earth's crust above and below sea level. Deep trenches scar the ocean floor. These stem from weaknesses in the earth's crust, which cause earthquakes and volcanoes. The Pacific Rim has 81 percent of the world's inactive and active volcanoes, and every year more than 80 percent of world seismic activity takes place in the Pacific. Most of these earthquakes occur below sea level. Nevertheless, the Pacific Rim's vulnerability to earthquakes is high: 53 percent of the world's major earthquakes between 1556 and 1964 occurred in Pacific Rim regions, and these accounted for 69 percent of all reported deaths due to earthquakes. In addition, monsoons cause massive flooding in Asia. All told, from 1970 to 1991, ten of the world's twenty-eight natural disasters that killed at least 5,000 people occurred in Pacific Rim countries.

A further source of instability is a meteorological phenomenon known as El Niño. Every seven to fourteen years the surface temperature of the normally cool waters off Peru and Ecuador is raised by warm ocean currents. El Niño—the name given to this ocean warming—affects weather patterns throughout the Pacific (and possibly across the globe) by altering wind patterns. Higher oceanic temperatures increase the amount of moisture in the atmosphere, and wind changes direct this warmer, moister air toward the eastern Pacific Rim. In 1982–1983 El Niño brought severe heat and storms and heavy rainfall to California, Ecuador, Peru, and Bolivia. At the same time, drier air masses in the western Pacific created one of the most serious droughts in Australia's recorded history, affecting virtually the whole of eastern Australia. In 1990–1991 the El Niño effect returned, but the drought, although longer-lasting than in 1982–1983, was confined mostly to southern Queensland and northern New South Wales. Because of El Niño, severe weather changes can be expected in many parts of the Pacific every five to ten years. However, the timing and severity of these changes cannot be predicted. El Niño and the Rim of Fire define an environment of risk and uncertainty to which inhabitants all around the Rim have to adjust or suffer the consequences.

There is a certain symmetry in the climatic zones between north and south and between east and west. In the northeast the existence of the huge Eurasian land mass disturbs the symmetry, creating the area of the so-called monsoons. Here the different rates of warming and cooling of land and sea create seasonal problems, winds that blow alternately from the dry interior of the continent during the winter and from the moist ocean during the summer. The monsoonal winds blow off the sea and drop a deluge of rain on the land, a deluge to which Asian farmers must adapt. The result is a set of climatic circumstances in Asia that is very different from those at comparable latitudes in the Americas or Australasia.

The range of climatic conditions throughout the Pacific region is enormous: from hot deserts (as in Central Australia and the Atacama Desert in northern Chile) to freezing ice caps and tundra (Alaska and northern Siberia), from the steamy jungles of Southeast Asia to the cold highlands of the Rockies and Andes. Between these extremes, warm regions range from those with a Mediterranean hot summer and wet, mild winter climate (California, much of southeastern Australia, New Zealand's North Island, and Central Chile) to those with cold winters and hot, wet summers (China). The cooler regions vary from those where warm oceanic currents provide a pleasant, if wet and cool, climate (as in British Columbia, Oregon, Washington, southern Chile, and New Zealand's South Island) to those where cold sea currents and inland winds give colder, drier winters (as in

Korea and Manchuria), and inland regions with short summers and cold winters (such as Siberia and the Canadian prairies).

The Meaning of the Pacific

Until the early sixteenth century Europeans had very little knowledge at all of the area, and its various inhabitants only local knowledge. The term "discovery," used for example in such labels as the "Age of Discoveries," is presumptuous since there were large numbers of local inhabitants living in the area before the European intrusion. These people did not, however, comprehend the Pacific as a whole; they knew only their own small areas.

Although the Pacific was first so named by the Portuguese navigator Magellan in 1520, the name did not receive immediate general acceptance. The Europeans did not usually call this ocean the Pacific for a long period after the first intrusion. The Pacific remained for nearly three centuries the South Sea, not only in common speech (especially that of seamen) but very generally on maps and in learned discourse.

As we have seen, geography has its ambiguities, but in any event geography is not enough. Just as resources are only resources when perceived and defined as such by humankind, so the Pacific in one sense really existed only when it was thus named or, as some historians would have it, *invented*. The Pacific therefore has two separate but related manifestations: first, as a physical presence, a set of definable geographical characteristics—in the short-run largely fixed—and second, as an idea found in the minds of those concerned with the area. On the one hand there was a long process of gradual exploration and identification of the physical area; on the other there were particular and changing meanings given to the Pacific as an idea or mental construct. The Pacific therefore has real meaning only in terms of the human relationships and activities that have the potential to bind it together; these activities and relationships have been largely economic. One problem is that they have not been, and still are not, coextensive with the geographical area, nor confined within that area. In what sense can they be defined as properly Pacific at all? For most of its history they certainly could not have been usefully assigned that label.

Since it was Europeans who were first concerned with the area as a whole, the name Pacific became invested with the meanings they imparted to it: as an area potentially a part of new empires, as an inventory of resources awaiting exploitation, as the home of a native population demanding to be converted to Christianity, employed in useful work, or subjected to European notions of a worthwhile life. It is not difficult to see the Pacific, or at least the idea of the Pacific, as a Euro-American invention, part of a world capitalist system ready to add the resources and people of the area to the inventory of exploitable assets. Such a world economy had a center, albeit a moving one and one that was for a period dominated by two or three powers. In the course of the nineteenth century the center clearly moved from Western Europe to the United States. The Pacific itself went through successively dominant phases as a Spanish lake (during the sixteenth and early seventeenth centuries), an English lake (during the eighteenth and nineteenth centuries) and finally a U.S. lake (from the late nineteenth into the twentieth century). The absorption of the Pacific into the European or Western world system was a protracted affair.

On the western side of the Pacific there was always a rival economic system with its core in China, although the Sinitic world extended well beyond the boundaries of China proper to include, for example, Korea and Japan. The Asian orientation of the economy of the western Pacific never completely disappeared, although there was a sense in which the region briefly (if several centuries can be called brief) became a periphery to the European core. The region's recent and loudly proclaimed entry into the "Pacific Century" has meaning only in terms of the emergence of a twin core within the Pacific itself and the relationship between its American and Asian arms, between the United States and Japan in particular.

There can be no meaningful history of the whole Rim or Basin, since there has never been such an integrated unit. There can be no real history of an entity that does not exist. It is necessary, therefore, to present a history of its regions. However, this book is not intended to be a balanced collection of textbook economic histories of the various societies of the Pacific. There is no aspiration to be comprehensive, since such a collection would inevitably be fragmented and incoherent.

The book is much more a history of the process by which, in some periods and in some important respects, certain societies have taken a leadership role in economically integrating significant parts of the Pacific Rim. Since integration has reached its highest level in the recent past, this history has a pronounced recent and present orientation. What is balanced in terms of this objective is by its nature unbalanced from the perspective of more conventional historical goals. Defining the Pacific in the context of such recent relationships can impart a teleological bias to history—that is, an interpretation made with hindsight based on end results.

Most attention here is devoted to the histories of China, Japan, and the United States, reflecting their significant leadership roles. In such a pursuit it is easy to forget the very societies to which the Pacific owes its origins as a defined idea. In particular there is a tendency to exclude from the definition the former Spanish colonies of Latin America, which were largely responsible for the initial European exploration of the area and for the first linking of the Americas and the Philippines; also the Russians, whose Russian-American Company brought together another part of the area, the northern Pacific; and the Pacific Islands, which often served as the bases of Euro-American trade activity and helped bind the Pacific into a looser kind of whole. This book gives a lesser but important place to these earlier contributions.

The Regions of the Pacific and Plan of the Book

The individual chapters of the book cover the economic and historical experience of particular regions. At the same time, they are ordered in a definite chronological sequence. However, there is a pronounced chronological overlap between chapters that reflects the coexistence of separate units of integration. Moreover, different regions passed through similar phases of economic development at different times; a common integrative process involved asynchronous sequences. This is the way history unfolds. There are as a consequence significant and necessary elements of backtracking both within and between chapters. There is a chronological structure to the chapters taken as a whole, in the sense that we move from the early civilizations of China through all the main periods to the present, concluding with prospects for the future.

Within this geographical and chronological framework, we cover two main themes. The first of these is where economic growth has occurred and reoccurred around the Pacific Rim in the past and present. Growth in a long perspective has taken place in cycles, not necessarily concurrent, in each Pacific region; these cycles, perforce, have taken place in real time, which justifies our chronological treatment. The second theme concerns the increasingly frequent efforts to integrate Pacific Rim economies. We therefore examine the ways in which both these trends have worked themselves out and are still working themselves out around the Pacific.

The grounds for seeing the Pacific as divided into different parts are geographical, cultural, political, and economic. A strictly pragmatic approach is unavoidable, since a consistent application of any one criterion produces anomalies and allows much of the messy historical experience to escape notice. Location, language or origin of settlers, prevailing political system, religious or cultural orientation, degree of reciprocal interaction, level of economic development—all these factors might be considered relevant. Moreover, the boundaries of the different regions are not fixed for all time; some changes are substantial. Part of the relevant historical experience is change over time in the *criteria* of regionalization and therefore in the nature of the partition itself.

There are five broad groupings. First, there is Asia. We use the term "East Asia" for China, Japan, Korea, and their immediate neighbors—Taiwan, Hong Kong, and Macau (or Macao). Japan is Asia's largest and wealthiest economy (see Map 1.2), but growth rates and levels of gross domestic product (GDP) per capita are also high in the "Little Dragons" and the provinces of southern China. Southeast

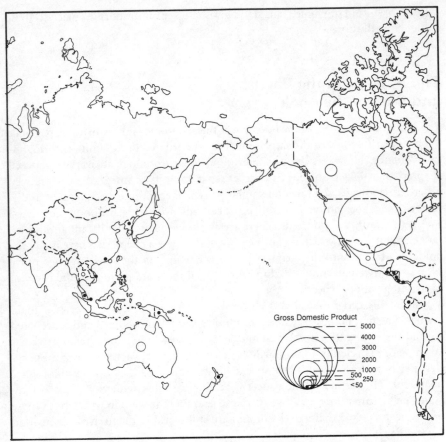

MAP 1.2   *Gross Domestic Product (U.S. $ billions) of Pacific Rim Countries in 1988*

Asia (we use the term with the *south* and the *east* run together because U.S. usage has made this standard) is much more diffuse, including the members of the Association of Southeast Asian Nations—Indonesia, the Philippines, Malaysia, Singapore, Thailand, and Brunei—as well as Vietnam and Papua New Guinea. This subregion is extremely fragmented, both topographically and in culture, including Muslim, Catholic, and Buddhist elements. It does, however, share a colonial inheritance and a relatively low level of economic development. Moreover, it contains significant Chinese minorities and has for a long period interacted closely with East Asia. In a region of poor economies, the relative per capita wealth of Singapore (and to a lesser extent Malaysia) is striking (see Map 1.3).

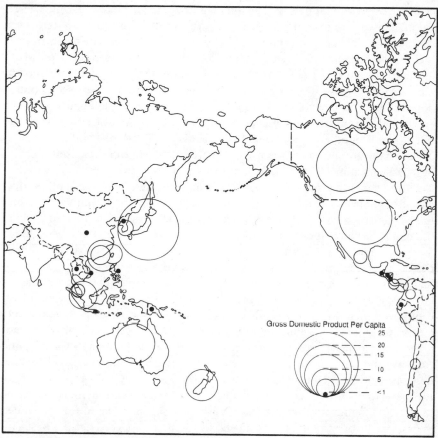

MAP 1.3   *Gross Domestic Product Per Capita (U.S. $ thousands) of Pacific Rim Countries in 1988*

In chapters 2 and 3 we deal with the Pacific area before the European intrusion. In Chapter 2 we discuss the interaction of people and environments and the emergence of the first settled societies in the pre-European era. The largest of these societies was China. In Chapter 3 we consider economic aspects of the Asian empires that rose and fell in this period, concentrating on the economic revolution in Song China. We then consider the long Ming-Qing period, during which China seems not to have surpassed its Song heights, and also address economic change in Tokugawa Japan.

A second group comprises the Latin American countries, once part of the Spanish empire and to a varying degree containing a population descended from settlers originating in the Iberian Peninsula. The nature and impact of the Euro-

pean intrusion into this region is analyzed in Chapter 4. Different in language, religion, and culture from the English-speaking countries, Latin American countries have operated at a much lower level of economic development for most of
their history. In some cases, such as Mexico, the population is mestizo, or mixed;
in others the surviving native population is relatively large and has retained its
separate identity, as in Peru or Ecuador. Chile, with a largely European population, still has much more in common with the Latin than the English-speaking
group. Other countries in the Latin group include the small Central American
states, plus Colombia. A case could be made for including the Philippines in this
group on the grounds of its Spanish colonial history. None of these countries had
in 1988 a per capita GDP of more than $2,500 (see Map 1.3).

Third, there is a group of English-speaking countries, largely the end product
of settlement from Great Britain, although there was significant immigration into
these countries from non-British sources. Great Britain's replacement of Spain as
the major European power in the Pacific is explored in Chapter 5. The United
States, Canada, Australia, and New Zealand are characterized by marked similarities in culture, political system, and level of economic development. The United
States has the highest gross domestic product of any nation that borders the Pacific (see Map 1.2). But Canada approaches its southern neighbor in terms of per
capita wealth, and Australia and New Zealand also enjoy high average incomes
(see Map 1.3). There is significant interaction between adjacent countries, and it is
a result of particular political histories that the United States and Canada, and
Australia and New Zealand, are separate. The United States and Canada have borders on both the Atlantic and the Pacific. The "Pacific region" or "Far West" of
the two nations is conventionally defined as the states and provinces bordering
the Pacific: California, Oregon, Washington, Alaska, and Hawaii in the United
States, and British Columbia in Canada. In Chapter 6 we consider the westward
movement of economic and political hegemony both within the world at large,
from Europe to the United States, and within the United States itself, from the Atlantic to the Pacific.

A fourth region is Northeast Asia, where Russian rule still officially prevails.
Despite the area's relatively small population, its long coastline—the second lon-
gest on the Pacific Rim, after Indonesia's—justifies a separate treatment, as do
particularities of location, culture, and political system. The Russians briefly
pushed the boundaries of this region into North America, but the natural geographical divide between Asia and North America reasserted its influence. This
Russian intrusion is considered in Chapter 5. Russian Asia is the real Northeast
Asia, although the label Northeast Asia is often given nowadays to what in this
book we call East Asia.

Chapter 7 is an analysis of the East Asian economic miracle, with focus on Japan and the mix of indigenous and external factors explaining its economic rise.
We also discuss the Little Dragons of the East Asian region and the experience of

Southeast Asia as a frontier of developed East Asia. In Chapter 8 we consider the more troubled experience of China.

The four regions outlined above include the modern nation-states that border the Pacific Ocean, forming what is conventionally referred to as the Pacific Rim. Note that the concept excludes the fifth group: the small Pacific islands, mostly in the South Pacific. The thousands of islands that make up Oceania are normally divided into three groups: Melanesia, Micronesia, and Polynesia. An adequate treatment of these islands' disparate histories is beyond the scope of this book. The region is therefore considered only in a general sense, which explains the emphasis on the Pacific Rim in the title.

There are several broad issues that affect economic life in most parts of the Pacific Rim and exert an influence not confined by political boundaries. Any study of themes such as multinational investment, overseas migration, and agricultural change would have to be approached from a wider perspective than that of the experience of individual nation-states.

One such issue, urbanization, is explored in detail in this book. Cities play a major role in promoting economic development, but they also share common problems. For over a thousand years, the Pacific Rim's economically advanced societies have built cities and developed ways of coping with the problems created by urban growth. In most Pacific Rim countries today, the majority of the population lives in cities. In China, Indonesia, and Thailand, there is a substantial non-urban population, but these nations still have some very large, fast-growing cities. Several of the world's biggest cities are in Pacific Rim countries. There is no doubt that future economic growth in the Pacific will see an increase in the number and size of large cities. Many people envisage that these cities will be overcrowded, be poorly serviced, have vast areas of poverty, and cause heavy environmental damage.

The economic impact and associated problems of urbanization are best studied through a broad framework showing comparisons among cities throughout the Pacific region rather than through a series of case studies. In Chapter 9 such a framework is used to examine the role of cities in the economic development of the Pacific Rim and assess the ability of those cities to cope with the problems of population growth. The history of city growth offers important lessons for today's planners and policymakers by revealing how some urban problems have been solved and why some persist because of how cities have attempted to solve them in the past.

In the conclusion we discuss the implications of history for understanding the Pacific at present and in the chapter "Prospects" offer a reading of the future.

2

The First Settlements
Around the Pacific

The arrival of the first human beings on the western margin of the Pacific Ocean was one of the most momentous events in the history of mankind. It led to the conquest of the world's largest ocean, the occupation of four huge continents, and the diversification of the human species into some of its most numerous, energetic and colourful cultures.

—Alan Thorne and Robert Raymond,
Man on the Rim: The Peopling of the Pacific (1989)

Humans and the Pacific

The early interaction of humans and the environment within the Pacific area is clouded in uncertainty. Controversy surrounds the issue of where and when humans originated. Answers have been gleaned from archaeological evidence, which is inherently incomplete and from which researchers have drawn conflicting conclusions. Thus, whereas some scholars believe that humans may have arrived in North America at least 40,000 years ago, others put the date of earliest human habitation at about 15,000 years ago. Estimates of the first aboriginal occupation of Australia range from 140,000 to 40,000 years ago. On the issue of when humans first made use of fire, the estimated dates vary from 1.5 million to 50,000 years ago.

For millions of years the world has experienced marked climatic swings between cold and warm periods, which have affected the extent of the world's ice sheets. A major cooling began around 100,000 to 90,000 years ago during the so-called Great Ice Age. The ice caps grew big enough to smother northern Europe, Asia, and Canada. Sea levels fluctuated, but the trend was clearly toward lower levels, as more water was trapped and held as ice at the poles. Sea levels today are an estimated 425 feet higher than those of 20,000 years ago. As the Pacific shrunk, new shelves of coastal land were created, notably between Siberia and Alaska; Japan and the Asian mainland; the Malay Peninsula and Java and Borneo; and Australia and New Guinea. Around 15,000 years ago, the ice sheets began to melt. Within 5,000 to 7,000 years, seas approached modern levels, again flooding continental shelves and isolating Japan, the Americas, and many of the islands of Southeast Asia.

Falling sea levels created new coastal territory for plants and animals and in turn for groups of hunter-gatherers. New islands poked up, in a few centuries developing vegetation, fish, and bird life. When the ice caps started to melt and the sea level rose again, life was displaced. Humans had to move on to find food—either across the sea to a visible island or inland. Natural disasters and conflicts between hunting groups over scarce food may also have forced migration.

During the Great Ice Age, groups of hunter-gatherers were able to walk from Asia to what are now the islands of Japan. It seems likely that humans made the sea crossing to New Guinea and Australia about 60,000 to 40,000 years ago, that they mastered the extremes of Siberia from around 35,000 years ago, and that around 15,000 years ago they crossed to the Americas. As noted previously, these dates are a matter of continuing dispute. The islands of Polynesia, in particular Hawaii and New Zealand, were colonized very recently, between A.D. 400 and 900.

The Emergence of Settled Societies

The spread of people around the Pacific turned up a bounty of food but also serious environmental problems. When the ice caps began to melt, the retreating glaciers of northern Asia and North America begat forests and tundra of lush vegetation, which sustained a large population of big game. These large animals were ill-adapted to the menace of human hunters. The temperate regions were free of the microparasites that afflicted humans in tropical areas. As a result, most species of large game were exterminated very quickly by ruthless and efficient hunters. In the Americas, mammoths, giant sloths, mastodons, sabre-toothed cats, giant armadillos, giant bears, long-horned bison, camels, horses, and other species disappeared in a remarkably short period of hunting, estimated at around only a thousand years. Overhunting may well have been responsible for the extinction of a number of Australian marsupial species, such as giant emus and wombats, and kangaroos up to ten feet tall. On the Australian mainland, thylacines (the Tasmanian tiger), and Tasmanian devils became extinct. Further climatic warming may well have played a contributory role in these extinctions by drying out vegetation upon which certain species depended for food. In New Zealand the megafauna (there, very large birds such as the moa) was wiped out by Polynesian immigrants—the Maoris—in relatively recent centuries, though before Europeans arrived.

Once the large species of a given region became scarce, humans could wander to new territory in search of a game-rich environment not already staked out by other hunters. If big game was not to be found, hunters could diversify by seeking new prey and trying new foods. Hunters in Siberia and Canada's Pacific Coast became expert boat-builders and fishermen. In Australia, they turned to smaller game, fish, and shellfish. Big-game hunting persisted only on the American plains, where a smaller bison evolved, thriving on short, low-nutrient grasses and capable of breeding right through winter. These bison bred too quickly to be overhunted until horses (reintroduced to the Americas by Spanish colonists) and rifles made bison-killing much easier for hunting tribes and European traders.

Big-game hunting bands customarily allocated the main tasks—preparing for the hunt, stalking and killing animals, and dividing up the flesh—to men. Women's work was more routine—tending campsites and fires, making clothes and baskets, caring for children, and foraging for edible seeds, nuts, berries, fruits, roots, grubs, and eggs. In so doing they would have acquired knowledge of how plants grew from seeds or cuttings. Dropping seeds or throwing away the unwanted parts of plants would accidentally plant new crops. People may have thinned out useless plants to make room for those bearing food. But for nomad groups, moving frequently to new hunting grounds, there was little incentive to spend much time cultivating plants.

Incentives began to change when rich areas of unhunted territory diminished and groups stayed on the spot areas for longer periods. Clustering of people made cooperation and self-protection easier. Groups that came to depend on the sea for food needed a fairly permanent base to shelter and repair their boats. The discovery at a large number of sites around the Pacific of clusters of shell middens, discarded tools, flint workings, and thick layers of ash is evidence of early permanent settlement. These protovillages were the hub of diversified food-collection systems, with work a mixture of hunting, fishing, simple craft-making and manufacturing, food gathering, and, eventually, cultivating. For instance, around 2500 B.C. people along the coast of Peru began to abandon nomadic life and live in villages near beaches and rocky points. They hunted birds, gathered fish and crabs, and grew small areas of crops to supplement their diet. From around 1900 B.C., when the best land close to the Pacific was occupied, people started to move inland to establish new settlements. They became full-time farmers and exchanged their surplus with that of the fishermen and hunters of the coastal villages. Such trade was of mutual benefit, and with specialization came greater efficiency and productivity.

In areas where plants grew easily and game was increasingly scarce, there was an incentive to cultivate rather than simply to gather. Slowly, knowledge of when and how to sow and harvest accumulated. Communities of farmers were self-selected: Those unwilling to work at farming or to save seeds for sowing the next crop became undernourished and were eliminated. The multiplying population of settled farmers marginalized the remaining groups of hunter-gatherers, whose numbers were limited by the availability of wild game and plants. Only in limited regions around the Pacific, such as Australia, Siberia, and the Eskimo, Athapaskan, and Great Plains regions of North America, did hunter-gatherer groups survive into recent times. By 2,000 years ago the estimated population of the main hunter-gatherer regions made up less than 2 percent of the total population of the Pacific Rim.

On some accounts this survival was due to a natural abundance or an easy accessibility of resources. For example, there are those who stress that a vast range of foods was available for collection in parts of Australia. Near Cape York 73 different species of fruit and 76 other kinds of plants were eaten by aboriginals. At Wilson's Promontory in Victoria, there are 120 edible species of plants; virtually all of these are known to have been eaten by aboriginals. Yet there is clear archaeological evidence of malnutrition and associated diseases in skeletal remains for this area. The bounty was seasonal. Many of the areas where hunter-gatherers survived were also areas of high risk where natural conditions were dangerously unstable. Risk-managing behavior often proved incompatible with advance into an agricultural economy. Behavior was probably adjusted to suit the worst possible conditions.

Once wild crops and animals became domesticated (that is, grown, tended, and fed to increase yields), humans loosened a basic constraint on economic growth. Now that humans could with some certainty *produce* food for their own use, rather than simply kill or gather what nature had to offer, populations could grow substantially without exhausting food supplies. McEvedy and Jones estimate that world population reached 1.7 million at 100,000 B.C. and that by 10,000 B.C. numbers had risen to around 4 million. These are rough estimates but acceptable as an order of magnitude. As agriculture became established, rates of population growth accelerated: from 5000 B.C. to 1000 B.C. the global population approximately doubled every millennium. From 1000 B.C. to A.D. 1, numbers increased from 50 million to 170 million.

It appears that domestication took place independently in a number of regions around the Pacific and throughout the world. There were many areas around the Pacific where useful plants and animals were tamed and tended: Central America (home to corn [maize], beans, chili peppers, squash, pumpkins, tobacco, and turkeys), South America (potatoes, tomatoes, pineapples, coca, and other crops), Southeast Asia (spices such as cloves, nutmeg, ginger, and tumeric, as well as mangos, bamboo, cotton, chickens, water buffalo, and geese), and the Philippines and New Guinea (coconuts, sugarcane, yams, sweet potatoes, and bananas).

Some highly specialized agricultures emerged that survive today only in fairly remote pockets. For example, "archipelago" farming linked together very different niches at varying altitudes in the Andes. Today a whole host of long-neglected crops, such as amaranth and quinoa, are being rediscovered. At surprisingly high altitudes several tubers were grown in addition to the potato.

The region of the Pacific most naturally suited to agriculture was China. Once farming communities began to settle its vast areas of fertile and easily worked soil, China's population grew quickly and substantially. By A.D. 1, 53 million people lived in China, 86 percent of the total population of all the countries bordering the Pacific. From about this time settlers from Korea and China began to arrive in Japan, introducing wet rice cultivation (hitherto fishing, the gathering of seaweeds, and buckwheat cultivation had been the mainstays of Japanese communities).

With the development of agriculture, a demographic concentration around an East Asian growth pole took shape. In A.D. 1000, 73 million people lived in East Asia: this was 82 percent of the total Pacific Rim population and 28 percent of the world population. In 1500, 83 percent of the Pacific Rim population (159 million) lived in East Asia (31 percent of the world total). The only other major centers of population along the Rim were in Southeast Asia (14.5 million) and in the Aztec and Inca empires (possibly as many as 30 million to 40 million, but probably many fewer). By 1800, nine out of every ten persons living in Pacific Rim countries (398 million) was an East Asian. In the last two centuries Southeast Asia and the Americas have increased their share substantially, yet in 1988 East Asia still accounted for 54 percent of the Pacific Rim's population of 2,459 million. China alone accounts for 22 percent of the world's current population.

The first Chinese villages seem to have been established near areas of undomesticated grain, which was harvested wild and, after a long period of experimenting, sown and cultivated. To date, the earliest village sites that have been found are along the Yangtze River and are at least 7,000 years old. It is estimated that by about 4,000 years ago, hundreds of villages covered a wide area of the Huangho River basin. These communities worked collectively to open up and farm areas using slash-and-burn methods. The initial staple, millet, was grown until the soil was exhausted, whereupon the villages would relocate. Life was a mixture of hunting, gathering, fishing, and cultivating.

Rice appears to have been domesticated in the Yangtze River basin around 6,000 years ago, and between 4,500 and 5,000 years ago in the Huangho River basin. Because rice thrived in wet conditions, farmers could use irrigation to flood their fields to retain moisture for the crop and to kill off competing weeds. Once farmers had invested substantial effort in irrigation, there was a reason to stay put and maintain the fertility of the soil. From about the seventh century B.C. rice fields began to be fallowed and manured and worked more productively with iron tools.

Once the balance between hunter-gathering and cultivating had tipped in favor of the latter, there was no turning back. Farming populations put down roots be-

nomadic
hunter-gather v. farm
⇒) org of defense

cause the investment in land clearing, improving, and irrigating created a disincentive to wander off to new areas. As greater productivity encouraged population growth, farming areas spread and reduced the areas of wild territory suitable for hunting. In good times, nomads might trade meat and hides for farmers' surplus food, but when food became scarce the farmers were vulnerable to the incursions of nomad raiding parties. The fundamental need for protection encouraged political organization. Agrarian societies became dependent on military regimes that collected taxes (surplus food) in return for keeping the peace.

These regimes created suitable conditions for *extensive* economic growth (where output grows, but only in line with population growth). But it was easy for them unintentionally to create disincentives for peasants to increase their productivity and per capita output and thus not achieve *intensive* economic growth. Any surplus might be taxed away to pay for monuments, royal tombs, or larger armies.

For instance, war between the Chinese and nomads from the north and between China's rival kingdoms was a costly business, made more so by the introduction of the crossbow and mounted archery from the fourth century B.C. The crossbow was a precision weapon that required skilled labor to manufacture. Mounted archery was to the advantage of the horsemen of the steppe tribes, which forced the Chinese to build long walls to help defend themselves. War placed extra strain on the peasantry, which provided the state with the tax revenue and manpower needed to run an expensive military machine. Political strife and ever-increasing military expenditure placed a great burden on the economy. When the emperor Wang Mang (A.D. 9–23) raised an army of over 300,000 men to fight the Hsiung-nu, a northern barbarian tribe, the resulting heavy taxation and conscription of labor drove people in the countryside into famine and bred rebellion against the regime.

The periods between China's great dynasties—the Han (206 B.C.–A.D. 220), T'ang (A.D. 618–906), Song (960–1279), and Ming (1368–1644)—were troubled times during which large military expenditures were required. Warlords clashed and divided the Han empire; invaders from the north brought down the T'ang, Song, and Ming dynasties. The need for regimes to obtain resources for self-preservation has been a continuing theme of Chinese history.

Intensive economic growth occurred as a side-effect of attempts by rulers to build up their tax base. There being only so much pie to be sliced, rulers could increase their wealth only by encouraging growth—in other words, the baking of larger pies. Greater productivity and an expansion of mercantile activity meant that more taxes could be collected, permitting a growth of military resources for defense and expansion. Rulers might offer peasants the security of land ownership to attract population from rival kingdoms (as was done in the states of Wei and Ch'in in northwest China before the fourth century B.C.). The kings of Java attempted to develop their hinterland (and thus increase their tax base) by granting peripheral land to loyal followers. Tax collection might also become less capricious. Trade and commerce might be fostered, providing extra revenue and encouraging the growth of cities large enough to act as major markets and centers for innovation and technological change. Chinese, Arab, and Indian traders in search of spices did business with the Southeast Asian states, which provided port and storage facilities, suppressed piracy, and levied tolerable rates of taxation.

From a modern, developed-world perspective, it all seems so simple. But such arrangements were not always forthcoming nor always maintained long enough to become established modes of political conduct. Having broken free of fundamental ecological limits to growth, humans faced political obstacles to improved well-being. These obstacles were slow to fall and were often built up again.

3

Early East Asia

*I still recall, after twenty-five years, the sense of exhilarating release with which
... I first came into contact with a great and ancient scheme of values in which
everything did **not** go back to Plato, Aristotle, and the Bible.*

—Oskar Spate, *Islands and Men* (1963)

In this chapter we will cover East Asia until the middle of the nineteenth century, when striking changes took place in its life. We will discuss the long-run experience of the Chinese economy, emphasizing the Song "economic revolution" and considering the debate about why for centuries afterwards, under the Ming and Qing (Manchu) dynasties, China did not regain the heights of those days.

Early China

We find in early Chinese civilization an impressive performance—great technological change betokening widespread creativity and, if nothing more, considerable population growth. A good question with which to start, then, is why were there so many Chinese? Why have the Chinese people constituted a sizeable fraction of the world's population since early prehistoric times? Most of the relevant history is the history of agriculture: The success of the Chinese is that they secured a productive heartland, began to farm it intensively, and have done so ever since.

The origins were in north China, on the *loess*. The loess is a windblown soil that forms level land, is even in texture, and is very fertile, retaining many of its minerals and sustaining cereal production without strain for thousands of years. Yields are high enough to offset the cold climate. The loess was not much covered with grass and was relatively easy to dig up with sticks. The Shang, a dynasty that established itself in the second millennium B.C., was the only civilization anywhere to occupy a large stretch of open grassland. On grassland elsewhere in the world, the dense vegetative cover made breaking through the turf difficult; farming began in various places, but only in patches scattered through the woods. The Shang, however, could soon rule over a population that multiplied on the basis of big, unbroken tracts of cereal crops.

What is more, it was learned how to grow rice in marshes on the loess and how to keep the growing plants irrigated. This method made for high yields of a particularly nutritive foodstuff. Wet rice cultivation came to typify Chinese agriculture. It spread southward. The movement south went on at varying speeds as late as the nineteenth century A.D., by which time most cultivable land, except that having absurdly low yields (mountaintops, say), had been taken up throughout the area that China occupies on modern maps. China had expanded south and west, in the process clearing vast, rich forests on clay soils. The clays were hard to plow but the warmer southerly climate and longer growing season compensated for that.

During the thousands of years throughout which the Chinese occupied more and more territory, intensive methods of farming were discovered. They were spread from region to region, in part by textbooks called *nong shu*. These books were written by a learned elite that depended for its income on rent and taxes levied on the peasant farmers. Chinese peasants themselves may have been unable to read and write, but their masters made sure they heard of new methods and new crop strains that could raise output. Especially important from the eleventh century A.D. were successive types of earlier-ripening varieties of rice. These gave higher yields. They resisted drought better and helped lessen the impact of the famines that constantly buffeted the peasant economy. The existence of written texts helped preserve "best practice" methods of farming through bouts of turmoil and disaster in Chinese history, such as times of invasion.

The Shang civilization emerged in a north Chinese "cradle of civilization." Few intrusions from other developed regions to the west—the Middle East or India—caused disturbance. There were one or two, however. Later cultural contacts, such as the arrival of Buddhism from India, did alter Chinese life. On the whole Chinese civilization was indigenous, and for such a large system it was unique in its degree of isolation. This was a primary civilization that retained elements of Bronze Age technology and village organization until the present century. Whereas other early civilizations vanished or were totally transformed by outside contacts and new waves of technology, this one survived.

On the face of it, organizing the Han Chinese farmers on the loess plain into a single social and political unit may not seem a difficult chore. China did become a single empire and remained one despite recurrent conquests by other dynasties. Whether they were invaders from the steppe or successful Chinese rebels, the upstarts took over the existing system and ran it for their own benefit rather than replacing it. Although geography may make some solutions easier than others, it does not dictate political results such as this. China, after all, was not always an empire on a plain: The political structure was decentralized in the period of the Warring States from 475–255 B.C. That was, incidentally, a creative period: One of the surprising, perhaps disagreeable, truths of history is that times of disorder tend to throw up more creative ideas than most periods of stability.

However, one warring state eventually conquered the others. The successful emperor did his best to make sure that China would not subdivide again. In 220 B.C. he burned the records of the local administrations he had overrun. China has been one state most of the time since; whenever it has been fragmented by fighting, a single victorious group has put Humpty-Dumpty together again. This unitary system housed archaic ways of life virtually until the present.

The state has been ruled from above by an elite that lived by administering society and taxing the peasantry. The elite wrote of the peasants that they were its "meat and fish." Nor did the elite have any reason to want to change a structure that guaranteed them prestige and a good living. Beneath them, a society of isolated, immobile villages persisted. The whole world was once like this, indeed even more separatist: At least China was unified enough below the political level by the Han people. China escaped the Babel of the thousands of local languages common in premodern times (and up to the present in Papua New Guinea).

The imperial elite in China did make some important investments that brought about certain kinds of change. From time to time there were bouts of canal-building and river improvements. Waterborne transportation was far cheaper than overland transportation in the ages before the railway, and canals eased the collection of taxes taken in bulky rice. Nevertheless, the tax system was not super-efficient, viewed in a broad sense. The productivity of China's farming was largely absorbed in population growth. Taxes supported an elite that remained a small minority. As mentioned, this rich, literate group had little reason to change things; the peasants did revolt quite often, but neither group had enough experience of other societies to think in terms of remodeling China on any other basis.

Expeditions by junk fleets that were mounted from China in the fifteenth century A.D. reached as far away as East Africa but found only less developed societies. These societies could be pressed into paying tribute to the emperor but were not suggestive of better modes of political or social organization. China rather smugly saw itself as the Middle Kingdom, with all else tributary and its emperor—in any dynasty—ruling with the "mandate of heaven." The famous symbol of this attitude is the Qing emperor's snub of Lord Macartney, the British emissary who arrived in 1799. The emperor declared that China produced all it needed and saw no point in trading for inferior barbarian products.

Chinese agrarian civilization was not merely big and centrally ruled; it also was creative enough to come up with and use the most advanced technologies of the premodern world. Before 475 B.C., under the late Chou, long-distance trade, city growth, and a wide use of money already existed. During the Ch'in (256–207 B.C.) iron farm tools, especially plows, were widely adopted. A single ironmaster employed a thousand workers.

China's technological inventory was a long one. It included the abacus, which was as swift at reckoning as the older hand calculators; iron-chain suspension bridges; drills for brine that could reach depths of 2,000 feet; porcelain ware; and paper. The ancient art of making decorative papercuts illustrates how handicraft industry was capable of a certain measure of mass production. As many as twenty copies could be made at a cutting. For clever designs in which the template cut out and the stencil remaining were both saleable as pictures, forty items could be produced at one time.

Some of the technologies traveled westward right across Eurasia. By the early seventeenth century, Francis Bacon proclaimed far away in England that the three greatest inventions known were the compass, printing, and gunpowder; all three were Chinese in origin. However, it is easy to exaggerate the role of China's technology in the Western world. Invention took place in Europe, too. Even more significant was the fact that although Chinese did use their inventions, they did not use them to the same extent as Europeans used what was available to them. Gunpowder impelled more projectiles in Europe than in Asia, printing copied more volumes, and the compass aided navigation farther and farther afield. The key difference between China and the West was not really technological—it was in social organization, which in Europe extended the use of advanced methods and pursued their further development.

Strikingly inventive potential was sometimes displayed in other East Asian societies. Fifteenth-century Korea provides an illustration. There, under the direction of King Sejong, a new twenty-nine-character alphabet and writing system called Han'gul was devised to order, in three years. Linguists consider this to have been one of the greatest inventions ever made in the sphere of literacy. Han'gul was put together with a moveable metal type. Together, moveable type and a phonetic syllabary were capable of bringing about an explosive increase in the production of printed books. This could have meant a steep drop in the "price of information," which would have encouraged development.

Unfortunately, Sejong died quite young. Although the use of Han'gul has been revived in modern Korea, it was marginalized soon after the king's death and kept in the shadows for centuries. The scholarly elite of traditional Korea was protecting its investment in the complicated Chinese script its members had spent so long learning. Easy access to literacy by the people would have undercut its monopoly.

The Korean example is typical of the problems besetting innovation in premodern times. Note that the difficulty lay less with invention than with innovation. When an inducement was offered by an individual with resources and vision, unsuspected reservoirs of human talent proved to be available. Discoveries were made. That it took only three years to devise Han'gul should be noted. There are other examples, especially from East Asia, suggesting that the problem in the premodern world was less the intellectual difficulty of invention than the lack of incentives to invent and above all the circumstances surrounding the decisions to invest enough to put techniques, even techniques already known, into the productive system.

With reference to "software," there are surely several holes in the linguistic determinism that says that without a phonetic alphabet, with nothing more than pictograms or ideograms, certain societies were at a dead end as regards developing linear thought, science, and advanced technology. That line of argument rests on a number of dubious assumptions, notably that premodern societies could not have reshaped their systems of writing given the incentives to do so. After all, Korea did.

Technical change is less important than the circumstances that permit or block its adoption. Not only did Koreans produce a flexible syllabary that could have reduced "software" costs, the Japanese simplified Chinese script to use it for purposes other than those of high culture or terms derived directly from Chinese. The Japanese have available a forty-seven–character syllabary but prefer to use a complicated mixture of three scripts, without noticeably harming either their literacy or the modern economy of their country. The Japanese would rather fight than switch. In addition, plenty of Chinese students enrolled in Western universities speak several Chinese languages and read freely in both Mandarin and English, just as students in continental Europe, most of all in the Netherlands, read textbooks in two, three, or four languages.

The costs of learning more than one language and the higher transaction costs where several are in use may be offset by the intellectual gains, or they may simply be unimportant if society rewards these things or takes them for granted. The notion of cultural barriers, at least in the language sphere, is a fallacy entertained by monoglot English speakers. The fact that it does not ring true nowadays suggests that premodern cultures could have been modified in various ways that might have permitted economic growth had only some other circumstances changed.

Moreover, the equation of science and technology is not pertinent for the early stages of industrialization; technology in eighteenth-century Britain was substantially the creation of artisans rather than scientists. In any case, Song China made strides in economic development with neither a phonetic alphabet nor Western science, and when it fell it was because of a Mongol invasion, not because it reached some intellectual or conceptual limit.

Many premodern inventions were in weapons technology or architecture, since these were the areas of special interest to the powerful. But not all inventions were of these kinds.

Within China itself, the technologies had a limited or ambiguous effect. The economy grew in magnitude and complexity, but this growth in the *total* income of society—economic *expansion*—did not necessarily produce economic *growth* as it is understood today, i.e., a rise in *average* income. Perhaps there were episodes in which average incomes did go up as well as total income, but they are hard to detect in the Chinese sources available for this early period; there is considerable evidence of piecemeal economic activity, but it is hard to add this up. Premodern societies did not construct the national income accounts we would need in order to trace movements in aggregate or per capita income.

Economic Growth in China Under the Song

We reach the most likely case of real growth with the Song dynasty during the tenth through thirteenth centuries A.D., perhaps a little earlier under the late T'ang in the ninth century. Productive methods advanced further under the Song. There were innovations in ceramics and printing, plus inventions such as pound locks, sternpost rudders, and, most notable of all, a water-powered spinning machine for hemp and another coarse fiber called ramie. This did not just remain the brainwave of an inventor in an attic or a speculative drawing like those in the notebooks of Leonardo da Vinci in fifteenth-century Italy. The water-powered spinning machine was in widespread use. The mechanism compared favorably with anything in Europe up to the time of Diderot's encyclopedia in the eighteenth century.

In certain respects later Western engineers were inspired by long-standing Chinese precedents—iron bridges, for instance. At the turn of the eighteenth and nineteenth centuries, when Admiral John Schanck planned the *Lady Nelson* to explore the coasts of Australia, he borrowed the Chinese idea of keels that could be raised to permit sailing in shallow waters.

Beyond its novelties, the Song period saw a peak in ironmaking. Tools and the other producer goods that are better made of iron than of wood became cheaper than at other times in the history of China or anywhere else until the England of the late eighteenth century.

As far as we can tell, the Song period was a "flowering," when the economy as a whole became larger and more varied. More to the point, income per head probably rose—that is, the average person became better off. We cannot strictly be sure that average real incomes did rise—there are no national income accounts for such remote periods and no censuses to tell us among how many heads to divide the national income. The indirect evidence is, however, quite persuasive, especially because it refers to a period of three centuries (longer if the rise of incomes began under the T'ang) and because it turns up in descriptions by general historians who have no special interest in the topic of economic growth.

The indications come in three parts. First, there were widespread consumption gains, mentioned in reports of how people lived. The capital, Kaifeng, was full of fast-food shops; a range of mild luxuries were in popular use (such as pepper and tea, items uncommon or unknown in Europe until the British "Commercial Revolution" of the late seventeenth century). The state made persistent efforts to restrict the consumption of prestige items, intended to mark *social* status rather than vulgar wealth. For this purpose sumptuary laws were passed, but their frequent repetition suggests that little notice was actually being taken of them.

Second, there was the scale and novelty of activity in the realm of technology, already mentioned.

Third, there was structural change. A fraction of the population was moving out of primary activities, mainly farming, into secondary (manufacturing) and tertiary (service) occupations, where individual productivity is higher. This change means that agricultural productivity per worker had risen, releasing labor from the land. Perhaps that analysis is too neat: Although there was urbanization during the period (Kaifeng had a population of two million) and although there was a standing army of one million men, much of the release of labor from agriculture was really the release of labor time. A hidden structural change took place in which peasant families devoted more of their total labor to manufacturing petty goods for sale, remaining in the countryside and farming the remainder of the time. Peasants had always made in the home many of such consumer and domestic items as they could afford to use themselves. Now they specialized much more and made goods for sale. The specialization drove up productivity, too, by the division-of-labor effect—it is so much more efficient for a person or family to concentrate on doing one thing than to do a whole range of things.

What was the underlying cause of Song prosperity? Again, we can make three suggestions. First, a type of privatization had begun during the late T'ang period and continued during the Song. The government seems to have retreated from demanding taxes in the form of labor services to taking taxes in cash or kind and from taking almost all extra output to accepting a fixed share. Once the tax obligation was met, therefore, the farm operator could keep anything else produced, and this was an incentive to raise output. A market developed in land and labor. The reasonable assumption is that this development would have increased efficiency because, instead of being held on a kind of service tenure, land would be acquired by those who thought they could squeeze the most out of it. Labor would be employed on a similar basis and would move to where its earnings were highest. Factors of production—land, labor, and capital—became more mobile. The system became more flexible and productive. The reasons for a shift toward the market economy during the late T'ang are rather obscure, but the Song reaped the benefits.

Second, the Song dynasty appears to have responded with unusual creativity for any premodern regime in encouraging the freeing of the economy and taking only a *share* of the greater total revenue thus generated. The customary reflex of a regime faced, as was the Song, with an urgent need for resources to fight off aggressors was to seize whatever assets it could from whoever had them. This emergency behavior, exhibited throughout premodern times, was like drenching the economy with a bucket of cold water. Needless to say, the uncertainty and disincentives created by such short-term actions harmed things for a long time. The Song, however, seem to have understood that even a fixed share of tax revenue would go on getting bigger if the economy were growing. Faced with a need for resources to fend off threats from steppe invaders, the Song undertook an emergency marketization. They were able to hold off the threat for a long time, and although the Mongols under Genghis Khan did eventually overwhelm them, very few societies were ever able to defend themselves against land attack from that particular quarter. Meanwhile, the economy of Song China went on growing.

Third, there were at least two physical reasons why the economy under the Song did well. Population shifted substantially down to the delta lands, where there was no water problem and the warmer climate extended the growing season. These benefits were an unexpected bonus from what was in essence a retreat from northwesterly areas threatened by nomads from the steppes. Agricultural productivity seems to have risen a lot. In addition, the Song improved canal and river navigation. This effort was aimed at making the collection of tax rice easier, but it created "positive externalities" for merchants, who could use the waterways to transport rice and other commodities more cheaply. This second bonus was important given the high costs of carrying bulky goods overland before the invention of steam locomotives and railroads.

The Failure to Surpass the Song for Many Centuries

The Song achievement was rudely terminated by an invasion of the Mongols from the steppes. The Mongols were expanding in several directions from central Asia in the thirteenth century, and China was their biggest prize. They are said to have slaughtered one-third of the native Han Chinese population in the course of capturing the country. They contemplated exterminating the Chinese and putting the entire land down to grass, recreating a steppe homeland for themselves and their horses. Less genocidal policies prevailed, and the invaders imposed an imperial system of a familiar kind, co-opting a Chinese elite to carry out the administration and taxing the rice-growing peasants. Pasture would have been much less productive than rice-growing, and far fewer people could have been supported.

Within a century the Mongol Yuan dynasty was ruling over an elaborate, renewed economy of rice paddies, cities, and trade. This was the gigantic society described to westerners in the writings of Marco Polo. Although the Venetian may not really have visited China, instead piecing together the tales of Persian travelers who had done so, there is no doubt that the Chinese empire he described was the outstanding economy in the world. When rebels reestablished a native Chinese dynasty called the Ming (1368–1644), the empire continued in essentially the same form: centered on an emperor, staffed by a small tier of literate bureaucrats, and containing large cities, extensive trade, and much household or workshop manufacturing. Above all the system was founded on a rice-growing peasantry whose numbers continued to swell but whose social position was fixed.

This "traditional" China continued for centuries without much by way of further structural change. Internal upheavals, such as peasant rebellions, were not absent, but the basic form remained. For several centuries, until the nineteenth, the country was fundamentally undisturbed by foreigners. The best-known contact the Middle Kingdom had with the outside world came in the early fifteenth century with large-scale expeditions by fleets of junks. Admiral Cheng Ho carried whole shiploads of soldiers around many Asian shores and exacted "tribute" gifts for the emperor from what the Chinese thought of as less civilized peoples. Cheng Ho even brought back a giraffe from East Africa, but no real trade benefits followed from the expeditions. In 1430 the emperor stopped them. He was powerful enough for his word to be law.

Fifty years later, plans to restart the voyages were quashed. It was an ironic date for China to abandon maritime activity—1480, only sixteen years before the first European vessels, under the Portuguese Vasco da Gama, passed around the Cape of Good Hope at the foot of Africa and landed in Asia at Calicut, India. In the little kingdoms of Europe no single ruler existed who could have stopped the progress of the "discoveries"; the Pope did try to divide the outer world between Spain and Portugal, but other countries mounted expeditions anyway. Early in the sixteenth century the Portuguese reached China, and later that century they and the Dutch were active in Japan.

The Europeans had little direct effect on China. Ming China was in an isolationist mood. Its response to pirates from Japan, who were preying on its southern coast, was a scorched-earth policy. Villages were burned and people relocated inland to deny the Japanese bases, supplies, and loot. The Ming were able to withdraw from the sea and from maritime trade because Chinese agriculture was so productive. There was plenty of rich southern forest land belonging to neighboring tribal peoples that they could seize and bring into cultivation without venturing more riskily overseas. China thus colonized, but only next door. The empire went on doing so into the nineteenth century, first under the Ming and then under the following dynasty, the Qing-Manchu, which invaded China from steppe Manchuria in the mid-seventeenth century.

The Qing created an empire so similar to the one they had overrun that it is convenient to group the dynasties as the Ming-Qing state. The Qing took on a Chinese gloss. They were an inland people who easily acquired the attitudes of self-sufficiency and self-satisfaction that had typified the Ming. Although foreign trade was permitted from the late seventeenth century on, the Qing themselves were not interested in "outer barbarians" such as European missionaries and traders.

Nevertheless, the Europeans did have a major *indirect* impact. They quickly brought in crops they had discovered in the Americas. This was part of the "Columbian Exchange," in which the Europeans had acquired such food plants as white potatoes, sweet potatoes, and peanuts. These crops do not require irrigation. In China they made productive many upland areas too high to be brought under artificial irrigation for rice. The effective land area increased substantially, and food supplies did not act as a check on population growth. Oddly enough, what these novelties did was to reinforce the capacity of the agrarian state to go on expanding without forcing a change in its character. Given the southern lands to colonize and the new dryland crops, China could swell out, providing fresh land for its peasant families and fresh provinces for its young bureaucrats to rule. The ambitious were not frustrated and tempted into the sort of military rebellion so characteristic of less developed countries. Agrarian China, the Chinese empire, could go on expanding and consolidating as long as a fertile frontier remained.

From the thirteenth to nineteenth centuries the countries of Europe underwent real and continual economic growth. They began to invent and improve productive technologies. Eventually they industrialized. They spread out to found empires over much of the world, and although they did not really succeed in colonizing East Asia, they did in the nineteenth century shake to the core its apparently solid but actually brittle political systems. Change was the order of the day in Europe, including several transformations in occupational structure, waves of rising productivity, and, despite a sizeable increase of population, finally a persistent, widespread rise in real incomes.

The same cannot be said of Ming-Qing China, for all the promise of its origins, especially the preceding Song economic revolution. Chinese society swelled up and rumbled ominously within much the same political and economic framework. It put on fat, not muscle. The sheer physical room that was there, next door, into which the Ming and Qing could overflow goes some way toward explaining the apparent paradox of Chinese history: how a society that had been so productive and innovative so much earlier than Europe, on so much grander a scale, could ultimately be eclipsed by the Europeans. Yet there was a sadder paradox. The European achievement was more or less independent. Contrasting China with Europe (though irresistible, given what actually transpired in the nineteenth century between expansionist Europe and resistant East Asia in general) is not the main point. It is more pertinent to ask another question: Why did the Chinese economy, which experienced unprecedented growth in Song times, fail to surpass its *own* historical achievement during the following centuries?

Writers on Chinese history lead us to believe, as a working hypothesis, that income per head stagnated in Ming-Qing times. Clearly this possibility is unlikely in a strict sense. There will have been some fluctuations even at the level of the whole empire, just as there were political ups and downs. Older Western writers saw the fluctuations as canceling out, as mere "Cycles of Cathay" with no particular direction. It is as if there were hidden stabilizers and the students were assigned to find out what they were.

Over the next few pages we will review a number of the suggestions that have been made to account for the expansion without growth that seems to have characterized Ming-Qing China. With respect to one common argument, the answer almost certainly is not that the empire was so efficient that it was able to tax away any surplus, removing spare funds from merchants and peasants who might otherwise have invested them in productive ways. Truth to tell, there was a great deal of investment. Admittedly, merchants were under pressure to opt out of business and "buy degrees," i.e., buy scholar-bureaucrat certification so that they could take up the status of landed officials and collect their share of state revenue. But for families outside the charmed circle of administrators, wealth-getting remained attractive, perhaps for the very reason that it pointed the way up the narrow but intensely desirable route to social status. As some successful merchants moved up, other individuals took up trade and replaced those who were busy faking their family trees and moving on to higher things.

There had, of course, to be innumerable investment decisions simply in order for the existing economic system to replicate itself so that it could support a 500 percent increase in population between 1400 and 1900. This was no *stagnant* economy—it was demonstrating remarkable *extensive* growth. What it does not seem to have done was to expand fast enough to overtake the continual increase in population.

Levels of taxation were not high enough to have held back all prospects of a return to *intensive* growth on Song lines. There is a gray area in terms of the unknown share of revenue milked from the peasants by local scholar-gentry, the bureaucrats, but it was unlikely to have been dominating. The share of all tax revenues that filtered to the spider in the center of the web, the emperor in Beijing, was not large enough to have permitted the central government to reconstruct such a vast agricultural economy—even had such an improbable, modern-sounding goal crossed its collective mind. This issue should be thought of in terms of the massive investment that would have been needed to bring about economic development. Enormous personal wealth in the hands of the emperor and his court could easily have coexisted with insufficient funds for this huge task. China was so large that a tiny percentage of its resources would have made one outrageously rich.

In reality the imperial system was a sort of protection racket, a ritualized arrangement whereby the elite lived off the people. In this system one role of the emperor was to act as broker, legitimizing the arrangements, concealing their function behind ceremonial and fancy dress, presiding over a mechanism for levying taxes and sharing them out, ensuring that individual administrators did not get too greedy. The amazing features are how long the system lasted and that it did not fly apart for good in regional strife.

The function of a state is defense and the provision of justice, to which may be added in the case of premodern China a very important "insurance" function of guarding against famine by organizing grain stores. Beyond these primary activities the Ming-Qing state scarcely went. There was rather little provision of a public infrastructure that could have helped or sparked development. Some authorities think the state periodically withdrew even from some of its simple functions and left their provision in private hands. This particular "privatization" sounds very modern and it is made to sound a deliberate way of deregulating the economy. If so, the moves were not sustained long enough to jump-start the private sector and get it back to a vigorous growth path.

Among other explanations offered of the stasis of Ming-Qing China, we can discount the idea that the Confucian values of the society were hostile to economic growth. Western travelers in the nineteenth and early twentieth centuries sometimes thought that Confucianism was inimical to economic vigor, but they were largely reacting to the gap between the industrial productivity of their own economies at that particular phase of history and the difficulties besetting late Qing China. If we are to think critically about these matters, it is best to have a range of historical periods available as examples; otherwise it is too easy to take for granted the relative positions of economies at the moment of any one comparison.

Some writers now think of Confucianism, or at any rate up-to-the-minute post-Confucianism, quite the other way. They see it as exceptionally favorable to growth because they regard its values of hard work, thrift, and concern for education as the root of modern growth in East Asia generally. In reality Confucianism and other value systems are not fixed and unchanging. They are as likely to be altered by change in the economy as economic change is likely to be produced by them. General cultural explanations cannot account for differences in performance from region to region or from one period to the next. The Song had been Confucian, too, and during their rule scholars had found it acceptable to draw a more flexible message out of the ancient texts. A similar rewriting was attempted towards the end of the nineteenth century, when growth was once more the goal. Although values are important and may hang over from one period to the next, they are not independent of other changes and should not be thought of as a bedrock on which everything else has to settle.

Another common explanation offered for the Ming-Qing stasis is that China failed to have a scientific revolution of the kind Europe had in the late seventeenth century. This observation is not quite to the point. To recover its Song vigor, the

investment

country need not have made intellectual advances of a completely unprecedented kind. In any case, even during the eighteenth-century industrialization of Britain, which is the comparison most writers have in mind, there was only a weak connection with scientific thought. British artisans with little or no formal abstract scientific knowledge made many of the inventions. Chinese artisans were very capable. They had made the water-powered spinning machine. They succeeded in reproducing the technology of British warships about 1840. Had the right incentives prevailed, there is no reason to suppose that they could not have constructed early industrial equipment.

In China's case the lack of appropriate incentives is certainly something to explain. The heights of Song iron output per head were not reached again in Ming-Qing times. Most startling, the water-powered spinning machines were actually given up, and textile production went back to handicraft methods. But these changes had to do with what happened to investment, not to high science. Furthermore, although technical change slowed down, it did not come to a complete stop. Despite what happened to the spinning machine, there were applications of water power to papermaking in 1570, sawmilling in 1627, and silk-winding in 1780. One interpretation is that we are partly seeing an illusion: Early modern Europe had started to change faster than the rest of the world—faster than anywhere had in the whole of history—and this created the false impression that civilizations such as China's had halted or were going backwards.

Commoner still is the explanation that blames China's considerable population growth for its slide into "backwardness." The rise in the number of people from about 75 million in 1400 to 450 million in 1900 was definitely huge by premodern standards. Attributing all sorts of ills to excessive rates of Third World population growth, enormous total numbers of inhabitants, or high densities of population (it is not always clear which is being blamed) was especially fashionable during the 1960s and 1970s. Alarmism makes good copy.

Yet, as with many of the arguments about Confucian culture, an extreme fixity of human institutions is actually being implied here, as if people cannot change their behavior given the incentive to do so. Natural scientists in particular are prone to argue that the exponential growth in the number of fruit flies in test tubes shows what is happening to the number of people on earth, not seeing that people are better able than fruit flies to adjust their family sizes to circumstances. (That they do not always want to do so and may be slow about it creates the fine grain of real history and current affairs; there are plenty of problems for us all there. But we are talking here about the underlying relationships and tendencies.)

Far from reversing economic growth, under some circumstances an increase of population may spur it. Professional demographers have become less concerned about the "population bomb," noting that larger numbers mean larger markets and (on simple assumptions about a normal distribution of intelligence in any population) more potential geniuses to help solve humanity's problems. Rather

Politics & institutions most important

than being the *cause* of poverty, Ming-Qing population growth may have been the *result* of too little economic growth. At least it offered the family more hands to work.

In addition, we may note that the population did not merely trend upward during Ming-Qing times; it fluctuated a lot. In the seventeenth century the total population fell a very long way below the sixteenth-century peak, recovering during the eighteenth century. If we put the total on base 100 in the year 1393, for which there is an estimate, it had risen to 328 by 1592 but was down to 114 by 1657. By 1776 the index number was back up to 439, but the intervening movement had obviously been a roller coaster. A lot of land had been emptied for the taking in the seventeenth century, yet historians of China do not emphasize any strong recovery of average incomes. If such strong population movements did not produce a big effect on incomes or spark a renewed search for labor-saving methods (such as bringing back the water-spinning machine), population does not seem to have been a major determining factor in economic life after all.

Politics and institutions are more likely influences on the economy. The feat of the Chinese in coping with the great population growth of Ming-Qing times and the myriad investment decisions required merely to keep a premodern economy expanding on such a scale was not trivial. China's institutions were not dead. We may reasonably suspect that they were adequate for the task of expansion, which meant replicating the same type of system, but were not up to re-creating an economy growing as it had under the Song, during the later Yuan period, and even during the phase of recovery after the Ming seized power. This "limited adequacy" appears to be the crux of Ming-Qing developmental history.

One respect in which the imperial government was active and effective was in minimizing the impact of the famines to which frequent floods and droughts made China vulnerable. Building on a system that had been developed in Song times, the Ming-Qing state improved the network of "ever-normal" granaries. The principle involved was to even out year-to-year fluctuations in the availability of food. Instead of permitting the peasants to gorge the excess after the better harvests, the government insisted that the stores be topped up. They were there to be opened in bad years. This system of social insurance was on a bigger scale and by all reports more effective than the efforts at containing famines made by governments in Europe. The system was at its height during the eighteenth century under the commanding Ch'ien Lung emperor, at a time when China was buoyant and expanding its sway over neighboring regions. This, however, was a stabilizing function, not one driving for growth.

Government was not very active in productive affairs. We now know that many of the large reclamation projects that, so it was once argued, required coordination by the central state were in reality organized by local gentry on behalf of peasant clients for a fee. By and large the state was content to preside over the whole economic system, over society and the polity, and take in revenue for the purposes of consumption by the elite and the imperial court. Little was provided in the way of infrastructure or services. Notably, there was no independent legal system, no protection for valuables carried over the roads, no policemen to guard the standing crops against people sneaking out at night and helping themselves to part of the harvest. Villagers had to form their own associations to guard the crops.

Private substitutes for certain actions we would nowadays expect of a government were not ineffective. Chinese merchants belonged to the native place association appropriate to their original home, and producers belonged to the appropriate trade guild. These bodies looked after their members' interests and largely determined with whom they would have business dealings. Sanctioned by government as alternatives to a large civil service, the guilds could impose severe penalties up to actual execution for cheats. In the growing economies of Europe, the opportunities of doing more business meant that the guilds were bypassed, and no doubt this would have happened in China had the economy grown strongly there, too. As it was, guild restrictiveness probably had some effect in curbing competition by ambitious members, preventing them from enlarging their firms and taking business away from their fellow members. It is doubtful whether this was a prime limitation on growth.

There were formal courts of law, but they lacked systematic procedures involving such nuisances as real evidence. Contracts were not readily enforceable. The informal and capricious system (magistrates could have accusers and accused beaten in court to extract confessions) worked astonishingly well on a day-to-day basis. The economy could not have expanded otherwise. The chances are that together with a sleepy government, the absence of contract law and other features of a secure environment for commerce tended nevertheless to limit the scope of economic activity. Business dealings tended to be face-to-face or confined to groups with which the merchants or artisans were already affiliated for nonbusiness reasons. At the margin the market may have been unable to acquire sufficient momentum of its own to put the economy back on a path of real growth. In the end, then, the most likely explanation of the Ming-Qing experience of "limited adequacy" is that the society could reduce transaction costs only so far, not far enough to put the economy on a course for sustained *intensive* growth. China's expansion was impressive, but high transaction costs prevented it from tipping over into growth of that kind.

Premodern Japan

Today, Japan's economy looms larger than any other in East Asia. Among Pacific Rim competitors, only California, if we treat it as a separate system, comes close.

Japan's society is much older than that of young, modern California, but its present prominence is much newer.

Japan easily absorbed the principles of Confucianism and of Chinese administration, government, philosophy, and culture. Japan also adopted the Chinese form of writing. In the thirteenth century invasions by China (under Mongol rule) and Korea were attempted. When the last of these was beaten off in 1281, Japan adopted a policy of isolation in an attempt to develop and strengthen its own culture and national identity. What had saved Japan from invasion was a giant typhoon that wrecked the Mongol fleet. This divine wind, or *kamikaze*, became Japan's symbol of the need for personal sacrifice for the sake of the nation.

Japan's economic life during the period known to the West as the Middle Ages is obscure, but from late Heian times, around A.D. 1050, it seems to have become quite active. This surge has been attributed to a reduction in the epidemic shocks that had repeatedly hit population, output, and the tax base. Eventually enough resistance was built up for smallpox and measles to become endemic instead of epidemic. After the eleventh century, then, population growth was less interrupted than it had been. Shifting cultivation could be replaced and better technologies of irrigated rice cultivation learned: bigger ponds, more iron tools, water wheels. The subsequent growth may be seen from the increase in population—from 5 million in the eleventh century to 10 million by 1300 and 18 million by 1600—as well as from the increase in the extent of rice paddy (arable) land, which (indexed at 100 units in 1450) had risen from 91 in 930 to 173 by 1600.

Despite the fact that emperors ruled, for a long time economic life was localized. The centralized state had a hard time establishing itself (on Chinese models) in Japan, being restricted before the late Heian period by the low productivity of agriculture and being subject after it to conflicts. During the sixteenth century the provincial lords, called *daimyo*, fought violent civil wars. The ultimate victory of the Tokugawa in these clan struggles was what brought that family to power. Its absolute determination to hold on to power, not to be ousted in turn, explains many of the features of the Tokugawa period, which lasted from 1600–1868.

Despite the civil wars of the sixteenth century, the importance of securing supplies caused the areas of paddy to continue to grow; there was a skillful armaments industry exporting swords to Southeast Asia, and other signs of energy were evident. The economies of the individual *daimyo* thus developed under the stimulus of war and the need to prepare for it. But the lordships were separate. A major gain was accordingly reaped when the Tokugawa took over and unified the country, making it a single market. Not only did they bring about unification and an end to the conflicts, but early in the seventeenth century they went further, dissolving some conservative guilds of producers (who would have restricted output in the interests of their own members) and throwing down toll gates, which made it costly to do business between one province, or *han*, and the next.

> shipping
> & trade

In the larger national market, economic distributions could realign themselves as far as the poor roads and limited transportation methods of the period allowed. However, Japan is an archipelago, and much of its land abuts the sea. With the new prospect of interregional trade, there was an incentive to improve shipping. The Japanese invented what was for the time a large, specialized, unarmed cargo ship, the *bezaisen*, or *sengokubune*, a development not unlike that of the *fluit* ship, which had appeared just a little earlier far away in Europe, in the rising economy of the Netherlands.

Now that the opportunity had arisen, some *han* began to buy elsewhere part of the basic foodstuff, rice. Some trade in goods can be traced back in many societies into distant prehistory, but it is always a watershed when regions or countries start to rely on "foreign" sources of staple foods. It implies that people think the level of commercial risk has fallen.

To pay for purchased food, certain *han* began to expand the production of cloth for sale or, in some coastal areas, of salt, the former being a major product anywhere in the world where manufacturing had started, the latter being indispensable for preserving food before the invention of refrigeration in the late nineteenth century. Tokugawa Japan benefited early from the reallocations of production that followed the unification of the market. Different regions were able to specialize and trade on their comparative advantage—that is, to produce the goods for which the payoff was greatest, not necessarily what they did best in absolute terms. (Someone else might have done better absolutely; the trick is to work where the gap between you and other producers is most in your favor.)

No given *han* needed any longer to produce the entire range of commodities it consumed. Output rose and resources were increasingly devoted to crops other than staple foods. The population grew during the first half of the Tokugawa period, to about 1720, after which it stabilized. Japan developed a varied, stylish economy, full of clever devices and clever designing, though no machines.

With output probably still growing, the slowdown or standstill in population growth meant that average incomes could go on increasing: Real economic growth was taking place, though in late Tokugawa times it may have begun to evaporate. In any case, this was a premodern economy; we are speaking of slight gains by modern, industrial standards. Furthermore, the gains in premodern times are partly hidden by greater yearly fluctuations than developed economies usually suffer. There were no chemical industries to make artificial fertilizers or pesticides. Yields were not secure enough to prevent bad weather or pests from reducing the harvest below adequate levels from time to time. *Average* yields could be rising overall while year-to-year fluctuations about the mean could still plunge the country into occasional famine. Late Tokugawa Japan did experience some very severe famines.

The Tokugawa replaced the old imperial capital, Kyoto, with a capital of their own. They chose the tiny fishing village called Edo, which today is Tokyo. Within a hundred years it had become that rarity in the premodern world, a "millionaire" city—i.e., with one million inhabitants. The construction and subsequent growth of a city of that size created a great demand for goods and services of all kinds. Edo remained an active market where the inhabitants, real city slickers, boasted of spending each day's wages before breakfast the next day. This was a great city, yet built by a secluded society.

Japan's self-isolation was, however, never absolute. Contacts had been fairly wide, extending to Japanese settlements in the Philippines, for instance. But from the start of the seventeenth century to the mid-nineteenth century, the government deliberately tightened the isolation. It ejected the Portuguese traders and missionaries who had arrived early in the sixteenth century, as well as almost all the Dutch. A handful of Dutch and Chinese merchants were permitted to live on an island at Nagasaki, a tiny window on the remainder of the world as far as Japan was concerned.

Otherwise the Japan of this period, the time of the Tokugawa shoguns, kept Europeans out. The isolationist policy was so sternly administered that one reason Western nations wanted to open Japan to the world in the 1850s was that Japan would not even return shipwrecked seamen. The motive for the original expulsions and the subsequent isolation was state security. The Tokugawa were determined that they would not be overthrown in turn. They soon became keen to avoid the disturbances that conflicting Christian missionaries seemed to bring about.

To further their overriding goal of securing internal order, the Tokugawa reorganized the political geography of Japan by settling the *daimyo* in approximately concentric rings centered on the new capital. Relatives and close supporters came first—they were settled to administer the better land nearby. They formed protective belts near Edo. Former enemies of the Tokugawa clan were assigned to *han* much further away, on land less suitable for rice-growing, in the mountains away in the west. They were the "outer *daimyo*."

The matter was not left at that point. Like other domineering but slightly insecure rulers elsewhere in the world, the Tokugawa wanted to restrict the chances of disgruntled *daimyo* building up enough resources to fund uprisings. They obliged the *daimyo* to live regularly for long periods in Edo, where they had to build palaces and live in sufficient style to put them in debt. This was the *sankin kotei*, or alternate residence system. It forced the *daimyo* to spend their land rents in the city and in that way added to demand. The lords could be watched and spied on in the city too, especially the outer *daimyo*, who were thought to be less loyal. Since the outer *daimyo* urgently needed cash during Tokugawa times to maintain the lifestyle associated with *sankin kotei*, they encouraged among their peasants specialist crop-growing and petty manufacturing as alternatives to rice-growing. Paddy field construction was in any case difficult in many of the more remote mountainous areas.

After about midway during the Tokugawa period the regime became more relaxed and probably weaker relative to the other lords, though it did not give that appearance. Having set tax levels based on the capacity of each district to produce rice in the seventeenth century, the regime was not able to raise the level of taxation. As a result, the outer *han,* whose economies were improved under the supervision of their lords, became steadily better off relative to the old, established areas, such as those in and around the Plain of Japan.

Left unchanged, the political and tax distributions insisted on by the Tokugawa fused with changing economic distributions to bring about their undoing. The new, distant areas under the control of *daimyo* families, which were the hereditary enemies of the Tokugawa, were the ones that were becoming rich. As it turned out, the Tokugawa had correctly identified the enemies of their house at the time they established *sankin kotei.* Two and a half centuries later, after Commodore Matthew Perry had opened up Japan, some outer *daimyo* were prominent among those who overthrew the Tokugawa shogunate and brought back the emperor.

A common problem in developing countries is how to demobilize the military, especially if a regime has ridden to power on the back of an army. Getting off the tiger without being eaten is tricky, and the Tokugawa faced the additional difficulty that the Japanese military formed a warrior caste, the samurai. The Tokugawa succeeded in buying out this caste. The samurai were settled in castle towns and permitted to keep up martial appearances and standing, but in reality were made pensioners, paid by a rice tax levied on the peasantry. Provided that the peasants could respond to the challenge of producing even more food, which they were exceptionally able to do, the samurai gained purchasing power and were pacified.

Security considerations, then, ruled the Tokugawa. An unintended consequence of the policies they undertook to dig themselves in as the rulers of Japan (they kept the imperial line to carry on ceremonial functions) was the expansion of market demand. It is one thing to argue, however, that there were numerous reasons why the market should have expanded, quite another to explain why the Japanese peasantry responded so energetically. The burden of production certainly fell on peasant shoulders; we can make some suggestions as to why they were responsive, but it has to be admitted that the reasons are not as clear as the changes on the demand side.

Peasant responsiveness seems to have been increased by the breaking up of the old communal or clan system of farming and the centering of production on the family farm. In principle, this restructuring helped reduce both the monitoring problem and the free-rider problem. That is, once the unit of production became the individual family, the head of the household could oversee the work more closely and ensure that everyone worked his or her hardest. And once individuals could tell rather better that making an effort paid them and that they could capture the full return for their labors rather than seeing it shared under the communal system, there was a greater incentive for them to work flat out. Once the incentives existed to keep people working at rural domestic manufacturing, these trades grew considerably. Cottage industries usefully occupied time that might otherwise have been frittered away when there was no field work.

Unlike many peasantries, the Japanese was or became surprisingly literate. Instruction in the temples helped. A number of peasants wrote books on how to farm, which even more peasants read. Forty percent of Japanese males in 1840 were literate and, more surprising in such a society, so were 15 percent of the females, a proportion not reached in every Third World country today.

To organize the supply of food, building materials, and other items for the towns, as well as to provide finance, the merchant class expanded. All told, it might not be impossible to present the economic history of Tokugawa Japan as a real success story. Granted, specialists in its history are inclined to think the regime stalled rather badly, yet there can be little doubt that this was an exceptionally productive and, for much of the time, a genuinely growing economy.

Why, then, should Japan not have gone on to even greater heights of creativity and sustained high growth rates? Two considerations that may be mentioned are consequences of the isolationist policy, this time negative ones. First, Japan did not interact with other states. Unlike the countries in the European states-system, Japan did not receive the stimulus of competition. Second, the country was almost entirely dependent on its domestic market. Isolation did away with any hope of adding from a foreign trade sector an increment of demand to that market. Being a set of islands meant that its economy could not creep out like an ink blot, as China's did. Behind the calculated standoffishness of the isolationist policy, Japanese technology outside farming ceased to advance much.

When in the 1850s Commodore Perry of the United States and his "Black Ships" arrived to present the Japanese with a request, backed by force, to open their country, the land whose people had once been able to improve on European muskets found that it had done little in the interval since the sixteenth century to preserve its security. Japan was a bustling, commercial economy, but it was essentially archaic, unable to defend itself against the European intrusion.

4

The European Intrusion:
A Spanish Lake

[I]n the last resort the warranty for what seems crazy over-regulation by the Crown may be that without such legislative promulgation of an ideally overriding law, ever ill-enforced but ever-asserted, the Indies might have split up into independent dominions and lordships, internally autocratic and probably in a state of anarchy between themselves.

—Oskar Spate, on the Spanish empire

In this chapter we trace the impact of the European intrusion into the Pacific from the sixteenth to the nineteenth century. First we consider the general nature of the intruders and their interest in the Pacific, then focus on the dominant European power in the area, Spain, and its American empire.

The Nature of the Intrusion

In the course of almost five centuries, Europeans played a very significant role in refashioning the Pacific Rim, radically changing the culture of native societies, inserting new settlements and redistributing old populations, and drastically modifying existing ecological systems. On occasion the influence was intended and the changes were deliberate; at other times the results of the European intrusion were inadvertent, and for a long period many of its main elements were unrecognized. Although the timing and extent of direct or indirect influence has varied, its impact has been all-pervasive.

Before the so-called Age of Discoveries there had already been a continuing interaction between Europe and Asia, largely across the broad Eurasian land mass. The highly crafted products of the Orient—high-value textiles such as silk, fine porcelain, beautifully wrought lacquer or jade work and more exotic products such as spices or tea—flowed westward, and, in the absence of a significant demand in Asia for European products, precious metals, notably specie such as gold and silver, moved in the opposite direction. More intermittently, but with more long-run significance, new technologies and diseases accompanied the traders, again more often moving westward. However, the connection between the Pacific Rim and Europe was mostly indirect, carried out through intermediaries, and fragile. Indeed, there had been no contact across the Americas, whose presence, discovered by the Vikings, had been largely forgotten in Europe and was unknown in Asia. The direct European intrusion into Asia by sea was to change the whole nature of the relationship.

Initially, given the limitations of the prevailing technology of transport and communications, remoteness from Europe protected the Pacific Rim from significant change. The lack of any precontact integration of the different regions of this vast area, together with the lightness of the European touch early in the contact period, helped minimize the impact. The European exploration and demarcation of the Pacific Rim was to be, at least relative to the discovery of the Atlantic or Indian ocean surroundings, a very long, drawn-out process, stretching over a period of about 300 years. The pace of change resulting from the movement of the European frontiers of exploration, political control, and settlement steadily gained momentum, sustaining itself even after the closing of these frontiers and the halting and reversal of the extension of the direct European presence. For the first four centuries of the European intrusion there was to be no real integration of the Pacific, economic or political. Although the Pacific Rim came to share a common relationship to the European world, this conjunction necessarily involved an outward- rather than inward-looking orientation. Furthermore, it was a fragmented orientation, since different European powers established influence over separate parts of the Rim and often sought, at least initially, to monopolize economic relations with their particular areas of influence or control. Not even the Spanish, with the most extensive early interests and the East-West link of the annual Manila galleon, managed genuinely to integrate the whole ocean.

Two comments help to place the intrusion in a long-term perspective. The direct intrusion ought to be placed in the context of a two-way traffic. First, Europe received as well as gave, borrowed as well as lent. According to A. R. Hall, one of the main elements in Europe's rise was its ability to assimilate inventions, ideas, and institutions from Asia, in particular China. He says about Europe, "No other civilization seems to have been so widespread in its roots, so eclectic in its borrowings, so ready to embrace the exotic. Most have tended (like the Chinese) to be strongly xenophobic, and to have resisted confession of inferiority in any respect, technological or otherwise."

Second, since some parts of the Pacific, notably New Zealand, were settled as little as 500 years before the arrival of the Europeans, the European intrusion represented only one further stage in a continuing movement of people into the area.

During the Age of Discoveries, the Europeans for the first time entered the Pacific by sea, displaying a newfound superiority in the type of ships used, in techniques of navigation, and, most significantly, in gunnery. The entry from both the Atlantic and Indian oceans was almost simultaneous, with a slight precedence to the Portuguese in the East Indies over the Spanish along the American coast. The motives for entry were no different from those elsewhere—in, for example, Africa or the Americas: The Europeans sought knowledge, power, profit, and souls, in a mix varying over time and among nations. On the one hand they sought to observe, sketch, preserve, and classify in a restless quest to understand and perhaps ultimately control the forces of nature. On the other they imposed themselves on native populations, organizing and reorganizing, exploiting resources and labor, and converting the heathen.

The enterprise engaged in was therefore a multifarious one. Like conquerors from all successful civilizations "on the rise," the European intruders usually assumed their innate superiority over technically inferior people and in this differed in no way from the rulers of the Pacific area, whether the people of the Middle Kingdom (China) or the Aztecs and Incas. Despite the initial reluctance of the Asian peoples to accept the Europeans' material products, the interlopers assumed a superiority of both visible and invisible baggage, of religious, political, and economic ideas as well as material culture. Further, they often assumed a self-consciously progressive role of bringing civilization to the underprivileged, although this attitude was by no means universal. There were also those, such as the Spanish cleric Bartolomé de Las Casas and his supporters, who deliberately sought to protect, study, and record for posterity the rich, alien native cultures.

When the Portuguese Magellan in the service of Spain began the first circumnavigation of the globe in 1518, Europe was already in the midst of one of its expansionary phases, with total population and individual economies growing rapidly, particularly on its western edge, fronting the Atlantic. In the west of Europe there was to be no major reversal of this process of expansion, only temporary setbacks and longer periods of slower growth. Spain and Portugal led the way in two important aspects of this expansion: in the commercialization of their domestic economies and in the relentless probing and exploration of the world outside Europe.

In a quest to establish direct contacts with India and the East by rounding the African continent, Portugal had been exploring the west coast of Africa for most of the fifteenth century. Spain—behind its Iberian neighbor in the race to open up the new trade routes—stumbled onto the Americas by accident with Christopher Columbus's arrival in October 1492. Portugal staked a claim to a trading monopoly with the territories discovered by its explorers; Spain reacted by demanding monopoly control over the American continent. Pope Alexander VI sought to mediate between the rival interests. In 1493 he traced an imaginary line along the meridian, passing 100 leagues (300 miles) to the west of the Cape Verde islands (themselves at 25° N 15° W, 500 miles west of Dakar), slicing the world into two equal portions. To Portugal the Pope allocated lands east of the meridian and to Spain the lands to the west. It seemed inconceivable to the three parties involved in these negotiations that other nations might not respect the agreement. After some further bickering both parties finally signed the Tordesillas Treaty on June 7, 1494, whereby they agreed to shift the demarcation line to a position 370 leagues (1,100 miles) to the west of the Cape Verde islands.

Such a monopoly could never be fully protected against the infringement of other powers. Europe was made up of a growing number of nation-states vying for political preeminence and economic dominance. There was a fierce and aggressive competition between these states, a competition magnified by the divisions created within Europe by the Protestant Reformation and the Counter-Reformation. Within a largely benign physical environment, relatively free of major capital-destructive shocks and reasonably well endowed with resources, the Europeans walked a tightrope between the anarchy of excessive political fragmentation and the stifling oppression of a highly centralized empire, the latter being unavailingly aspired to, for example, by Philip II of Spain in the second half of the sixteenth century. Competition frequently resulted in armed conflict, both within and outside Europe, such conflict often breaking out within the Pacific Basin itself.

The age of mercantilism saw these states—initially Spain and Portugal, later Holland, France, and England—compete to establish control over the potentially lucrative trades between Europe and the rest of the world, notably the spice trade. In the early seventeenth century the Dutch, on the crest of a rising commercial wave, displaced the Portuguese from the East Indies and the lucrative spice trade, then held on against later pressure from the British. Subsequently, regulated companies such as the Dutch East Indies Company were set up to take advantage of trade possibilities and to promote both private and national interests in environments of high risk.

The gains to be made from trade were large given the complementarity in factor endowment between the European metropolis, well supplied with capital and labor, and the periphery, including the Pacific Rim, better endowed than Europe in land and resources. The "ghost acres"—land newly acquired, held, and exploited over the next few centuries and equivalent to extra territory in Europe—became an object of acquisitive desire.

In practice, nobody was completely clear where the Pope's dividing line was located, but the Pacific was without doubt defined as a Spanish lake. While the

Spanish established themselves in the Americas and the Philippines, the Portuguese gained a foothold on the eastern boundary of Asia, notably in the East Indies, possibly even exploring the coastline of New South Wales and Victoria in Australia, although secretly. Spain remained the dominant European power in the area, retaining control of the whole American coastline until the early, and the Philippines until the late, nineteenth century. Portuguese activity in the Pacific remained slight, being largely limited to Macau in China and to the East Indies.

What was the nature of the intruders and what was their lasting legacy to the Pacific Rim? Such questions can only be answered after defining what the Europeans shared in common. It is difficult to make such a definition since the heterogeneity of the newcomers, which has been neglected, is so striking. Yet there was a core of shared characteristics: common values often associated with Christianity; self-conscious participation in a common enterprise motivated by profit, power, and proselytization; similarities of institutional and behavioral background; and, perhaps more important, a common pool of knowledge and resources arising from increasingly frequent interaction within Europe itself.

The two major institutional legs of the European economic advance were the nation-state and the market, complementary institutions that emerged simultaneously, if haltingly and unevenly, particularly during the sixteenth and seventeenth centuries. Where economic development was most significant, governments and commodity and factor markets interacted positively. The competitive pluralism of Europe, which underpinned conflict within the Pacific as elsewhere, also promoted innovation, imitation, and adaptation in a whole series of different realms, not least the economic. Already by the time of the Discoveries, at least in western Europe, there had begun the long, unsteady, economic ascent widely referred to as the Industrial Revolution (but better characterized as the "Great Economic Evolution" since it was neither wholly industrial nor compressed into a period short enough to be described as genuinely revolutionary). Change was becoming an integral part of the European world, albeit at very different rates in different regions at different times, cumulatively transforming European society in a manner that, judged by its eventual results, was truly unprecedented. The focus of the most rapid change moved from the Iberian Peninsula, first to the Low Countries and then to Britain and France. The transference of technical or economic hegemony was reflected in nations' ability to penetrate new areas successfully, notably in the Pacific.

The main characteristic of the European intrusion was therefore heterogeneity, a heterogeneity of source country, of timing, of route of intrusion, of period of stay, of nature of colony. At different times the Spanish, the Portuguese, the Dutch, the British, the French, the Germans, the Russians, and even those neo-Europeans—the Americans, Canadians, and Australians—stamped their influence on the area. The period of expanding European presence stretched from Vasco Nuñez de Balboa's first view of the Pacific in 1513 right through to the

United States's seizure of the Philippines in 1898 and its detachment of Panama from Colombia shortly before the First World War in order to secure control of the Panama Canal. Initially intrusion was by sea, but for some the Pacific represented the back door of newly settled societies, only established after a long transcontinental movement. The easiest crossing was made by the Spanish in Central America. Elsewhere the crossing of large continental land masses was slower. The Russians arrived on the Pacific in the mid-seventeenth century and over the next two centuries established a significant presence. The British in Canada and explorers from the United States further south did not reach the Pacific Coast until the early nineteenth century but then built up strongholds in a relatively short time.

Colonies of Sojourn and Colonies of Settlement

On parts of the Pacific Rim Europeans settled only rather briefly; they sojourned. Elsewhere they settled permanently, creating in the process what Crosby has called neo-Europes. The permanent colonies of settlement came to occupy a significant portion of the Rim. Together Chile, the United States, Canada, the far east of Russia, and Australia and New Zealand accounted for an enormous area. Other Latin American nations are largely of native and mestizo character, bearing the imprint of both precontact and European populations. These represent an intermediate case. European settlement began early in the Spanish Americas but on a minuscule scale. It accelerated at the end of the eighteenth century but reached substantial levels only in the nineteenth century.

Elsewhere the Europeans established political control for only a brief period, although their impact on political, social, and economic life was dramatic. Temporary European control was concentrated chiefly on or near coasts in Southeast Asia, where Indochina, Malaysia and Singapore, the Philippines, and the East Indies eventually came under French, British, Spanish, and Dutch rule, respectively, for varying periods of time. Some colonies were of long duration, such as the Philippines or the East Indies; others were a product of the much later imperial competition of the second half of the nineteenth century.

It is intriguing to note the contrasting powers of resistance to the European political intrusion in different parts of the Rim. In the Americas the political organization of the Incas collapsed and that of the Aztecs crumbled before the determined onslaught of a handful of Spaniards. In the sixteenth century, European expansion terminated any independent experiment at civilization in the New World. A long line of societies of some size and complexity had risen and fallen for thousands of years in Mesoamerica and the Andes, culminating in the rise of the Inca and Aztec empires at the end of what was in European terms the Middle Ages.

Other societies, largely located in East Asia, managed to resist direct intrusion completely. Japan is the most notable example, although the interior of China represents another largely no-go area. However, the Europeans ultimately ended the self-imposed isolation from outside influence that had characterized these societies. European influence was experienced in two waves—an initial early contact during the sixteenth century, which resulted in self-imposed isolation, and a later, more brutal intrusion in the nineteenth.

What determined the location of colonies of settlement and of sojourn? Indeed, what made possible successful resistance? Two major elements deterred European settlement—physical checks, particularly harsh or unfamiliar climatic conditions (often associated with a virulent disease environment), and/or political checks in already densely populated areas with long-established civilizations having some potential for economic development and a significant immunity to Eurasian diseases. Where native population density was low and climatic conditions acceptable to the Europeans, they were quick to settle, once an improvement in transportation and communication linked these areas to the rest of the world. A good endowment of easily exploited and valuable resources such as gold helped.

The area regarded with the most dread by the Europeans lay in the tropics, particularly in the heavily forested tropics. Here was a pool of lethal fevers that raised death rates among European soldiers well above levels elsewhere, such as in Australasia. Improvements in hygiene and medicine made possible a dramatic fall in mortality among soldiers during the nineteenth century and allowed a later occupation of such areas by white settlers, as the experience of the colony of Queensland in Australia shows. However, disease clearly influenced the pattern of settlement.

The most-favored areas were those blessed with the Mediterranean type of climate, characterized by relatively short winters, generally warm and wet, and long, hot, dry summers. Symmetry dictated the location of such areas at the same latitudes in both the Northern and Southern hemispheres, between 30 and 40 degrees, and on either side of the Pacific—that is, in southern Australia and across the Pacific in central Chile and to the north in California, but not on the Asian side. Areas adjacent to the Mediterranean climatic zone also shared climatic characteristics similar to parts of Europe, temperate and moist.

On the northwest shore of the Pacific there was no such area because of the influence of the broad Eurasian landmass and its central mountain system, which created a large monsoonal area stretching from Japan to northern Australia. This climatic factor tended to inhibit European penetration. Moreover, in this area major civilizations had long since developed, well adapted to the environment and resistant to takeover because they had been exposed by ancient contact to the Eurasian disease pool.

There were precontact civilizations in the Americas, too, but they did not develop as far or resist European intrusion as well as the Chinese civilization. What was it that made the pre-Columbian civilizations of the Americas so brittle? Was it mainly the vulnerability to diseases, from which they had been shielded for thousands of years by virtue of their isolation from the Eurasian landmass? Recent literature seems to suggest so. However, the Aztec and Inca empires were probably vulnerable in other ways. A discussion of the pre-Columbian empires will help to contrast their low resistance to the European intrusion with the much more successful resistance in some Asian civilizations and permit us to analyze the forces that promoted or checked the process of early economic development in general.

Native American civilizations built cities, great temple mounds, and stone monuments; they grew maize on the reclaimed margins of lakes and along hillside terraces; they wove textiles; they had a well-developed hierarchy of classes; and they created an outstanding body of astronomical and mathematical knowledge. Situated in isolation in the New World, they offer "controls" on theories based solely on the experience of the Old World, including Asia. What we mainly want to know about them is why they did not become larger and spread out over more of the Americas; why they did not develop further complexity in the way China (as well as South and West Asian, Near Eastern, and ultimately European societies) did; and why they lacked a capacity to resist outside intrusion, as did Japan. They were of course responsible for great economic achievements. There was the possibility of further development on both sides of the Pacific, though as things turned out it went much further, much earlier, in China.

Neither the Inca nor the Aztec empire lay in easy territory. Both were in the tropics, though mountain chains did give them a range of climates. The Inca capital, Cuzco, was at an elevation of 11,380 feet and could hardly have been further from the sea. There was not one navigable river. Transportation was made possible only by carving roads through sheer rock. In contrast, the Aztec city of Tenochtitlan was built on an island in Lake Texcoco, probably in 1345. This site made sense in terms of water transportation. In any case, this was a region of the world that lacked robust animals able to be domesticated for draft purposes and where no society adopted the wheel other than for toys.

The Incas emerge into historical light after about 1440, when the Inca Pachcutec rebuilt the city of Cuzco. The empire expanded during the late fifteenth century into a vacuum created by the fall of two other groups. Much of the population had retreated to hill forts, and the Inca organized a movement back to formerly occupied lands. Agricultural development took place by the *mitmaq* system, whereby the ruler supervised the relocation of colonists. There was plenty of social mobility as well, almost any glimmering of (male) talent being recruited for the provincial bureaucracy needed to oversee *mitmaq*. The resultant empire may have been six times the area of France.

In the expansionary phase, population grew rapidly. Cuzco may have exceeded 100,000 inhabitants, and by the time the Spaniards came the total population of the empire may have been over nine million—though the estimates of demo-graphic historians vary so wildly as to be almost laughable. Fortunately, for our purposes the absolute number matters less than the indications that, given the rather limited technology, the farming system may already have been showing signs of strain by the time of the Spanish conquest in the early sixteenth century. This strain does not really imply a problem of population pressure, although the difficulty may have seemed to show up as too many mouths to feed. The deeper historical problem was inadequate technological change in agriculture.

In the settled pockets the population was dense. The new empire was laid out in separate areas based on what were in effect extended families, called *ayllu*. Lo-cal political boundaries were redrawn to enclose different ecological zones, be-tween which there was some occasion for trade because vertical zones—up the mountains—were complementary: they produced different products. At higher levels the main crop was the potato, and there was some grazing by the wool-bearing animals, llamas and alpacas. Lower down maize was grown, and because it stores better than potatoes the population of those regions built up most. There was some irrigation, though farm tools were of poor quality. Game belonged by law to the state, and most hunting was forbidden. Not a lot of meat was con-sumed. Even maize production was liable to fluctuate, and the uncertainty about supplies of food seems to have given rise to a number of nervous religious cere-monies associated with the prospects for society, the crops, or the harvest. Large complexes of food stores, as many as 2,000 buildings each, are now thought to have been largely ceremonial in function rather than part of an organized market-ing or redistributive system.

The intended self-sufficiency of each *ayllu* limited trade outside its bounds. Commerce would have been costly in any case, since there were no suitable draft animals. Despite outstanding feats of engineering in which the Inca built over 3,000 miles of mountain roads—some through tunnels, others spanning chasms with rope bridges—communications were limited. Whether this limitation was a significant check on Incan growth is another matter: The steep slopes of the An-des restrict communications even with modern trucks, yet growth has still taken place in the region.

This topic brings us to the issue of the obstacles to development in the Incan empire. There are many hypotheses about these and no clear guidance as to how we may choose among them. Evidently, there was to some extent a self-limiting character to economic growth in a country organized in small, separate, and eco-logically self-contained units, where expansion came about by replicating the units. Even so, Inca society may have been capable of more productive activities, but like many ancient civilizations its main organizational drive was aimed (be-yond the road-building projects and grain stores) at putting up large monuments.

Paradoxically, there may be relatively little to explain, if the question is why the Incas did not reach Song Chinese or later European levels of productivity and income. There was the competition for power and privilege endemic to such societies, but until the arrival of the Spaniards no sharp change in external circumstances changed the balance of forces. The problem of the succession to the ruler was not solved here (it has been solved seldom enough in world history), giving rise to much conflict. When the conquering Spaniard, Pizarro, arrived in 1532, he found the Inca empire in political disarray, with the succession not yet firmly established. This state of affairs helped him dissolve the empire and terminate one part of the pre-Columbian American experiment at building large-scale economies; the overthrow of the Aztecs ended the other.

The limited economic development of both the Inca and Aztec empires would thus have been the outcome of the political system. This theory is not the same as a *cultural* explanation. Some writers do proclaim that non-Western cultures (embracing polities) have their own goals and are not necessarily tending toward "modern" economic development, but this is almost certainly a misconception: Too many civilizations in the world, certainly more than the Western one, have sought advanced technologies and high levels of economic activity for development to be considered an improbable goal, although the precise route by which the goal is reached may vary and the movement may sometimes fall back.

For the Aztec empire the population estimates vary wildly, some suggesting totals as high as 20–30 million, with only 100,000 or so inhabitants in Tenochtitlan. A severe run of famines in 1450–1454 spurred the extension of irrigation works, and the subsequent growth of population may have come to press hard against food supplies. There is a vigorous debate about the possibility that protein scarcity explains the practice of human sacrifice and cannibalism. Mere religious fervor, it is said, could not explain such extreme behavior; only dire need could do so. This is surely too materialistic a view. The existence of a fairly abundant wildlife resource that was not fully exploited argues against the idea of a protein scarcity so severe that it caused cannibalism. More likely, the institutions of a very hierarchical state restricted the expression of creativity and meant that the problem of food scarcity was not properly attacked; certainly the farm tools in use were merely stone ones.

A particular problem in understanding the limited development of the pre-Columbian empires is that so much of the evidence is purely archaeological and can bear only indirectly on matters of social, political, and economic organization. With too little direct information, speculation is unusually rife.

There are four main categories of explanation for the failure of pre-Columbian development. One invokes dramatic change from the outside. This hypothesis is usually presented as though Western imperialism was the whole problem—it is implied that the Spanish invaders who captured Central America in the early sixteenth century destroyed civilizations that, left to their own devices, would eventually have performed economic feats as great as any performed in the Old World. This possibility is not to be dismissed out of hand; what can be said is that, although the premodern empires of the New World possessed many social forms in common with those of the Old World, there was no sign of further significant development taking place at the moment Spain burst in.

The remaining types of explanation refer to internal features—material, cultural, and political. The material hypothesis finds a check to Aztec or Incan growth (as to that of the earlier Mayan civilization on the Atlantic side of Central America) in some environmental limitation or catastrophe, or at least in population stress. One suggestion, a kind of mammalian or geographical determinism, points out that the range of mammal species available for domestication as beasts of burden or for traction in plowing was much narrower in the New World than in the Old World. The New World was therefore at a disadvantage in rates of social change compared with the Old World, calamitously so once the Spanish invasions brought societies from the two worlds into collision.

A refinement of this idea is that the main axis of the Eurasian landmass is east-west, permitting the diffusion of useful plants and animals along lines of latitude, whereas the Americas run north-south, which slows down the necessary acclimatizations. On the time-scale of history and prehistory, the gap in social and technological development, though fatal for the less developed system if the two worlds were to fight, does not seem large enough to persuade us to give enormous weight to this kind of determinism. Both the Old World and the New World were surely at a sufficient level of complexity by 1492 for the remaining differences to have been the result of differences in forms of social organization—that is to say, to have lain in the realm of social science rather than natural science. In general, natural disasters bring about the collapse only of societies that are already too brittle to cope or recover. The population-stress argument is also improbable. Given the extent to which the population sizes of those days have been exceeded in later times, the idea of overpopulation cannot mean that there were too many Incas or Aztecs for the land to support. We reiterate that it can mean only that there was too little agricultural innovation.

That limitation brings us to cultural obstacles of the kind that would depress the rate of innovation. This theory is often phrased to suggest that from the start pre-Columbian societies took a cultural track that had no hope of leading to the types of logical thought that gave the West its record-keeping, numeracy, science, and eventually the technology that underlay its economic growth.

There is no certainty in this kind of interpretation, either, and we should note that, contrary to a common supposition among writers on cultural matters, culture is not necessarily distinct or independent: The forms of economic life can react back and change the culture. Nevertheless, it is interesting to speculate whether some peculiarity of the pre-Columbian systems really did prevent them, say, from devising modern science. Societies in Mesoamerica or the Andes might, however, have reached far higher levels of productivity than they did before an inability to invent science would have checked them. Much relevant technology did not need to be science-based. There is simply no compelling reason to suppose that, having developed as far as they had by 1600, the Americas could not have eventually improved their technologies in response to population growth and military or political unrest. As far as going on to attain an equivalent of the British Industrial Revolution is concerned, since high science was not greatly involved in this anyhow, the matter is both speculative and beside the point.

The Aztecs had their own attitudes to time and the individual. For them, time moved with endless repetition in sacred cycles of fifty-two years; there was no open-ended forward motion; and current events were a replay of what had gone before. Thus Tenochtitlan was perceived as the reemergence of the previous Toltec empire's capital of Tula. Similarly, the Aztecs had a limited sense of their own individuality, seeing themselves as members of groups, the fate of which was ordained. It has been suggested that these things militated against invention, but this proposal is not easy to accept given that Aztec society was far from static in many respects.

The most precise version of the culturist line of argument is that neither the Incas nor Aztecs discovered phonetic writing. The Incas kept their records in the form of knotted ropes. This sounds clumsy and perhaps it was, yet almost four thousand knots are listed in Ashley's *Book of Knots,* so there may have been no effective limit to the information that could have been stored. Aztec writing, like Chinese writing and the systems discovered independently in three other Old World civilizations, was in the form of pictograms, with discrete, nonrepeatable, nonstandardized components. Alphabetic writing systems, conversely, derive from one Semitic discovery 3,500 years ago. It has been suggested that only alphabetic scripts are flexible enough to form a basis for abstract thought and systematized knowledge, which the Aztecs accordingly could not develop. The assumption is that pre-Columbian Americans could never have made the conceptual leap, say, to industrial technology. Perhaps they could not; but the Maya *had* discovered the concept of zero, which was done independently only in one other case, in a single other culture, in Hindu India 2,000 years ago. Were New World minds really so constrained?

Ultimately, all these cultural-bottleneck theories are unpersuasive. They do not help us think about what was likely to have happened if the circumstances had changed—that is, to think about the true potential of these native Americans. Some of the theories confuse necessary and sufficient conditions. It is too easy a step from observing that no society without alphabetic writing "developed" independently (a dubious proposition anyhow, since it ignores the achievement of real economic growth in Song China and some other places) to implying that only societies with alphabetic writing systems can generate growth. Although it is problematical to explain precisely how change might have happened, it is just as unclear why we should believe that the pre-Columbian New World was doomed to stay on the tracks along which it had started.

To return to the Aztecs, there is no reason to believe that they were incapable of invention. We know that to say so would not be true. But there is reason to think that, as in most premodern societies, those Aztec groups with political authority had narrow, self-serving goals, whereas most other people had little chance or incentive to risk either inventing or innovating.

Yet, although such societies tended to cycle, we should not confuse this pattern with a tendency to return to an equilibrium fixed in all respects. The best approach, then, to explaining the rate of New World development, is a third one that refers to the internal structure of the pre-Columbian empires, an argument relating to the political structure and reward system to which we made reference earlier. Premodern economies were mostly prisoners of narrow political elites; change commonly took the form of the violent replacement of one unprogressive elite group by another rather than anything more fundamental. Political life trod water, so to speak, restricting the incentives for invention and innovation. Yet the population continued to grow—there was thus trend as well as cycle in pre-Columbian history.

Both the Inca and Aztec empires had experienced only about a hundred years of rapid expansion before the Spanish arrival, an intrusion so unexpected and so brutal that it was like the landing of hostile Martians. The internal conflicts detectable just before the conquests may have been "teething problems," may have been endemic to local politics as the states clashed with rising aristocratic groups, or may have been deeper symptoms of empires in decay. It is hard to tell. Certainly it was difficult to accumulate capital in states that required tribute from the nobility. It was harder still to think of taking risks on novel forms of investment.

Development may have required rewriting history and rethinking the calendar, replacing bloodthirsty gods with a deity or deities that fostered the unique capabilities of the individual, secularizing the view of the natural world, creating new criteria for prestige, and introducing a phonetic alphabet. In short, a total restructuring of hierarchical political systems and political goals may have been needed. Of course, these things were needed before Old World civilizations could change, too. Alternatively, if growth came about anyhow, for some other reason, it may have reacted back and remolded these political features. Either way, such changes surely were not impossible, though they did not seem close in pre-Columbian America at the start of the sixteenth century.

As a consequence, even the relatively advanced civilizations of the Aztecs and Incas—that is, advanced by the standards of the Americas—did not have the capacity to resist a technologically superior civilization effectively. Disease gave the coup de grace.

The Nature of the Spanish Empire

The Spanish empire was remarkable for two main features: first, for the speed with which a small band of soldiers conquered very much larger armies; and second, for the long period—almost 300 years—during which Spain retained political control over a colossal area stretching from California to Chile.

The assaults of Hernan Cortéz on the Aztec empire in Mexico (1519–1521) and Francesco Pizarro on the Inca empire in Peru (1532–1533) proved quickly decisive. They continued the traditions of the *reconquista,* or reconquest, of the Iberian territory previously lost to Islam, a process completed in 1492 with the retaking of Granada. The speed of victory was assisted by divisions within the existing pre-Columbian empires and the havoc wreaked by European diseases on the hapless natives. The centers of the former empires became the focal points for the viceroyalties of New Spain and Peru, at Mexico City in the former case and at Lima in the second.

Military seizure by the *conquistadores* led to a demand for the kind of rewards that would raise the status of the recipients to that of an *hidalgo,* or gentleman. This reward most commonly took the form of the *encomienda,* a feudal-type grant not of land but of tribute-paying, labor-supplying natives. The reciprocal obligations of the *encomendero* were to look after the economic, social, and most of all religious welfare of the natives. Such grants not only encouraged exploitation of native labor but also threatened to build independent power-blocs within the growing Spanish American empire.

Military seizure was followed by a centralist coup d'état, in which the government in Spain created an administrative and judicial structure to control the empire directly and simultaneously legislated to dissolve the *encomiendas.* As one authority has it, "the crown's problem ... was to conquer the conquistadores." This objective was achieved by the extension of the Castilian bureaucracy to the New World and by the promulgation of the New Laws of 1542, which did abolish the *encomienda* in an effort to prevent the emergence of a hereditary aristocracy in the New World. In Peru this measure provoked a rebellion in which the viceroy was murdered, and civil war followed. The New Laws were revoked, but the government had made its point. Within a remarkably short period Spain had asserted its authority, although more easily in Mexico than in Peru.

The process of conquest spread outward from these centers, and lesser concentrations of Spanish population were established in areas remote from them—along the Pacific Coast in Central America, in the Quito region, and in central Chile, for example. Such concentrations became the bases for the *audiencias* into which the viceroyalties were divided (and incidentally the nuclei for later independent states). The *audiencia* was the judicial tribunal that exercised administrative authority within defined jurisdictions. By the end of the sixteenth century there were eleven in all, of which seven were relevant to the Pacific Rim. Mexico City and Lima speak for themselves but there were also *audiencias* in Manila, Panama, Guatemala, Quito, and Chile. Each *audiencia* was treated as an independent jurisdiction directly linked to the king of Castile.

The assertion of strong Spanish control led to the imposition of highly centralized political and economic structures. The Spanish empire was run by a series of
councils. The Council of the Indies was the governing body for the Americas.
Economic life, notably trade between Spain and the Americas, fell under the Casa
de Contratacion, located in Seville (much later Cadiz). Clearly the level of centralization varied, de facto if not de jure, according to the competence and motivation of particular governments or ministers. In theory all power flowed from the
monarch in Spain; the system was patrimonial—that is, the monarch acted as
owner as well as sovereign. Though bureaucratic, it was not hierarchical, consisting rather of a series of overlapping authorities whose competencies checked and
restrained each other, which allowed the monarch maximum scope for the exercise of power.

Moreover, under the *patronato*, the Pope allowed appointments within the
Church to be made by the monarch. Consequently, despite disputes within the
Church concerning the treatment of the native population, the structure of the
Church buttressed the strong central authority. The Church quickly emerged as a
major landowner, a major source of capital, and a very significant actor in most
areas of economic activity.

There were all sorts of reasons why central control could not be complete. Poor
communications and an ignorance of local conditions acted to check its authority. In practice there was significant devolution of decisionmaking. Under the tag
"*obedezco pero no cumplo*"—"I obey but do not comply"—adjustment of instructions to local circumstances occurred without subversion of royal authority.

Another aspect of centralization was the dominance of towns. The Spanish empire was an urban civilization in that most of the Spanish population lived in
towns that were administrative and military centers rather than market towns.
The peculiarity of this characteristic is highlighted by James Lang, who saw the
symbol of Spanish colonization as the *adelantado* pacing out the grids of a Spanish town rather than the frontiersmen so characteristic of British colonization.
The *cabildo*, or town council, ran the towns; rural areas were organized into
corregimientos.

The economic structure was fashioned to promote the interests of Spain, with a
strong emphasis on regulation of economic activity and markets. For Spain, mining lay at the core of the domestic economy. The development of sectors producing commodities competitive with Spanish imports was discouraged. The whole
trading system was organized to support the flow of output from the mines to
Spain. A convoy system moved the silver. The government took its "fifth" and also
charged a convoy tax. Labor was organized on a vast scale to work the mines. After the introduction of the amalgamation process, mercury became a crucial in-
put and its production a government monopoly.

Not only did the government intervene extensively, it also tried to deter the officials who ran the empire from developing local attachments. Laws prevented in-

termarriage of *peninsulares* with creoles—that is, between home-born Spaniards and those of Spanish origin born in the Americas—and the former's involvement in local business enterprises. The *ascenso,* or ladder of preferment, also encouraged mobility and a speedy turnover of incumbents.

As a result, the working of markets, already imperfect because of vast distances, high levels of risk, and information deficiencies, was further hindered by government regulation. Nevertheless, these regulations were often observed in the breach. It was impossible to hold the economy in a straitjacket. Smuggling, the illegal purchase of position, and out-and-out corruption became commonplace. A diversified economy began to emerge in spite of government wishes. The economic emphasis shifted from town to country. The hacienda, or country estate, emerged as a typical unit of agricultural and pastoral output, its owner also often engaged in mercantile or manufacturing activity.

Ironically, the prelude to the securing of independence in Latin America, as in North America, was an attempt by the royal government to reassert its political authority and revive its revenue flow. In 1767, under Charles III, José de Galvez was sent from Spain to reform the administration, reassert central control, and rebuild Spain's economic interests. Stronger political control, however, was now associated with a distinct movement toward free trade. For the first time legal restrictions on much intra-empire trade were removed.

Three great themes characterize the colonial history of Spain: first, the changing relationship between native and settler; second, the relationship between *peninsulares* and creoles; and third, the long, drawn-out retreat of Spain before the fast-rising power of Great Britain and later the United States.

The first theme raises the issue of the demographic collapse of the native population and its significance for later historical developments. The degree and timing of both collapse and recovery varied from region to region. However, all underwent a similar process, by which the entry of Eurasian diseases decimated unprotected populations, reducing them to as little as one-tenth of their original size. There is great controversy about the exact size of precontact populations, but there is no disputing the demoralizing impact of the combined onslaught of Spanish *conquistadores* and new diseases. In most areas decline continued well into the seventeenth century.

The contraction of the native economy over this period was only partly compensated for by the expansion of the settler society. After all, initial inflows of Spanish settlers were very small. There emerged a growing problem of labor scarcity, met to some degree by the import of African slaves. Populations became polyglot, mixed and stratified by race. Elaborate distinctions of terminology were developed to describe the status rankings associated with the changing racial mix. The capacity of native populations and separate economies to survive varied greatly. Native cultures survived best in the more inaccessible parts of the Andes.

The second theme raises the issue of the degree of both economic and political development. There was an attempt to prevent the creoles from gaining any real experience in self-government and to exclude them from the higher reaches of trade. The ability of the government to achieve both purposes steadily declined until the Bourbon reforms temporarily reversed this trend late in the colonial period. The result of government action was to impose additional costs and risk on decisionmakers. (The mix of government and market in the economic development of the Spanish Americas is discussed in Chapter 6.)

Third, the Spanish found it increasingly difficult to keep the Americas as Spanish as they would have liked. Resistance to ruling groups, fragmentation of political unity, and the penetration of foreign economic interests into the empire all had their origins in the colonial period.

The Beginnings of Integration

How far did the Spanish succeed in integrating significant parts of the Pacific Rim, notably the Americas, or in linking the two sides of the Pacific?

Within the Americas, in an era when overland movement was expensive, slow, and risky, the coastal route represented the only link between different parts of the empire. The coastal route had its problems. Disadvantageous wind patterns, vast distances, thin coastal strips with restricted hinterlands, difficult access into the Pacific from the Atlantic—all these factors created obstacles to the expansion of an interregional trade. Even more significant was the limited number of good natural ports. Only a handful of ports existed within the Spanish area; Acapulco, Panama, Guayaquil, Callao, Arica, and Valparaiso stand out.

It was no accident that both the pre-Columbian and Spanish empires were located away from the coast, despite the enormous difficulties of communication and transportation. To a significant degree resource location dictated the pattern of settlement. Moreover, the Pacific Coast was a singularly unattractive place for much of its length. Fever-ridden within the tropics—particularly after the introduction of African diseases to supplement Eurasian ones—arid for long stretches of both the north and south, and restricted in area, it offered little to the settlers. Only in initially remote areas in the far north—what is now the northern United States and southern Canada—and in the far south—specifically, central Chile—was disease a lesser problem and the climate attractive. The central valleys of California and Chile offered large areas of potentially high fertility. However, distance imposed its own constraints on the opening of these areas.

There were problems apart from disease, some of which affected both upland and coastal areas. Geophysical instability affected the whole coastal area; volcanoes, earthquakes, and the resulting landslips or tsunami (tidal waves) posed enormous problems. Moreover, the ports of Spanish America became subject to attack by pirates or the navies of rival colonial powers. For these reasons it was not unusual for important cities to be relocated a number of times, as was for example the capital of Guatemala, or Guayaquil, the port of Quito.

The route from Arica via the port of Callao, Lima's outlet, to Panama in Central America constituted one step in the carrying of silver from the silver mountain, Potosi, high in the Andes, back to Spain. The galleons of the Armada del Sur (the Southern Armada) tended to hug—as much as the prevailing winds allowed—the west coast of South America. A typical convoy consisted of four or five vessels, two or three of which were royal ships, and carried something like 40 percent of the silver annually arriving in Spain. The high value-to-bulk ratio of silver made such costly transportation feasible. It also made a convoy system necessary to protect the ships.

In any given year during the seventeenth century there were also thirty to seventy vessels, most privately built, owned, and operated, plying the Pacific coastal trade. Within Spanish America, trade was legal along only a small number of routes and through defined ports. Although intercolonial commerce was first regulated, later outlawed, it could not be prevented completely. For example, New Spanish textiles, usually woolens, were early exported from Puebla—in what is now southern Mexico—to Peru, but the number of permitted journeys was greatly restricted after 1590, and a complete ban was imposed on the New Spain–Peru trade in 1634.

As Peruvian and Quito workshops developed they began to export woolens to Chile, where the Araucanian Revolt of 1599 and interregional competition had destroyed the workshops. Chile increasingly specialized in ranching. There was much scope for this kind of specialization.

By the middle of the seventeenth century the monopolistic system was breaking down. Smuggling became rife. Focusing attention solely on the American trade with Spain gives a misleading impression of economic depression within the Americas during the seventeenth century. Intra-American trade grew to compensate for intercontinental trade reductions. Domestic production of such food staples as grain, beef, wines, and olive oil grew to significant levels. Silver production did not decline in the way that the flow of silver to Spain suggests; much silver seeped away to finance illicit trade. Small workshops began to substitute domestically produced textiles or leather goods for imports. Construction materials and naval stores were also produced. Cash crops such as cacao, sugar, tobacco, and textile dyes made their appearance. As import substitution permitted Latin America to become self-sufficient in the production of foodstuffs and other commodities, there were bound to be some surpluses. It was logical to trade such resources. From a relatively early date there developed along the South American coast a trade in such items as wheat, wine, and sugar, from surplus areas in Chile or Peru to deficit areas elsewhere. To support this trade, a ship-building industry grew up in the area of Guayaquil, in what is now Ecuador.

The first significant medium of integration of the whole Pacific Basin was the Manila galleon, an annual voyage linking the Spanish colonies in the Americas with the Philippines, Spain's only colony in Asia. This voyage continued from the 1580s right to the early nineteenth century. The round-trip from Acapulco to Manila and back could last as long as three years; it was dangerous, time-consuming, and sustained only with government assistance. Despite the regular losses the government incurred on the voyage, private trade, and in particular smuggling, was very profitable. Perforce, such a voyage had to fit into the framework of Spain's attempt to regulate and control trade among the colonies in such a way as to maximize the revenue for Spain itself. At the Asian end of the voyage, Chinese traders linked Manila to Chinese ports and their highly desirable commodities; at the American end, Asian spices and silks were distributed along the Pacific Coast. Therefore, the galleon essentially linked the markets of China and the Americas. As elsewhere, the flow of Chinese goods and East Indian spices represented a demand on the bullion of the Americas. It is likely that the significance of the Manila galleons in assisting Europe to meet its persistent and large deficit on trade in commodities has been underestimated. The flow of bullion was large, but nobody will ever know exactly how large. On one account, 15,000 tons of American silver flowed through Europe to Asia and 13,000 tons across the Pacific.

This trade established only a fragile bond between the two sides of the Pacific. Moreover, it had little impact in stimulating either settlement in or economic development of the Philippine colony, and although it did improve knowledge of the geography of the California coastline, this was not of a kind to stimulate interest in settling there until the late eighteenth century.

There is a second sense in which the Spanish did integrate the Pacific; the Spanish silver dollar became the main medium of exchange. The dollar was minted in the Americas from American silver. Being of uniform shape, weight, and fineness, it was often more convenient and less risky to use than local currencies. For example, in China the Spanish silver dollar—first the piaster ("pieces of eight") and later the Carolus dollar—entered the economy as a result of the Manila galleon. By the late eighteenth century it circulated widely in south China. By the early nineteenth century the Spanish dollar was the standard coin in Canton (Guangzhou), circulated as far north as Peking (Beijing), and was even accepted as payment for taxes in some regions. (The Mexican dollar inherited this role after Independence.) The silver dollar passed ever more widely as an international medium of exchange. In the colony of New South Wales (Australia), the local currency was nearly placed on a silver dollar standard during the 1820s.

It is easy to give a premature dating to these developments. It is easier to exaggerate the scale and significance of all this activity. The upshot of Spanish trade amounted to very little. Only superficially, at least with respect to commodity flows, was the Pacific a Spanish lake. The degree of integration achieved until the early nineteenth century was extremely limited.

5

The European Intrusion: *Pax Britannica*

Europeans and their commensal and parasitic comrades were not good at adapting to truly alien lands and climates, but they were very good at constructing new versions of Europe out of suitable real estate.

—Alfred Crosby, *Ecological Imperialism* (1986)

In this chapter we consider the way in which the British took over from the Spanish as the main European influence on the Pacific and conclude by summarizing the lasting legacy of the European intrusion.

Great Britain's "Swing to the East"

British interest in the Pacific began early and increased slowly. Initially British incursions into the Pacific were piecemeal, the attacks on Spanish trade and colonies sporadic and unsystematic. In this early period exploration and the discovery of potential resources could not be disentangled from piracy. Trade with established empires such as China and exploitation of the whale fisheries of the Pacific became important in the eighteenth century.

British interest in the Pacific increased dramatically with the so-called swing to the East that followed the loss of its American colonies (1776–1783). The foundation of New South Wales (Australia) represented both an attempt to dispose of unwanted convicts previously sent to the American colonies and, at the same time, the creation of a port of call and supply base facilitating the extension of

British influence to China and the northeast Pacific. Independence in Latin America also opened profitable opportunities for British economic involvement.

It is often forgotten that decolonization began early. The beginning of decolonization overlapped very significantly with the process of colonization. The first wave of decolonization affected the colonies of settlement, although it also had an indirect influence on colonies where European settlement was insignificant. It began with the War of Independence (1776–1783), or the Revolutionary War, as U.S. historians prefer to call it, in which the British colonies in America asserted their right to run their affairs without interference by the imperial authorities. That war represented a rebellion against British efforts to reimpose central control. After the French and Indian War (1754–1763), the colonists no longer faced a military threat from other colonial powers and therefore no longer felt the need for British protection, though they gained greatly from the way in which the Royal Navy kept the oceans free for trade throughout the nineteenth century.

The first wave of decolonization continued with the assertion of independence by most parts of the Spanish empire, though not the Philippines (which passed from Spanish to U.S. control in 1898 and gained independence only in 1946). This struggle was drawn out, occurring over the period from 1810 to 1824, when the Imperial Army of Spain was finally defeated at the battle of Ayacucho. It also had as a background a Spanish attempt to recreate strong central control over its American empire. Armies largely composed of creoles had faced armies composed of troops brought in from outside and *peninsulares*. The opportunity for the initial assertion of independence was the Napoleonic invasion of Spain (1808) and the installation of Napoleon's brother Joseph as monarch in place of the Bourbon emperor, Ferdinand VII. Rebellion was often raised either in the name of the legitimate emperor or in the name of the liberal democracy at Cadiz. Such military conflict revealed significant underlying divisions in Spanish America (in some cases remaining more or less unresolved to the present). In many parts of the old empire there followed long periods of civil war and anarchy.

In the U.S. case, independence led to the separation of the thirteen revolutionary colonies from loyalist Canada. The British colonies in the West Indies also went their own way. The old unity was lost, and attention turned to the transcontinental crossing; in the process a sizeable United States was created. The former British restrictions on movement beyond the Appalachians were removed. The Spanish empire in North America broke up into a much larger number of units. There was some correspondence between the new nations' boundaries and those of the old imperial administrative units, the viceroyalties and *audiencias*. Attempts to preserve a more unified system in Central America, centered on Guatemala or in the northern part of South America (Gran Colombia), failed. Fragmentation was at its greatest in Central America.

Decolonization created as many opportunities for Great Britain as it did constraints. It certainly changed the whole pattern of Great Britain's relationship with the different regions of the Pacific. Nor was this change limited to the promotion of free trade and the securing of an open door for foreign investment. Settlement of Australasia and military intervention in China represented more proactive policies.

There has been considerable debate about the motivation for the British settlement of New South Wales in 1788, following soon after James Cook's "discovery" of both New Zealand and the east coast of Australia in 1770 during the first of his three path-breaking explorations of the Pacific. The convict argument still holds sway; this view regards New South Wales as primarily a receptacle for British convicts who could no longer be deposited in the American colonies. The apparent potential for the supply of naval stores, notably timber and flax, was unrealized.

The settlement was costly, covering its needs up to the 1840s by selling its services as a jail to the British. As population increased, the colony became less suited to this purpose. The surprising feature of the new colony was the speed with which it developed a free polity and economy. Even the convicts, on "tickets of leave," were quickly allowed to seek their own employment. Within a short period, just over half a century, the colony acquired all the trappings of a democratic, free market system.

In practice Australia and New Zealand consisted of a series of separate colonies, independent creations or satellites detached from the original core. Van Diemen's Land (later called Tasmania) separated from New South Wales in 1803. Convict-free settlements were established in West Australia in 1828 and South Australia in 1836, the former several thousand miles distant from the East Coast. Until 1840 the New Zealand colony was an offshoot of New South Wales. In that year a number of independent settlements were established in New Zealand. Finally Victoria broke off from New South Wales in 1851, and Queensland followed suit in 1859. By the middle of the nineteenth century each of these colonies largely ran its own affairs, particularly its own economic affairs. Just as there was no unified Canada until 1867, so there was no unified Australia until federation in 1901. However, these transitions were achieved peacefully, with the blessing of the colonial power.

Until the gold rushes in the mid-nineteenth century, all these colonies remained minuscule in size. They differed in the timing of their settlement and in the structure of their economies but competed with each other for increasingly important free settlers. Because of the vast distances involved, most immigrants were assisted by government subsidies, financed initially by land sales. Within a short period the colonies developed economies much more diversified than might reasonably be expected given their size. The level of services or manufactures produced was high. Australia—an anachronism in any event—was not simply "a quarry and sheeprun," dependent on the success of export staples such as gold or wool. Even wool became a significant export only in the 1830s.

The nature of British interest in China was very different. It arose initially because of a significant demand for Chinese products—tea, porcelain, silk, and the like—unmatched by a reciprocal demand for British goods. The Chinese obstinately refused to purchase European imports in respectable amounts, so much so that the British appetite for their products led to a large deficit in trade. The interest intensified when the Chinese refused to establish even normal diplomatic relations. The British resorted to force and were able to impose their will on a China that was in a weakened condition, its capacity to resist impaired. However, there was no collapse, as had occurred to the pre-Columbian empires in the Americas. Weakness reflected the ever-changing relationship between the population and resources in China.

Traditionally strong imperial governments were active and effective in minimizing the impact of the famines to which frequent floods and droughts made China vulnerable. From about 1810, however, the empire ran into difficulties. The troubles brewed up into chaotic and massive revolt under a pseudo-Christian leadership. This was the Taiping Rebellion, which lasted from 1850 to 1865, being put down in the end only with bloody slaughter. Twenty-five million lives were said to have been lost. The government failed to avoid the catastrophe, which has been called the "greatest Malthusian crisis known to history" on the assumption that the underlying cause was hunger caused by overpopulation. But "overpopulation" at 400 million in 1850 was surpassed by a population of 450 million at the end of the century. The real issue, then, was not population growth, since more people went on being fed, but rather the response from the side of production and distribution, which was too sluggish to cope smoothly with the rise in numbers. The Qing court did survive, though in order to reduce the pressure it had to open its own homeland of Manchuria to Chinese immigrants in 1860.

European intrusions began to add to the confusion in nineteenth-century China, though they did not initiate it. Nor did the Europeans always destabilize the country—not *quite* always. The Qing used European help to put down the Taiping rebels. Yet one Western country after another, and in the 1890s a newly expansionary Japan, acquired trading concessions and large sums of money as reparations for real or imaginary losses at Chinese hands.

The outsiders were militarily stronger. They had steam vessels and cannons as a result of their industrialization. First among them was Britain. In the period 1839–1842 the British objected violently to the Chinese government's attempt to prohibit the export to China of opium grown in Bengal, part of British India. The opium was used to balance British trade with China. Mandarins were involved in the trade, too, for a cut, but the Qing central government was opposed to more and more of its subjects becoming drug addicts, as well as to the reduced tax receipts it would get from people who were smoking the "foreign mud."

For the British, pushing the issue of free trade (in drugs) at official gunpoint was one of the most shameful of imperialist actions. From the Opium Wars on, foreign interference in China continued to be mostly negative in a political and social sense, culminating in notices in European parts of Shanghai saying "No

Dogs or Chinese." On the other hand, economically speaking the contacts led to a transfer of technology from which the Chinese learned new methods of business and administration and acquired railways and industrial machinery they could have gotten nowhere else.

The Treaty of Nanking (1842) forced open the so-called Treaty Ports. Following the British example, all the main powers struggled for an economic sphere of influence in China. In turn the French, Germans, Americans, and Russians all asserted strong claims. Internal problems made it difficult for the Chinese to resist these claims, although violence often broke out, as in the Boxer Rebellion. The conflict resulted in the creation of a series of enclaves of foreign control subject to extraterritoriality (foreign law) and to frequent interventions in Chinese affairs and outside control over the customs administration. The 150-year lease of Hong Kong taken by the British, expiring in 1997, was one legacy of this process. Others are less obvious, including the Shanghai replica of the Liverpool waterfront, called the Bund, and a German type of beer in Shantung province.

The shilly-shallying policies of the Qing toward foreign powers and foreign ways are usually contrasted with the determined effort made by the Meiji government in Japan after 1868 to absorb Western industrial and military techniques. The Chinese elite could not fully decide whether to embrace Westernisms or to hide their heads in the sand. The problems could have been resolved at the top, if anywhere. There was no fundamental lack of technological skill in China. When the British pushed their way up the Chinese estuaries in 1842, they found complete replicas of their own warships built by the Chinese. The vessels were close to being launched. Whether the Chinese were well enough organized to have fought effectively is another matter, but the standard contrast between the ability of the Japanese to copy the West and the confusion of the Chinese can be overdrawn.

China could even have been seen as more likely to industrialize than Japan. The population, and hence potential market, was much bigger. The country had better natural resources. Chinese armaments were modernized in the 1860s. Some of the later nineteenth-century efforts at development were on a respectable scale. Students were sent overseas from the 1870s and colleges established at home. The talent was there. Only a consistent and open-minded political will was lacking. Unfortunately, that lack conditioned the history of weak industrialization during the remaining life of imperial China, which fell to a "liberal" revolution in 1911.

Intervention in China was important but untypical of British behavior. There was no such intrusion into Japan. On the whole the British preferred to operate through free but one-sided markets, exercising clear economic superiority and a little diplomatic suasion to get their way. Their interest in the Americas was strong but usually did not involve direct political action. Other European powers, such as the French and later the Germans, also had a presence in the Pacific Basin but exerted much less influence than the British. However, their competition eventually forced the carving up of the Pacific into a number of separate colonial preserves. Just as in China, each colonial power jealously protected its own sphere of influence and control.

Further Integration

Interest in the Pacific had increased even before the canal or railway ages when, during the seventeenth and eighteenth centuries, major productivity advances occurred in sea carriage. A high level of risk in international trade created high transaction costs. As these came down, the pace of integration around the Pacific quickened. One general index of shipping productivity indicates a rate of advance of almost 1 percent per annum, largely accounted for by a reduction in risk as a result of the elimination in many areas of piracy and a greater chance of obtaining full loads on regular runs.

Integration of the Pacific required the extension of markets for both commodities and the factors of production throughout the basin. In its turn this extension required the removal of obstacles to the distribution of commodities and movement of the factors of production. In the English-speaking societies a liberal policy of land distribution encouraged the development of an active market for land. For other markets a key step was the reduction of transaction costs. Such costs could take many different forms—protection, financing, merchanting, insurance, warehousing, and transport. The protective umbrella of the *Pax Britannica* helped provide a secure, low-cost environment for international trade in the nineteenth century. British naval influence in the Pacific helped promote exchange, just as the activity of British banks, insurance companies, and merchant houses also reduced costs by providing the auxiliary services underpinning trade.

The most dramatic influences in promoting market integration were improvements in communications and transportation. Before the advent of the electric telegraph in the nineteenth century, the speed of movement of information, people, and commodities was very uniform. One of the consequences of the acceleration in modern times in technical change—starting with the telegraph—has been to greatly reduce the cost and time of information transfer both absolutely and relative to transport of commodities. The effect was to reduce risk and uncertainty for those operating in the relevant markets, making price upsets less frequent and unexpected. Such a change was a precondition for the significant movement of capital into an area as overpoweringly large as the Pacific.

For most of the nineteenth century the Pacific remained remote from the main markets of the world in the sense of the time taken to receive and react to information about changes in market conditions. The building of the Suez Canal (opened in 1869) helped speed up communications between Europe and the Pacific, but the electric telegraph was the key change. The laying of telegraph lines was as significant as the construction of railroads, with which on land they were usually linked. In some areas the telegraph network emerged independently of the railroad network—for example, in the crossing of the harsh interior of Australia. Submarine cables extended the network internationally and were vital to the linking of continents.

By the mid-1870s links from Europe via the Suez Canal were made to the *entrepôts* of Singapore and Hong Kong and to Batavia (Jakarta) and Shanghai. The usefulness of these links was limited until internal telegraph systems were built in China in 1898 and in Malaya about the same time. By then Australia had already connected all its main cities, a network completed as early as 1872. Across the Pacific the first link from the Atlantic to the Pacific had been completed even earlier, from New York to San Francisco in 1861. Within a short period many more links straddled the continent. The crossing of the Pacific and joining of the Asian and U.S. networks was a much more difficult engineering feat not achieved in the nineteenth century.

The most visible aspects of transportation improvement were the advent of the railway and the steamship. By the 1870s, largely at the instigation of the Australian and New Zealand colonies, steamship services crossed the Pacific. However, they required a subsidy, which indicated the low level of traffic generated across the ocean, and they were repeatedly subjects for discussion at intercolonial conferences. It proved very difficult to support steamship services across the Pacific. However, there were myriad improvements in every transport medium, reducing cost, controlling risk, and increasing the regularity of service. The most graphic image of integration in the Pacific is probably the steamship, but for a time this invention promoted a competitive improvement in sailing ships, so that steam and sail developed side by side. This reactive development of an older technology is indeed called "the sailing-ship syndrome." The famous "clippers" cut the time required to sail from Australia to just over sixty days in the 1850s. So efficient were they that the early impact of steam on the longer routes was slight. The enormous needs of early steamships for coal kept their routes close to coaling ports. Sailing clippers were still taking grain from Australia to Europe as late as 1939.

The railroad networks were much quicker to be constructed. Very often they radiated from the export ports, such as Sydney, Shanghai, and Singapore. Such networks were being built from the mid-nineteenth century onward, first in the areas of European settlement and later in the Asian economies. More strategic in their significance were the railways built across Panama in 1855 to reduce the time and cost required for a transport from the Atlantic to the Pacific. In 1869 the Central Pacific and Union Pacific railways were joined, and the first transcontinental railway across the United States was completed. Within a quarter of a century there were five such links, terminating at Oakland, Los Angeles, Portland, Tacoma, and San Francisco. The Canadians and Russians were slower in constructing their own transcontinental lines, completing the Canadian Pacific and Trans Siberian links to Vancouver and Vladivostok, respectively, only in 1885 and 1902.

In areas of European settlement, such improvements in transport and communications were both a result of and a cause of population increase in the Pacific region.

Tentative trading links between the different Pacific regimes only slowly began to emerge—for example, the Australian colonies traded with Asia Pacific and with both parts of the Americas. Some of the trade in "first-generation" staples—that is, resources easily gathered and not readily subject to the assertion of full private property rights—was of long history. Examples include sandalwood and béche-de-mer. Overexploitation often ensured a brief life for such first-generation staples.

The result of the general and accelerating decline of transaction costs in the Pacific area was to draw an increasing number of commodities into the trading network of Europe and the eastern United States and later to increase the return to investment in the area. Increasing demand in Europe and North America also raised real prices, offsetting even more of the transaction costs. At first trade was limited to high value-to-bulk commodities: highly wrought manufactures, cash crops such as tea or sugar, precious metals, and maritime and coastal resources of high value. The Russians sought out the fur-bearing animals found along the North American coast, and British and U.S. hunters pursued the whales and seals found widely throughout the Pacific.

On the other hand, the high bulk-to-value ratio of the raw materials and foodstuffs most in demand during the first acceleration of industrialization largely excluded the Pacific from Europe's expanding hinterland. Coal and iron ore, even wheat, did not become significant parts of the trading network until much later, although wheat was traded intermittently to meet temporary deficits in Rim countries whenever high prices more than compensated for transport costs. For example, the Australian colonies occasionally drew in grain from Chile. Only later was wheat from the Pacific regularly sought after by Europe, and even then the risks in carriage around Cape Horn kept the grain in discrete loads rather than bulk.

One significant exception involved high-value textile fibers, such as silk and wool. Wool's value per unit of weight was on the order of ten times that of wheat, although the key variable determining its transport cost was volume, not weight, and the key element in reducing its transport cost was the hydraulic press, which compacted the bulk.

The first really dramatic stimulus to market penetration came with the gold rushes. Siberia had for a long time been a source of gold, but its transport routes lay outside the Pacific area. Elsewhere, the bunching of gold rushes in the mid-nineteenth century was not accidental. Previous pastoral or ranching activities yielded a good knowledge of the relevant locations. The rapidly rising importance of international trade heightened the demand for gold as a readily acceptable medium of exchange. The initial rushes occurred in California in 1848 and Victoria,

Australia, in 1851. The location then moved northward and eastward, although with less value and explosive force, to British Columbia and Otago, in New Zealand, in the 1860s and to the Yukon and Klondike in 1897–1898. The movement around Australia was in a counterclockwise direction, culminating in the 1890s rush to Coolgardie and Kalgoorlie, West Australia.

Such rushes generated an enormous increase in the value of output in the areas concerned. The prospect of a high return, albeit with high risk, prompted a large influx of prospective miners to the new ventures, not only from older fields but also from outside the Pacific. Large numbers of Chinese often worked over the mullock, or tailings, of a field when the first miners moved on. Others entered the industry to service the mines, providing foodstuffs, equipment, or transportation. The flow of people also entailed a flow of commodities. The massively increased demand and violent price rises of the time made it possible to make a fortune by supplying the goldfields without engaging in mining oneself.

When the population of particular goldfields passed a certain minimum size, the associated urban centers persisted beyond the gold rush era. The major long-term effect of the gold rushes was therefore to expand permanent population in the areas affected, which were usually located well inland. The growth of ports serving the goldfields, such as San Francisco, Melbourne, and Perth, was also promoted. Movement of gold and supplies accelerated the improvement in transport and communications, which began in the middle of the nineteenth century. However, the first effect was once more to link the regions of the Pacific Rim more closely with metropolitan centers in Europe. The market for Pacific commodities was growing rapidly in absolute terms.

The alluvial gold rushes were precursors of later rushes, involving minerals of lesser value and a transition to a capital rather than labor inflow. In gold extraction, quartz mining replaced alluvial mining. Tin was the only other metal subject to alluvial mining. The later "oil rushes" had similar consequences.

The settlement and commercialization of the Pacific by Europeans and the decimation of some of its native populations stimulated an expansion in the labor market. As levels of economic activity increased, the rising demand for labor could not be satisfied either by the use of slaves, since the slave trade was outlawed at the beginning of the century, or by an additional inflow of Europeans. The white settlers preferred to take the white collar and skilled jobs, leaving the unskilled jobs to others. Consequently, the labor market became strongly segmented, most of all between its tropical and temperate parts. European settlement in the Pacific may have been "thin and prosperous," but that level of prosperity, especially for wage labor, was only attained by the exclusion from temperate lands of "the poor and overcrowded"—that is, Asian and Pacific laborers. This segmentation was given formal approval by a policy of exclusion that began its legislative life in the 1880s.

The largest demand for unskilled labor came from mining, plantation agriculture, and construction, particularly in transport. Many workers were employed under fixed-term contracts and indentures and actually moved back and forth between home and workplace. Others were engaged in a more permanent relocation. The variety of people on the move is surprising. From Asia large numbers of Chinese, Japanese, and Indians spread throughout the Pacific Basin. The Chinese concentrated mainly in Southeast Asia but had a significant presence in areas of new settlement. The Indians were prominent in Malaya and Fiji, the Japanese in Hawaii and British Columbia. Pacific islanders could be found in large numbers outside their home territories, working as far apart as Peru, where they gathered guano (deposits of bird droppings shipped as fertilizer), and Queensland, where they cut sugar cane.

By far the most significant and numerous movement was that of the Chinese, who, against the wishes of their own government, began to emigrate in large numbers after the 1830s, particularly from the southern provinces in Fujian and Guangdong. Their emigration may be very old—certainly there was trade with Indonesia a couple of thousand years ago, and in the early modern period there was at least one big massacre of Chinese settlers in the Philippines. Chinese went on moving overseas long into this century, whenever local barriers were not thrown up either to keep them out of somewhere and exclude their "unfair" (i.e., cheaper) labor or to imprison them within communist China. Thus the Chinese sailed in the mid-nineteenth century to "Old Gold Mountain" (California) and "New Gold Mountain" (Victoria), where they excited hostility. They established large expatriate communities around the Pacific, especially in Southeast Asian countries such as Thailand, Malaysia, and Indonesia. In those countries they often excited resentment, too, and sometimes actually have been massacred in quite recent decades. Economic activity takes place within, and often despite, a much less healthy and "rational" political context.

In areas of European settlement the Chinese entry was often only temporary, partly because the initial movement was largely male and partly because the introduction of highly restrictive legislation in the second half of the nineteenth and early twentieth centuries curbed the dramatic inflow initiated by the gold rushes, preventing the reunification of families.

As soon as the outside presence threatened to reduce the wages of white settlers or to disturb the homogeneity of European populations, the barriers to entry came up. These became increasingly more stringent. The "White Australia" policy, quickly legislated into existence by the new federation in 1901 and 1902, was typical. Australia even legislated a tariff and bounty system to replace the Kanakas (indentured Melanesian laborers) in the sugar industry with white workers earning higher wages. Only in the last thirty years have such policies been reversed.

Cultural and political differences have ensured that integration in the Pacific would have economic roots. However, economic forces were not allowed to break down the cultural and political differences. The sheer size of the Pacific still acted as a major obstacle to integration, despite continuing transport improvement in the form of the motor car and airplane. The process described here was only a tentative one, one slowed significantly by two world wars (conventionally dated 1914–1918 and 1939–1945) and a major depression during the 1930s, events that impeded existing commodity and capital flows. Defensive policies such as the White Australia policy had already created major obstacles in the way of free movement of labor. The process of integration accelerated once more after the Second World War.

A Lasting Legacy?

No part of the Pacific Rim was left unaffected by the European intrusion. In the newly settled areas, almost completely European populations came to predominate because the sparse native populations were destroyed by microbes from which they had been isolated for centuries and to which they therefore had no immunity. The same process that afflicted Latin America was repeated in Siberia, then the Russian Far East and Alaska, in Australasia—although the Maoris in New Zealand fared much better than the Australian aborigines—and in Oceania, in island after island. Venereal disease lowered fertility, just as such diseases as smallpox, influenza, measles, and the like raised mortality rates. The white settlers outbred and outlived the natives; the outlook for the former was as favorable as that of the latter was unfavorable. Europeans therefore took the place of the native populations, very often inheriting cleared land suitable for agriculture or pastoralism and, because their numbers still remained low, bringing about development by substituting capital for labor. It is significant that European crops and domesticated animals also thrived in those regions that were free of major predators or disease.

Much of the Rim outside Asia was occupied by immigrants of European origin, although sometimes their move from Europe lay one or two generations back. The flow of migrants to the United States persisted from the sixteenth to the early twentieth century, to Australia from 1788 to the present. These flows only became large in the late nineteenth and twentieth centuries. As late as 1900 the total European population on the Pacific Rim did not exceed eight million. The European population became dominant in North America; in parts of Latin America, notably Chile; in the Russian Far East; and in Australasia. In much of the rest of Latin America the population also included a significant European element.

The Europeans were by no means always successful when they sought to settle permanently. There were evident failures in attempts at permanent settlement, notably by the Russians in the Americas and Hawaii, although the economic failure of one European group was often associated with the economic success of another.

The Russians possessed certain advantages. In the north the climate was harsh but in a way already familiar to European settlers. The Russians therefore were used to such an environment. The speed of movement of the Russian frontier, the "Wild East," as one historian has called it, was comparable with the transcontinental movement in North America. The Russian empire was to be the longest-lived of the European empires, mainly because it had a contiguous landed rather than a dispersed maritime nature. But once Russia changed from a landed to a maritime perspective, the usual problems of assuming control over far-flung possessions asserted themselves. Russian America proved a short-lived settlement of sojourn.

The Russians crossed the Ural Mountains only in the 1580s, but by 1638 they had reached the Pacific Coast. Over the next century they not only explored the Kamchatka Peninsula and fixed the political boundary with China for two centuries by the Treaty of Nerchinsk (1689) but also, in the persons of Vitus Bering and his men, crossed the Aleutian Islands and discovered what is now Alaska. As an explorer, Bering was the equal of a Cook or a La Perouse.

The economic lure in the trans-Siberian crossing had been fur—mainly in the form of the sable—just as it had been fur in the movement across North America, where the beaver was the particular attraction. The rapacity of trappers exceeded the capacity of fur-bearing animals to breed. The tendency was for overexploitation to impel ever faster movement of the frontier of the fur harvest. Trapper and trader were drawn on ever further into new areas. On the Pacific the sea otter and fur seal offered far more expensive pelts; as resources with higher value, they compensated for their distant location in an environment of greater risk.

The movement of the Russians along the North American coast after the establishment of Russian America (Alaska), with its capital at New Archangel (present-day Sitka), culminated in the founding of Fort Ross, about eighty miles north of San Francisco, first settled by the Russian-American Company in 1812, and in the attempted settlement of the Sandwich Islands (Hawaii) in 1815–1817. Despite attempts to diversify into other export staples, the main trade commodity remained fur, and these peripheral bases were intended to act as granaries and possible staging points for further movement south.

Ultimately the Russians failed to sustain American colonies. They were always reluctant to make a formal claim to the area for fear of offending potential allies. Fort Ross was sold in 1841 and Alaska in 1867, the former to the Swiss entrepreneur John Sutter, of Californian gold rush fame, the latter to the federal government of the United States. The reasons for failure included the competition of rival European powers, initially Spain, later Britain and the United States, but also the problems of integrating such a vast and inhospitable area into the Russian empire. The distances were enormous. Disregarding the enormous overland routes within Eurasia or North America, there were still 400 miles from the main center in Siberian Okhotsk to Petropavlovsk on the Pacific, another 1,100 miles to the nearest of the Aleutians, and a further 1,200 miles along the Aleutians before the North American continent was reached. All of this territory had to be traversed in small boats.

It is scarcely surprising that Russian America succumbed. There were far too many difficulties, which in microcosm illustrate the initial problems of any area of new settlement: foreign competition in the Chinese fur trade and in trying to sell manufactures along the American coast; unaccustomedly strong native resistance from the Kolashes, who destroyed New Archangel in 1802; labor shortages aggravated by constraints on migration and by disease or privation among both the Russians and the natives; the unfamiliar maritime mold of the colony; the restrictive monopolistic charter of the Russian-American Company, which controlled the colonies; and the traditional administrative and technical backwardness of the Russians. All contributed to the financial difficulties of the colonies and the decision to withdraw before possible ejection by rival colonial powers, but vulnerability to fluctuations in food supply was the key failure. Remoteness and the harsh environment led to a series of supply problems, with local food shortages becoming particularly acute at the very beginning of the nineteenth century, during the 1820s, and again in the mid-1850s. This happened despite the tiny size of the Russian population, which reached a maximum of 1,823 in 1839. Once the initial abundance of fur-bearing animals had disappeared, a high level of risk and a resource environment otherwise poor for the time prevented permanent Russian settlement.

It should not be forgotten that the arrival of Europeans was not the only lasting population movement to affect the Pacific Rim. Pacific peoples also moved around. Indeed, the latter dwarfed the former if we include the movement of the Chinese into Manchuria. The European presence, even if only temporary, often prompted significant movements of other people. These occurred on both a temporary and a permanent basis and were every bit as large as the European entry itself. In Southeast Asia cluster migration was as common among the Chinese as among the Europeans; family members, friends, and neighbors moved together and reestablished the traditional social and economic life of the region from which they came. A whole social structure was reproduced, with entrepreneurs and workers servicing the immigrant communities. Indians also settled permanently in Fiji and Japanese in Hawaii. Chinatowns and Asian communities of various kinds appeared throughout the new societies.

With the recent easing of immigration restrictions and the inability in places such as California to keep frontiers watertight, a fresh wave of migrants from both Latin America and Asia promises to change dramatically the composition of population. Hispanics are likely to become the largest single group in California

within a short period. Asian groups in the cities of Australia and British Columbia are rising as a proportion of total population. Even in New Zealand (with a
less catastrophic fall in the native population), the Maori birth rate, much higher
than that of the Pakeha (European) community, is changing the proportions of
the overall population. The demographic picture is a dynamic one, in which European origins are fading.

Despite the movement of other peoples within the Pacific Basin, the main
countries of European settlement remain recognizably European in their institutional characteristics, although they also bear the imprint of a successful adaptation to the local environment. For the most part they remain sparsely populated,
at least by the standards of the European source countries or the Asia Pacific region. Labor scarcity in the past helped keep income levels relatively high. Certainly a free labor market could have stimulated enormous labor flows from low-
income areas to these higher-income enclaves.

There has been a tendency to stress either the "invisible baggage" of the newcomers or the influence of a new and alien environment upon them. On the one
hand we find the thesis advanced that the new societies represented a fragment of
the home society in arrested development, the nature of the fragment being determined by the timing of settlement and the condition of the source country at
that particular moment of time. In Latin America, the United States, and Australasia, the full implications of Spanish feudalism, British bourgeois liberalism, and
British collectivism, respectively, are seen as unfolding in a way not experienced
in the source country. A variant of this approach also argues for continuity but
with the qualification that European society was simplified in the areas of new
settlement by the stripping away of the topmost and bottom-most elements of the
social structure. There was no imported aristocracy nor destitute *lumpenpro-
letariat* in these countries. Nor did brief flirtations with the use of forced labor, as
with convicts in Australia, make any permanent impression on the new societies.

An opposing viewpoint is represented by the frontier thesis, the notion that the
environment determined the nature of the new societies. The benignity and ma-
lignity of the environment are seen as affecting the nature of each frontier society,
encouraging individualism or collectivism, respectively, and thereby influencing
the relative importance of government and market in the opening up of the new
areas.

In practice, the new societies clearly were products of both their cultural background and the adaptation to alien physical and biological environments.

Within the countries of European settlement the native populations had lived
at levels of economic development well below those of the incoming settlers. In
some areas they were still only hunter-gatherers, particularly in the English colonies. Elsewhere there were sophisticated systems of agriculture, notably in the Aztec and Incan empires. In some areas farming techniques totally alien to methods

in Europe had been developed to suit different environments, from the thin, nutrient-deficient soils of the tropics to the high, often terraced plots of the Andes, with their short growing seasons, frequent frosts, and violent changes of temperature from night to day. Neither the wet rice agriculture of the former nor the integrated "archipelago" farming of the latter, with its vast array of cold-resistant tubers, was imitated by the white settlers. They adapted local foods that fit easily into their own regimes but really sought environments suitable for their existing crops or livestock. Some new crops were adopted—maize, tobacco, the potato, manioc (cassava), and the tomato—but the agricultural systems of the native populations were largely ignored.

There were two main reasons for this neglect. First, Europeans often disliked unfamiliar environments and their characteristic crops. Second, the decimation of native populations hindered the transfer of ecological knowledge from native societies and reinforced the break. However, in some Latin American nations, particularly the Andean nations of Ecuador, Peru, and Bolivia, significant native populations have survived and retained their own agricultural systems. Ironically, in Western nations research on the native crops is now revealing their qualities.

In general the settlers introduced their own agriculture, a European system with domesticated crops and animals alien to the native ecologies. The absence of significant predators and relevant plant diseases meant that these animals and crops multiplied very rapidly. For example, with no assistance from man, cattle became numerous on the Argentine pampas and horses on the North American prairies. However, there were difficult problems of adaptation in arid or semiarid environments or where soils were deficient in the appropriate nutrients. The wholesale introduction of irrigation systems or massive and continued addition of fertilizer to the soil could not help but change fragile native ecologies. Despite the emphasis on agricultures that were extensive rather than intensive—that is, adapted to a relatively abundant supply of land—the Europeanization of the environment was inevitable.

Much of this Europeanization was inadvertent. With the best will in the world, farmers versed in European techniques could not avoid altering the balance of flora and fauna. Crosby has detailed the rapid spread of European plants in environments disturbed by the economic activities of settlers. "Weeds" invaded those areas, carried in grain seed or in the mud on boots. Native grasses were often destroyed by the cloven hooves of domesticated livestock and the cropping of new shoots. Exotic grasses quickly invaded disturbed environments and within a few decades had begun to replace the native species.

Some change was deliberate—for example, the work of Acclimatization Societies, which introduced animals from home in attempts to extend the range of available species and recreate the environment of the immigrants' homelands. Enormous changes in the landscape were wrought. Sometimes these began to involve transfers between Pacific regions, as with the introduction of Australian eu-

calypts in California. Sometimes the results of the introduction of exotic fauna were potentially catastrophic, as with destruction of pasture by the rabbit in Australia. Overexploitation of particular resources also created its own problems. The disappearance of fur-bearing animals such as the sea otter along the North American coast, the removal of tree cover in clearing for agriculture, the destruction caused by early alluvial and later hydraulic mining—all these significantly refashioned the environment. The construction of large new urban centers and of a dense transport infrastructure, so characteristic of the "European" Pacific, compounded the changes. Where change becomes damage is of course a value judgment. There is no doubt that ecologies were changed beyond recognition, but in many cases this transformation was a precondition for the maintenance of a high standard of living for the newcomers and provided them with a more varied scene.

One enduring feature of the new societies has been the diversity of their economies. Although continuing to produce primary commodities on a significant scale, they also had significant manufacturing and service sectors from an early date. Initially, remoteness encouraged this development; later, technical dynamism reinforced it. The pattern of diversification of the economy spread to the whole of the Pacific Rim. Society after society has been drawn into the market economy and begun a process of modernization. The influence of Europe has extended to a whole range of different areas—to the establishment of the nation-state, to bureaucratic systems of organizing both government and private enterprises, to industrialization and urbanization, and to all facets of modern living, even such matters as dress and diet. Within the wet rice area, agriculture remained largely free from change until the process of mechanization began in Japan after the Second World War.

What parts of the overall package of what is called "modernization" necessarily go together? To what degree do the affected countries retain elements of their indigenous cultures? Whatever the changes in technology and organization, Western notions of democracy were not as readily embraced outside the English-speaking areas. Certainly the political systems of the other areas have tended to be more authoritarian.

The process of modernization was not limited to East Asia. Even in the former colonies of sojourn, a lasting impetus was given to the process of economic development. After decolonization, governments took over that were as committed to fostering a rapid pace of modernization as the former colonizers. The commitment was part of the reaction against colonialism, which encouraged a nationalism that was associated, as in Europe, with a policy of strengthening the relevant economies. How much the governments concerned had to build upon in the way of physical and human capital depended upon the net balance of positive and negative legacies inherited from the colonial era. There was a wide spectrum of legacies, from strong positive contributions to significant negative ones.

The net result of colonization reflected first of all the identity of the colonizing power. The Dutch and the Portuguese lay at one end of the spectrum, the British at the other. Somewhat ironically, the later Japanese conquest seems to have had a stronger positive influence than the European. In colonies of temporary sojourn, in contrast to colonies of settlement, the Europeans never represented more than a fraction of 1 percent of the population—a sprinkling of officials, a few entrepreneurs or merchants, perhaps some missionaries and to a varying degree their dependents. Ultimately these people were easily ejected or assimilated; the attitudes and institutions they brought with them had a more lasting impact. On the contrary, the Japanese represented as much as 5 percent of the population in Korea or Taiwan. Their physical presence was greater than was the Europeans' in *their* colonies, and more significantly the economies of the Japanese colonies were better integrated into the domestic economy. The result was considerable investment in plant and equipment and training of managers and skilled workers. The European powers never became so directly involved.

The balance of advantage and disadvantage of colonization for economic development is a complex one, not easy to evaluate without a clear specification of assumed objectives. On the negative, side there was the tendency of the metropolitan power to drain resources from the colonies in various ways, in remittances of profits or incomes and payment for administrative services. Often such a drain showed itself in a persistent and large trade surplus—in other words, an excess in the value of commodities dispatched relative to those received. Certainly the typical case was for such an export surplus to be maintained over long periods.

A second negative influence involved the placement of personnel from the metropolitan power at the apex of the political and economic systems. Newcomers filled the top posts in the public service, the professions, and, of course, the military. This substitution deprived the native population of experience relevant to the postcolonial period. Again, the degree of such substitution differed. In some cases even lower-level positions were taken by nonnatives—other Asian people, for example.

A third area of potential damage reflected the framing of policy in the interests of the metropolitan power. Particularly at key periods of stress, during economic depressions for example, macroeconomic policy was usually shaped in the interest of the colonizing power rather than the colonial society. Even in the era of laissez-faire and free trade, imperial preference was usual.

On the positive side, the colonial powers left significant infrastructures, both economic and social. Although the transport infrastructures might have been designed to serve mainly the plantations and mines producing exportable commodities, there is no doubt that they assisted in spreading the domestic market and training native personnel in a wide range of managerial and engineering skills. The mines and plantations themselves represented the core of a modern economy. There is little doubt that public health and educational facilities were improved. However, there may have been some element of initial deindustrialization resulting from exposure to competition from European factory-made goods. For example, local industry often suffered from the competition of British cotton goods. However, after a short time more mechanized factory-based production often began to compensate for this loss. Overall, from the perspective of economic development, the net effect of colonization was clearly positive in some places; in others it may have been negative, and much depends on what one thinks is the relevant period over which the assessment should be made.

There are those who regard formal empire, or formal political control, as irrelevant. Within an informal empire, they argue, Britain asserted as much economic dominion over Latin America, for example, as over Malaya or the Australian colonies. It is not uncommon to assume that such dependency has resulted in an unequal exchange between the periphery of ex-colonial societies and the metropolis of developed industrial countries and even to stress that underdevelopment is created by developmental links with the metropolitan power. Dependency is seen as a consequence of the exchange of primary commodities for manufactured commodities, the domination of the domestic economy by foreign capital, and the alliance of foreign capitalists, and later multinational companies, with domestic *compradors* (i.e., mere agents of foreign manufacturers) and exporters. Latin America is said to epitomize these relationships and Southeast Asia to fit the same pattern. It is often forgotten that such characteristics held for a large proportion of the first wave of decolonized societies, notably the English-speaking colonies of North America, and also the four Little Dragons of East Asia, which were at different times Japanese or British colonies.

Unhappily, a new European model, the Soviet model, influenced the pattern of economic policy adopted by those countries of the first wave of decolonization that have been slowest to develop significantly and practically all of the countries of the second wave. An inflexible policy of import substitution and a negative interaction between government and market hindered economic development. Conversely, where an informal Western empire exists it takes the form of an empire of ideas, in particular the domination of a wide range of European ideas over economic policy. This empire undoubtedly lives on.

6

The American Century

The Pacific Ocean is now our ocean. It never before was anybody's since the earth was formed. The Chinese of the great Central Kingdom never came down to the sea—they never built any ports, let alone ever set out across the stormy deeps. The British may have held a kind of sway as a part of their Rule Britannia. The Japanese, with ferocious industry, pretty nearly held it commercially and made, as we recall, a bid to establish their imperial sun in all its skies, but they were doomed to fail because of the United States. Now the Pacific is America's.

—Henry R. Luce, *Life* (February 23, 1953)

One of the most significant factors explaining the recent rise in importance of the Pacific has been the change in world economic leadership, or economic hegemony, as some prefer to call it. This passed first from Great Britain to the United States and threatens to pass from the United States to Japan. The latter transition is only half-finished and may never be fully complete. So fast is the pace of economic and technical change today that another leader may already be emerging.

The rise of the United States has also been associated with a shift in its demographic and economic balance from east to west. This shift is best symbolized by the publicity given each year to a mile-by-mile movement toward the west of the demographic center of the United States. Since 1790 it has moved steadily through Maryland, Virginia, leaving West Virginia during the 1850s, then Ohio, Indiana at century's end, and Illinois at the midpoint of the new century. On census day, April 1, 1990, the center had reached the farm of Garland Eaton, Sr., in Missouri.

These two tendencies merit careful analysis and are the principal themes of this chapter.

Regions of the United States

A country as large as the United States inevitably has regions differentiated by physical environment and by the particular interaction between humankind and environment. The classification adopted here is a three-region division—North, South and West. The relevant differences are large and important, and therefore the actual sequence of settlement by region is itself a principal factor in determining the nature of the overall economic experience. This is a clear case of what economic historians now call *path-dependence,* meaning that the history of a region in one period has a very substantial carryover effect in the next period. The following account summarizes the main characteristics of the primary regions and the nature of their interaction.

The North comprises two elements of the original colonial core, New England and the Middle Colonies, as well as an area settled shortly after independence, the Midwest. The region was originally characterized by domination of the rural sector by family farming on relatively small parcels and by a multitude of country towns with a smaller number of rapidly growing cities. It possessed a diversified, market-based economy and a democratic system of government initially very promotive of economic development at both the state and local levels. It was a pluralistic political system, naturally very egalitarian but with growing social differentiation.

The South included areas of the core that acted as the springboard for a second movement across the continent. Here, until the Civil War of the 1860s, the economy was based on export staples, initially tobacco, sugar, and rice but by the nineteenth century mainly cotton, produced on plantations using slave labor and on small farms with very few slaves. There was also a largely self-sufficient domestic economy, much less market-penetrated and diversified than the economy of the North. The level of urbanization was also significantly lower. Cotton culture carried the main features of the Southern economy right across the lower continent to Texas. The South therefore evolved a rival economic and social system to that of the North. The uneasy political balance broke down by the middle of the nineteenth century. The Civil War represented the triumph of the Northern over the Southern system.

There is little doubt that the risky natural environment of the South was a potent influence on the Southern economy. It was a malignant environment, and malaria, yellow fever, pellagra, hookworm, and many other diseases remained a special threat throughout the pre–twentieth-century period. Floods and hurricanes also presented a significant degree of instability unheard of elsewhere. However, its resource endowment—a warm and wet climate highly suited to lucrative cash crop production—offset the risks from the very beginning. In particular, this environment is important in explaining the introduction of slavery, which replaced the use of indentured white labor, and of the plantation system itself. Black slaves had a much greater immunity than whites to the fevers of the area, often introduced from their homelands in Africa in the first place. Interestingly, the Southern states were the only place in the Americas where the slaves consistently and rapidly reproduced themselves.

There is some argument in the scholarly literature over which half of the colonial core provided the dominant culture, whether the Yankee culture of New England prevailed overall. Undoubtedly the somewhat harsher and less fertile environment of New England encouraged a strong migrant stream into new areas. The victory of the North in the Civil War confirmed the introduction of its social system into the West.

The West embraces that vast area stretching from the rain shadow of the Rocky Mountains to the Pacific Coast. It has a number of distinctive characteristics. Most of it is arid or semiarid except for an area in the Northwest, in the states of Washington and Oregon. However, there does exist a plentiful if finite supply of water in the artesian basins east of the Rockies and in the rivers that collect the precipitation falling on the Rockies and carry it to the Pacific. Heavy investment is required to take advantage of these water sources.

The West is relatively disease-free but is subject to geographical and climatic shocks. Located along the Rim of Fire, the coastal area is known for its volcanoes (Mount St. Helens) and its earthquakes. Many of the largest settlements lie on fault lines, the most famous example being San Francisco, on the San Andreas Fault. Drought is a potential threat throughout the region.

A third characteristic of the West is that much of the area lay under Spanish and then Mexican control and was only acquired by the United States by force in the 1840s. One legacy of Spanish control was the recognition of the previously existing system of land grants, which complicated the issue of land distribution under U.S. rule and made impossible a simple creation of family farming. The attractions of the area lay in the abundance of resources—fur, fish, and timber, as well as gold, silver, and other minerals—and in the rich potential for farming as soon as the initial obstacles could be overcome.

It was perhaps fortunate that North American settlement occurred from east to west rather than from west to east. The transcontinental movement might have met significant obstacles had it begun from the Pacific. Such a movement would have been difficult had it come from Spain's colonies or (later) Mexico without assistance from the benefits of prior economic development in the East—the rich sources of capital, the markets that gave value to the West's resources, even the gold, and the technologies that allowed the surmounting of the greatest natural obstacles. After all, the Rockies represented a major barrier to movement; the Mexicans had found the Pacific Coast itself relatively difficult of access.

Formative Periods in the Two Americas

The rise to economic leadership of English-speaking North America, particularly the United States, and the relative decline of (mainly Spanish) Latin America requires an explanation. Such an explanation involves a comparison of long-run tendencies in the two areas.

Superficially, the initial advantage seemed to lie on the side of Latin America. Its resource endowment was clearly superior. Gold, silver, and labor were in much more abundant supply. Yet these apparent advantages could also be traps. The existence of large numbers of potential workers offered a temptation for the colonists in Latin America to become merely parasitic, to live on the backs of the native population. Various labor schemes were devised to do just that, whether they took the form of a semifeudal system such as *encomienda,* corvée labor in the mines under *mita,* or simply debt peonage.

Even gold and silver had both beneficial and harmful effects in that they stimulated a continuing interest by the Spanish in their empire as a pump for the extraction of revenue. Again, this activity was largely parasitic, since little was given in return. Economists explain the behavior of both the colonial government and the colonists as *rent-seeking*—that is, seeking the redirection of existing income streams toward themselves rather than the creation of new streams. In this way the potentially favorable effects of Latin America's greater resource abundance were counteracted.

However, it is still unclear why the thirteen British colonies, founded in an apparently unprepossessing part of the continent, managed to achieve a successful combination of political stability and economic prosperity. The two characteristics are notable in the respective histories of English-speaking and Spanish-speaking America by either their joint presence or their joint absence. In the former, it is clear that economic prosperity was achieved very early in the colonial period, if probate inventories are anything to go by. The statistical evidence that has survived shows the colonists enjoying at a very early date a material standard of living at least equal to that of the British. Well before factory industrialization became a significant force in the world, let alone in the United States, U.S. citizens were among the wealthiest people, particularly vis-à-vis income generated per head of population. Moreover, they achieved sustained *intensive* growth at a very early date, if at a rate slow by modern standards.

It is tempting to simplify the picture and offer one of two explanations. One has the United States abundantly endowed with just the kind of resources critical to economic development. Such an endowment characterizes both the core area of the nation at the time of independence and the new areas just about to be settled at that time across the Appalachians in the Midwest. This region yielded land of good fertility and usually good drainage; a moist and mostly temperate climate capable of supporting the cultivation of a wide range of foodstuffs and cash crops through long growing seasons; and an abundance of first-generation staples such as fish, fur-bearing animals, and timber, as well as industrial raw materials such as iron, coal, and cotton.

Equally important was a superb natural transport infrastructure consisting of a heavily indented coastline with rivers navigable for long stretches, the Great Lakes, and the whole Mississippi-Missouri-Ohio watershed as it impinged on this region. The water routes were easily linked by public works such as the Erie Canal (1825), which joined the Hudson-Mohawk river system with the Great Lakes and was probably the most profitable canal ever constructed.

Such a cornucopia was particularly characteristic of the North region. Movement either westward or southward eventually involved growing disadvantages, as one entered an increasingly arid or disease-prone region. Successful settlement in the resource-abundant and risk-benign environment of the North largely preceded settlement in the West. Settlement of the South was more or less simultaneous with that of the North, the high potential return from many economic activities compensating for greater risk exposure.

One highly respected U.S. economic historian has argued that resource abundance was a vital factor in the nation's economic success but that it was defined, perhaps even created, by technical dynamism and therefore by economic success itself. After all, there are no resources as such, only the possibilities of resources provided by nature in the context of the technology of a given society at a certain moment in its evolution. However, in the United States, nature provided a rich stream of possibilities, the absence of which would have been a major obstacle to such splendid economic development.

The economic development of the United States can be viewed as a continent's discovery of how to exploit its own resources. A dramatic decline took place in the share of total output traded with the outside world, reaching a persistently low level during the eighteenth and nineteenth centuries. This decline reflected the success of the learning process. The sheer size and resources of the United States allowed a degree of self-sufficiency unmatched by other "leader" economies, such as Great Britain or even Japan.

The second explanation for the United States's economic and political success rests on a form of cultural rather than geographical determinism. The nature of the migrants, or rather the nature of the societies from which they came, is seen as the key to understanding differences in economic performance between English- and Spanish-speaking America. The stress is both on attitudes and values and on knowledge of technology or institutions—that is, on the "invisible baggage" of the colonists.

The major early sources of migrants into North America were the most dynamic economies of the early modern period, particularly the British Isles, Germany, and to a lesser extent France, whereas the migrants into Central and South

America came largely from the Iberian Peninsula, an area in economic decline after the sixteenth century—if its economy had ever risen far enough to warrant the term *decline*. Key groups in northwestern Europe were developing mechanisms of problem-solving, as befitted economies changing fast enough to keep posing new problems. After all, once initiated, the process of economic development is usually self-reinforcing. The important baggage for a new society may be specific ecological or organizational knowledge relevant or adaptable to new areas of settlement. Some measure of preadaptation occurs, but it only requires one or two migrants. More important is a general problem-solving bias. Receptive settlers can pick up pertinent information very quickly. To some degree all migrants, by breaking their accommodation with the source society, make themselves open to new ways of seeing or doing things. Some, however, seem intent on raising their position or status by recreating the old society and placing themselves on a higher social rung.

The cultural argument has limited validity unless spelled out in detail. There seems no reason to believe that there are more potential innovators or entrepreneurs, more people prepared to take a risk, in one rather than another society. The key difference is in opportunity, or in where that opportunity exists. Opportunity may be limited by particular patterns of behavior or by institutional structures, but these need to be specified in some detail.

There are serious reservations about an argument based on either geographical or cultural determinism. A satisfactory explanation is likely to be multicausal rather than unicausal, incorporating something of each of the previous explanations.

As a heuristic device, we might assume that there is a natural tendency for economic development to occur, even in its *intensive* form. Obstacles to such an advance can be created by the environment or by the political system. Both are potential sources of risk or uncertainty for the key economic decisions, the investment decisions. A high-risk environment can be a major obstacle to economic development. To some degree, abundant resources compensate for high risk. Again, the market system, so efficient in attracting resources, can be impeded by high levels of risk inherent in its atomistic nature, notably opportunism and volatile price behavior. The key factor at the core of the process of economic development is the relationship between government and the market, particularly regarding the management of risk.

North America was characterized by both dense markets and dense government, each structure embedded in strong communities. Government in the British colonies was at its densest at the bottom level. Colonists did not like paying taxes to the British or even to local colonial masters. However, they did not mind paying at the local level in return for local public goods, an activity usually promotive of market development. Thereby they reduced the abuse of political power and also promoted commercial advance. The market was not simply allowed to flourish of its own accord; it was actively promoted by government.

Upon independence, the dense system of government was inherited with strong tiers at the state and local levels. The three main tiers—federal, state, and local—were buttressed by a fourth tier of multifarious informal organizations. These balancing institutions in the community straddled the divide between the public and private spheres, providing all sorts of noneconomic services as well as promoting information transfer, problem-solving, and risk management. No market can thrive without the support of a strong community, particularly before specialized auxiliary institutions exist to provide the services required to lower transaction costs in a market economy. The community also provides the underpinning of values that support market activity. Without these, frequent recourse to judicial enforcement of contract would be needed but would be too costly. In the Southern states and in Latin America, a hostile environment, the existence of slavery, and the short commercial life of some first-generation staples encouraged transience and lack of commitment to community. Laborlords had not the interest in community held by landlords. Good community institutions were vital.

Latin America lacked dense market and government structures. External links with Spain were created but were heavily regulated and controlled. In theory, all trade moved along well-defined routes; in practice, smuggling created a black market with high levels of risk. Domestic markets failed to blossom and were discouraged if they threatened to produce commodities competitive with those from Spain. Factor markets also failed to develop. Land was usually tied up in large holdings rather than distributed in plots accessible to ordinary migrant families and open to frequent exchange. Slavery and various other forms of forced labor were common. Slaves usually failed to reproduce themselves. The short time-horizon of those using slave labor is shown by their reliance on purchases of additional slaves rather than on the natural increase of existing slave populations.

The structure of government was highly centralized, with instructions originating from Madrid on all sorts of matters. Local government was almost nonexistent except as a reflection of the central authority. Creole, or local, representation in colonial government was kept to a minimum most of the time. Revenue raised was not reinvested in public goods. In fact, the government was often a new source of risk.

The key to successful economic development lies in a positive interaction of government and market that happened to be missing in Latin America. Structures are important but not sufficient; competent decisionmaking still matters. However, government can be overcentralized or excessively decentralized. There is a fine tightrope to walk between an inflated, rent-seeking imperial center and anarchic fragmentation. Without efficient markets it is difficult for government to raise revenue; without a dense structure of government, key public goods necessary to market operation will not be provided.

Transport improvement illustrates the point. During the colonial period the involvement of local government was critical to the improvement of transport, and such improvement was critical to the extension of markets. When railroads and canals were pushed inward from the Atlantic seaboard in the first half of the nineteenth century, transport improvement continued to be a product of "mixed enterprise." The key players were city governments and the local business interests they represented. Cities such as Boston and Baltimore, which were not located on major rivers, built railroads (with loans, subsidies, and land grants to private railroad companies) to gain control of their hinterlands. Competing cities with access to river traffic extended their commercial reach by building canals.

The major achievement for the Spanish was to retain central control of a large empire for four centuries. It would have been almost too much to have expected economic development as well. Left largely alone, the North American colonies were competitive, creative, and innovative in a way the monolithic control of the Spanish empire would never allow. In microcosm the British colonies recreated the multicell nation-state system of Europe. Spain and its empire looked more like the Tsarist Russian autocracy.

American Industrial Leadership

Given the relative advantages of the North American colonies, it is perhaps not surprising that the United States swept past Great Britain in terms of both leadership in industrial technology and the level of prosperity achieved. By 1914 U.S. superiority was very pronounced. Not only was the value of its industrial output approximately as great as that of Great Britain, Germany, and France combined, but within industry itself productivity levels per worker were about twice the British level, which reflected a capital endowment also double the British level.

The "American System of Manufacturing" differed significantly from the British precedent. The economy of the United States was characterized by features that also marked the other areas of settlement. The relative abundance of land and resources not only helped to maintain a significant export trade of primary commodities, even at the peak of U.S. industrial leadership, but also influenced the very nature of industrialization.

Underpinning the American System of Manufacturing was an abundance of energy sources. The new machine technology required large inputs of energy, and North America was well endowed with every conceivable type, soft and hard. The graphic image of the Industrial Revolution, the use of steam power, does not accurately describe the nature of most nineteenth-century U.S. industrialization. Where appropriate, steam power was used and used quickly, as in the transport sector, whether in the steamboats on the Mississippi or in the steam locomotives of the rapidly expanding rail network. But in the factories and other economic enterprises, steam was little used until the last third of the nineteenth century. Other sources of energy were lavishly exploited, probably with a generally decreasing degree of efficiency over time. Soft energy sources were used first: human energy from a young and healthy population (an often neglected energy source); then livestock, notably horses, supported by the extensive pasture available throughout the humid parts of the nation; and the abundant timber from the woodlands and forests. Hard energy sources ranged from water power, available at many sites in New England (the center of early textile industrialization), through anthracite and black coal to oil. The abundant energy more than compensated for the initially high price of the relatively scarce capital, which became cheaper and more readily available only toward the end of the nineteenth century.

Machine-using, capital-intensive technology economized on some labor, notably unskilled workers, but it required vast amounts of energy. Yet the most important sector of U.S. industry in the nineteenth century was the machine-tool sector. The use of precision instruments allowed the mechanization of the limited number of metal-using processes, such as boring, drilling, and planing. From this followed the production of machines by machines. Market opportunities and pressures spread the use of machines throughout the economy.

The widespread application of a machine technology was dependent upon the use of interchangeable parts. Traditionally the key figure in the British Industrial Revolution was the fitter, and the key tool, the file. Each part was unique to a particular machine. In such a system parts were not interchangeable in the way so successfully shown for firearms by U.S. manufacturers, at the Great Exhibition at the Crystal Palace in London in 1851. The whole machine culture was characteristically American, from the cotton gin to the combine harvester, from the Colt revolver to the sewing machine, from the bicycle to the Model T Ford. Machines increased substantially the productivity of labor.

At the same time U.S. businessmen pioneered the production line. As early as the late eighteenth century, Oliver Evans created a flour mill in Baltimore, the production line of which required no human labor. The basic principle was developed in the meat-packing works in Chicago and the Midwest, where overhead conveyors moved the carcass around to various points, at which it was progressively and systematically dismembered. This was, strictly, a *dis*-assembly line. The assembly line culminated in the making of the Model T Ford, where it was combined with an intensive machine technology.

However, U.S. industry did not stop here. The second wave of accelerated industrialization demanded explicit scientific knowledge, not just the skilled tinkering of engineers. High levels of literacy and the direction of significant educational expenditure toward science and technology created success in the new industries—chemicals, electronics, and automobiles. The United States seized the opportunity to exploit fully the possibilities inherent in the motor car and the use of electricity and new materials.

These technical breakthroughs were also associated with the rising importance of the large business enterprise. The capital-using bias in technical progress brought with it significant economies of scale. The problems of managing large numbers of workers and large quantities of capital for the railways prompted the use of new methods of organization. Such large investments also brought a high level of commercial and industrial risk.

The new enterprises sought to integrate vertically and horizontally, absorbing both suppliers and competitors. The goal was to take transactions out of the market and to internalize them—to reduce risks by keeping as many as possible within one firm. Conceptualizing the process of trust-building and amalgamation as an attempt to minimize transaction costs, however, slightly misses the point. Clearly the bureaucratic revolution allowed both an increase in efficiency, the result of specialization of function and the appointment of professional managers, and an increase in direct market control through the "visible hand" (rather than reliance on the "invisible hand" of market competition, as described by Adam Smith). It was also underpinned by the divorce between ownership and control, as ownership in the limited liability joint stock company was dispersed among large numbers of individuals and companies. Once again an important, if not the most important, motive for the new system of ownership was management of risk.

While the United States was forging ahead in perfecting the new machine technology, Latin America had slipped from empire into anarchy. Independence was followed by a long period of conflict before the revised national boundaries became fixed. New political structures emerged only slowly. In particular there was a continuing struggle between centrifugal and centripetal forces. After much strife the tendency to centralization reasserted itself, albeit in the smaller political units emerging from the Spanish empire. However, a tradition of "winner-take-all" politics was established, which made for frequent and often nonconstitutional changes of government.

After independence, therefore, the Latin American nations were afflicted by the twin, and related, problems of political instability and aborted breakthroughs to sustained economic advance. The latter reflected the proliferation of market imperfections and economic uncertainty. Economic behavior and institutional structures adjusted to an environment of extremely high risk. In particular, the market for manufactures was limited by the low level, unevenness, and volatility of income. How modest Latin America's degree of industrial development was relative to that of the United States is illustrated by the textile industry in Mexico. Mexico possessed the most developed industrial structure in Latin America, yet in the late nineteenth century the United States had roughly eight times the number of ring spindles (for spinning) per head of population.

There have been periods, as for example amid the favorable international conditions before the First World War, when a significant number of Latin American states appeared about to achieve an economic takeoff and rapid industrial growth was sustained for brief intervals. However, these proved to be short-lived interludes between periods of extreme economic difficulty and, by the twentieth century, renewed political instability. Debt repudiation, currency revaluation, and rising inflation were more typical of economic life in Latin America.

Economic Growth and the American Far West

The Coast and Cascade ranges border the Pacific from southern Alaska to Northern California. This long, thin strip of mountains blocks the weather fronts from the Pacific and gets soaked with precipitation. By the time the fronts have crossed the mountains they are invariably spent: In Northern California, the land west of the Cascades and the Sierra Nevada can receive up to 150 inches of precipitation annually, but on the interior eastern slope the figure drops to as low as 4 inches. In its natural state the San Joaquin Valley south of Sacramento is a desert, as is the coastal plain of Southern California, sandwiched between the Pacific and a chain of mountains.

Along the coast there is a poor match between the supply of good farmland and the natural rainfall. The desert soil in the south is wonderfully fertile but usually receives insufficient rainfall for successful agriculture. Irrigation is indispensable to the region's farmers. When the Spanish explored Southern California they found an arid wasteland they judged to be virtually useless. The high ground in the north gets enough moisture for farming, but the land, though fertile, is mostly hilly and heavily timbered. Areas better suited to cultivation, such as Oregon's Willamette River valley, are isolated by natural barriers, and marketing the produce has been difficult. Most of the rivers are short and flow strongly to the ocean. Furthermore, North America's Pacific Coast lacks natural harbors, the notable exceptions being San Francisco Bay and the waterways at Vancouver, Seattle, Tacoma, and San Diego.

The situation is best exemplified by California's Central Valley, a flat stretch of potentially very fertile land extending some 600–700 miles from the entry into the valley in the far north of the Sacramento River to the entry in the far south of the San Joaquin River. Flowing in opposite directions, the two streams find a confluence in San Francisco Bay, forming the largest contiguous estuary in the continental United States. Throughout its length the valley averages a width of about 100 miles, broadening somewhat at its central point. It is as large as England.

Outside the coastal strip and a few valleys opening directly from the sea, the Central Valley was and is the core of Californian agriculture. Large areas of the valley were originally prone to seasonal flooding; on many occasions almost the whole northern valley became a gigantic lake. The valley, located between the coastal mountains and the Sierra Nevada, is in a potential rain shadow; its rivers, however, collect the enormous amount of rain that sometimes falls on the mountains. Heavy precipitation on the mountains means that, although the rivers travel short distances to the sea, they carry enormous amounts of water, particularly during the spring thaw and during storm deluges. Often these rivers carry too much water and flooding results. The southern half of the valley, conversely, is much more likely to be subject to drought than to floods. The regular alternation of these two types of natural shock has exerted much more of a molding influence on economic behavior than have earthquakes, to which the region is also vulnerable.

The earthquake hazard arises from California's location on the Rim of Fire. Such a potential threat has been compounded by the construction of major cities on fault lines. There is some excuse for this placement, since it is difficult to avoid such faults in the coastal area. Moreover, San Francisco and Oakland have been built around the finest natural harbor along a coastline singularly deficient in this respect. Even the 1906 disaster failed to provoke an avoidance response—that is, the relocation of the city of San Francisco elsewhere. Since that date there has been an enormous increase in the scale of urban capital at risk to another earthquake. To offset this risk, there has also been a proliferation of both private and public risk-management responses, ranging from the adjustment of construction materials through the provision for an emergency fire-fighting capacity to the taking out of earthquake insurance. A rich society can afford to take enough precautions to make all but the largest of disasters endurable. However, a stroke of extreme ill fortune—a giant quake—would demand the support of all the resources of the U.S. economy.

In other respects the risk environment was and is less threatening. The biological shocks of disease—human, animal, or plant—were not much of a problem, although in the shantytowns of the gold rushes there could be epidemics of typhoid and the like. Generally the climate was attractive to settlers, and quickly a low mortality and long life expectancy prevailed. From the very beginning a certain amount of individual violence was endemic in Western society, but there was an absence of more organized violence such as brigandage, conflict with the native population, or outside invasion. California and the West emerged relatively unscathed from the Civil War.

In terms of resources California was always potentially very well endowed. It has been argued that in some areas the abundance available to the pre-European population was such as to encourage the establishment of private property rights even among them. The whole Pacific Coast was attractive to settlers because of its first-generation staples, resources available for gathering and requiring little processing. It is often difficult to impute strong property rights to such commodities and, even if such rights are imputed, to monitor their observance. The whole area was prolific in fur-bearing animals, the beaver on land and the sea otter along the coast. Dense stands of trees, some of immense dimensions and great age, such as the redwood or sequoia, existed, particularly on the hills and mountains and northern coastal strips, where rainfall was adequate. The rivers and sea were rich in fisheries. The meeting of warm and cold currents off the California coast created an abundance of food for a variety of fisheries, although the supply was subject to quite dramatic natural shifts.

Many of these resources were easy to exploit both by natives and newcomers. Less immediately useful were the alluvial deposits of gold washed down by the rivers from the mountains or the tar that bubbled to the surface in the La Brea deposits in Los Angeles. The whole Western area was rich in minerals and potential raw materials. Although many of these deposits might have a long life as the technology of extraction improved and became more capital-intensive, the alluvial deposits had a finite lifetime, like many of the other first-generation staples. Fishes, fur-bearing animals, and timber disappeared at a rapid rate.

The sunny and mild climate of Southern California was in itself very favorable to human settlement. It has supported a whole series of employment- and wealth-creating activities, such as moviemaking, tourism, and the testing of aircraft. The region's first economic boom was in agriculture. Fertile soils and a long growing season free of frost allowed the cultivation of a wide range of crops, even out of season. California could grow subsistence crops and a whole series of second-generation staples—that is, cash crops that were renewable year after year—from wheat to cotton, plus a wide variety of fruits, nuts, and vegetables. These are all grown on a stupendous scale. But without irrigation and transport links with potential markets within California and the rest of the nation, the land had initially been valueless. Some means of organizing and releasing resources to provide water supply and transport infrastructure had to be found.

The inaccessibility of California was at first largely responsible for its slow settlement, but once it was opened up by settlers its economy grew dramatically. Early on, the first-generation staples became a focal point of competition between different nations trying to establish political sovereignty and an economic presence in the area. Spanish settlement was a reaction to the interest of these other nations. The lack of good harbors, the apparent inhospitality of the desert coast in the south, and the general inaccessibility of the whole area had discouraged earlier colonization, even when the Manila galleon had familiarized at least some Spaniards with the area. Spanish settlement was part of a defensive reaction, which, however, proved weak.

New Spain, representing Old Spain, claimed all the land as far north as the Columbia River (a claim inherited by Mexico when it became independent in 1821). Russian activity in the North Pacific forced Spain, after a gap of about 160 years, finally to colonize and fortify Upper California. To this end the inspector general of Charles III, José de Galvez, led an expedition north from Baja California in 1768. As a result, at the time of the Russian intrusion there were four Spanish presidios, or forts, including one at the capital of Monterey and another at San Francisco. They were supported by nineteen mission settlements stretching from San Diego to the Golden Gate.

About 3,000 Spanish-speaking colonists, with the help of the presidio militias, ruled 20,000 Indians, using their labor on the missions. These religious outposts adopted a proselytizing role and produced a range of foodstuffs, from grains and livestock products to wine and olive oil. The population density in Spanish California was only marginally greater than in the Russian-held territories. The area remained extremely remote from the main centers of population in New Spain and from the main trade routes, its growth partly stifled by restrictions on trade with other nations.

Mexican control (after independence in 1821) was no stronger than that of the Spanish, so it is scarcely surprising that very little pressure was required to detach California from Mexico. U.S. intruders helped exert such pressure in the 1840s. The economic difficulties and political instability of the fledgling Republic of Mexico made the protection of such distant areas, only accessible across long and dangerous supply routes, an impossibility. There was a continuing tendency for the province to detach itself from its core. Rival governors appeared. Competing for support, they made large distributions of land. The missions were broken up as part of an anticlerical movement. Some Spanish or Mexican settlers threw in their lot with the newly arriving U.S. frontiersmen. By the early 1840s the province was clearly about to reject Mexico's control permanently. In a series of events analogous to those in Texas, an initial assertion of separate republican status in 1846 was followed by the absorption of California by the United States under the Treaty of Guadalupe Hidalgo (1848) and the declaration of statehood in 1850.

The California gold rushes accelerated these changes. Nine days before Mexico ceded California, gold was discovered at Sutter's Mill, near Sacramento. The resulting surge in population created a bigger market not only for the farmers in California but also for those in Oregon. In California, Oregon, and Washington, total population rose from 106,000 to 444,000 between 1850 and 1860. Oregon, which had no effective government until 1843 and no political boundaries until 1848, achieved statehood in 1856, as did Washington in 1889. The discovery of gold at Fraser River in 1858 lured diggers from the United States across the Canadian border, and the founding of British Columbia (1858) was an attempt to prevent U.S. demands to annex the region. There was a similar situation in Australia: The gold rushes encouraged immigration, and farmers and manufacturers benefited from a wider market. Furthermore, this immigration created an electorate that demanded that Crown lands be made available for small family farms rather than be used as large pastoral estates.

The U.S. gold rushes displayed elements that characterized all the later booms. There was a marked lack of government control. This absence differed markedly from the experience of the Australian gold rushes. In both California and Australia the government quickly asserted its ownership of the gold. However Victoria,

Australia, went on to regulate the size of claims and to tax gold production through a license fee, later replaced by an export tax. The income thus derived helped pay for the gold commissioners, who were responsible for law and order on the fields and for escort services that took the gold to the main export ports. Moreover, the initial monetary confusion caused by the gold discoveries was dealt with by the opening of a branch of the Royal Mint at Sydney in 1855 (and further branches in Melbourne in 1872 and Perth in 1899). The government was responsible for assaying and coining.

In California the situation was very different. At the time of the gold rushes there was no real existing framework of government. Consequently, the state was slow to react to problems, and there was much more self-reliance on the fields. The government was unable to siphon off as much revenue as the Australian state did. Policing of the fields, where the level of violence was almost certainly higher than in Victoria, was in the hands of vigilante groups. The initial reaction to monetary problems was to allow the creation of private mints; solutions to other problems were often provided within a context of free market operations rather than reliance on government.

The preference for free market solutions continued even after the initial period of alluvial mining. Technical improvements in equipment and the construction of elaborate systems of water control allowed the introduction of hydraulic mining, which tore away whole California hillsides in the quest for gold. There followed massive environmental damage and the dumping of enormous amounts of tailings into river systems. The introduction of similar systems into Australia was quickly countered by government action. By contrast, the fight to control hydraulic mining in California was a long, drawn-out process.

As elsewhere throughout the Pacific, there has been a problem in limiting the exploitation of first-generation staples to a sustainable level. The definition of private property rights, which might have made things more orderly, took time, as the case of alluvial gold illustrates. The economic exploitation of fur-bearing animals, the large herds of cattle left by the missions to run wild, timber reserves, and the fisheries off the coast all led to intermittent local booms and a rapid depletion of the reserves. Improvements in technology accelerated the process.

The second great stimulus to the settlement of the American West was public investment in railroad building and irrigation projects. The companies that built the transcontinental railroads were given by the federal government 400-foot-wide rights-of-way and grants of each alternate square mile of land adjacent to the track free of charge. Under the Homestead Acts, 160-acre sections of land were made available at a low cost for farming. Irrigation was first practiced by farmers who could divert water or afford to have it pumped from nearby streams. Private irrigation companies served some farmers, but federal government involvement was needed if all the homesteads of the desert region were to be provided with water. The water made Southern California blossom with orchards and vineyards and turned the San Joaquin and Sacramento valleys into the most productive farming region in the world.

In *Cadillac Desert*, Marc Reisner writes that the major federal government water projects were "as close to socialism as anything this country has ever done." In Australia, contemporaries described such public investment as "colonial socialism." In fact, the use of the word "socialism" is misleading here: Public investment was intended to create conditions that would encourage *private* investment. By organizing and releasing scarce resources, the public sector provided the infrastructure necessary for profitable investment in private activities. It was expected, for example, that once the public sector built railroads that reduced high transportation costs, the private sector would respond to new investment opportunities in fields such as agriculture or urban activities such as manufacturing, residential building, and real estate. The proceeds of economic growth were shared between the state (through increased revenue from taxes and land sales) and the rest of the community (through greater economic activity). This was not socialism, therefore, but a means of developing the country's resources through a symbiotic partnership between the public and private sectors. Of course, the appropriate mix changed over time; flexibility of structures allowed for appropriate adjustments.

By the time transcontinental railroads were being laid across the Great Plains and the Canadian prairies, hundreds of towns (many existing in name only) were competing vigorously to be included on one or more of the routes. The successful towns would be linked with Eastern markets and therefore be well placed to provide local farmers with transport, processing, and commercial services. It was thought that this battle would determine which towns would become the major cities of the American West; each individual settlement's future as a place of profitable investment was at stake. Thus, when Tacoma was selected as the terminus of the Northern Pacific line, nearby Seattle fought back and paid for its own branch line connection. The Seattle city government then lobbied successfully for improved rail services, and the Northern Pacific moved its terminal to that city eight years later.

Before the 1870s, Los Angeles was a small town competing with the likes of Wilmington, San Bernardino, and Anaheim as a service center for local farmers. The town was located fifteen miles from the Pacific on a minor river, and no natural deep-water harbor existed close by. San Diego, 100 miles to the south, had the only suitable harbor in Southern California and seemed perfectly placed to grow into the region's metropolis. To offset these natural disadvantages, Los Angeles merchants and landowners proposed that the city government provide a subsidy to the Southern Pacific railroad to pay for a costly detour of a new line from San Francisco to New Orleans through Los Angeles. Local voters approved the plan in a ballot. It was a winning move: Los Angeles became an important railroad center.

The city government followed up by improving the harbor at San Pedro and building major waterworks for the city and nearby farmers.

The use of "mixed enterprise" to develop North America did not arouse much ideological debate. Most people saw it as a cheap and convenient method of opening up the continent. Since the colonial period, U.S. society had upheld the right of each individual to follow market signals freely, in keeping with the principles embodied in Jacksonian democracy. Under mixed enterprise, the private sector used state subsidies to increase private rates of return; the state used the resulting increases in private investment to boost social rates of return. This system did not contradict the philosophy of individual achievement free of government interference. The settlement of the U.S. West was characterized by a continuing series of economic booms involving the rapid exploitation of available resources, which affected almost every sector of the economy. Individuals were able to harvest resources rapidly and largely unchecked by government oversight.

These booms occurred in the context of an extremely rapid development of markets. Initially, commodity markets were constrained by the sparseness of population and the problems of access. However, sharp population increase and transport improvements established close links with the large and quickly growing markets to the east. In addition, the telegraph made possible the immediate transmission of information concerning price movements and market opportunities. The West could also take advantage of auxiliary market institutions that had already developed in older areas of settlement.

Factor markets developed alongside the commodity markets. The initial ambiguity about land rights often gave a significant advantage to those who could afford good lawyers. Nevertheless, a land market developed that was capable of putting the acreage into the hands of those who could reap the highest returns. Last of the factor markets to develop was a capital market integrating California with the Eastern states. Only in the second half of the nineteenth century did interest rates in the whole nation begin to converge. The fragmentation of the U.S. banking system did not assist this process. High incomes generated high savings, and a significant amount of Eastern capital undoubtedly went to finance the opening of California.

By 1910 there were five major cities along North America's Pacific Coast: San Francisco–Oakland (population 687,000), Los Angeles (438,000), Seattle (239,000), Portland (215,000), and Vancouver (124,000). Tacoma (84,000) and San Diego (40,000) were the only other large cities along the coast. Each of the five major cities had established railroad networks to draw trade and commerce from their hinterlands and away from smaller, competing towns. Each benefited from repeated booms in agriculture—in wheat on the large bonanza farms, in fruits and vegetables that supplied Eastern markets out of season, and in cotton, where mechanization and large scientific inputs produced the highest yields in the United States. Each city prospered because its population growth was due mostly to immigration. Migrants were generally of working age (though Southern California did attract a large number of retired persons); their education had been provided by other regions of the United States; and they usually arrived with money to spend, adding to the total level of demand for goods and services. Building and servicing the cities increased the demand for labor. Labor costs were high, but this did not affect the cities' economic prosperity because agriculture in their hinterlands was so productive.

The Pacific Rim cities were basically commercial in function. They all increased their manufacturing capacity during the 1920s, but growth was most rapid in Los Angeles. New investment in diverse and profitable areas meant that the Los Angeles economy continually renewed itself, like a hardy plant. Oil, gas, airplanes, and defense industries were all California success stories. The climate and range of scenery drew filmmakers to Hollywood. The rate of black immigration increased, and labor costs fell. California also attracted outcasts, like John Steinbeck's Joads (in *The Grapes of Wrath*). People migrated to Los Angeles because of the range of jobs the city offered, and for those with skills and savings there was also the expectation of a congenial life in sunny suburbia. Even though the Great Depression hit house-building and real estate hard, oil production, agriculture, and the movies still thrived.

California is a perfect illustration of both the successes and the failures of a market economy. On the one hand, the California economy sustained the highest income per head achieved anywhere in the world through a long period of extraordinarily rapid growth. This economy operated with a highly capital-intensive technology at the frontier of best-practice. On the other hand, in California the market has yielded some of its ugliest aspects—corruption, exploitation of labor, unemployment, poverty, the squandering of natural resources, environmental damage, and a frequent failure to require private users to pay for public goods.

The difficulty of defining property rights or monitoring their enforcement often results in the overexploitation of resources such as timber or fish. From an early date governments and private individuals in California sought to preserve these, not always very successfully. The greatest difficulties arose with the finite supply of water. A common problem has stemmed from government's asserting a strong ownership right after an initial period of allowing private rights to prevail. The tendency of government to undercharge for the use of water has encouraged farmers to overconsume it. However, irrigation greatly increased the intensity of land use, multiplying its value manifold.

The maldistribution of the demand for water relative to its sources of supply necessitated enormous engineering works redirecting the flow to the arid south and to the rapidly growing cities. Enormous rivers such as the Colorado were controlled and used to supply electricity as well as water. The size of the projects tended to grow over time, from the local works of the San Joaquin Valley to the massive remaking of nature in the Owens Valley. Water was carried enormous distances. Yet water demands—domestic, agricultural, and industrial, and now for vast wildlife refuges—have increased year by year at an alarming rate. Today nearly every major river has been dammed, its water diverted, its normal flow changed. The impact on ecological systems—salmon spawning, for example— has been great. It is possible that the proper pricing of water would postpone for a long time the placing of an operational limit on the growth of population and the economy.

Some of the consequences of earlier unregulated water use were potentially cat- astrophic. Within the Central Valley the debris from hydraulic gold mining, par- ticularly on the American and Feather River fields, began to move downstream in the 1860s and to raise the bed not only of the tributaries but also of the main riv- ers. This process both impeded navigation on the rivers and greatly increased the risk of flooding. Such flooding was treated as a problem to be solved by individual action, despite the fact that nobody during the nineteenth century was in posses- sion of the relevant information on river flow. The consequence of individual ac- tion was a series of attempts to pass the problem on to somebody else. A competi- tive raising of levees was likely to be expensive, inefficient, and vulnerable to failure if as few as one or two holders of land along the river did not act. Coopera- tive action was required to solve the problem, both to gain the particular knowl- edge of river flows, their variation, and the appropriate measures needed for flood control and actually to implement the enormous engineering task. More to the point all this had to be paid for in the context of an obvious free-rider problem— each party hoped the others would have to bear the costs. It is difficult to know under what conditions cooperation can evolve spontaneously to resolve such problems. In most cases a government-imposed solution is more efficient.

In many areas, therefore, California illustrated the problems of a market econ- omy. Elements of high risk demanded government action. However, dramatic economic development created the financial resources needed to resolve the problems thrown up by growth itself. On balance the successes greatly exceeded the failures.

The Westward Shift

The westward shift took two different forms: a rising interest in the resources of, and the United States's strategic position in, the Pacific; and an increasing pres- ence, both demographic and economic, in the Western region of the nation, par- ticularly California. These two tendencies reinforced each other.

First, U.S. interest in the Pacific involved New England merchants and traders. That interest rose as U.S. traders displaced the British along the coast during the Napoleonic Wars. The merchant marine of the new republic was competitive in the whole Pacific area, invading the preserve of the British East India Company in

Australasian waters as well as trading in fur, sandalwood, and bêche-de-mer with China. There was also a significant trade with Spanish and Mexican California, notably in hides. Yankee traders were prepared to deal in anything that was in demand in the area.

The interest in trade was supplemented by a growing attention to whaling and sealing. As the whale fisheries of the Atlantic were worked out, whalers from Nantucket and other New England ports began to move into the Pacific. The first whaler to reach the Hawaiian Islands arrived in 1819. For forty years whaling was the most important factor in the islands' economic life. The first visit of a U.S. naval squadron came in 1826. The interest in whaling continued to grow throughout the first half of the nineteenth century, until by midcentury the United States had a fleet of about 900 boats in the Pacific area, centered on Hawaii.

The Hawaiian whale industry was the most significant in the history of the Pacific. It was destroyed by the overexploitation of the whale population, the side effects of the U.S. Civil War, the destruction of thirty-three ships by pack ice in 1871, and the substitution of inorganic for organic oil. The replacement of sail by steam, in which the British were far more competitive, also temporarily undermined the U.S. position.

However, a temporary setback in one sector did not prevent the success of the United States in establishing the preeminence of its interests along North America's Pacific coast. Under the Monroe Doctrine, framed in 1823 the basic principle of U.S. policy had become "America for the Americans." At least for the time being, this motto implied slight interest in the world outside the Americas. Manifest Destiny, as it was called, would eventually have carried the United States to the Pacific Coast even in the absence of the gold rushes. However, the latter accelerated the whole process and began to focus attention on such issues as the crossing of the isthmus of Panama to avoid the long, dangerous rounding of Cape Horn. What at the end of the eighteenth century had been an equal competition between the United States and a number of European powers became by the mid-nineteenth century a very unequal contest. There was a major defeat inflicted by the United States on Mexico, which lost half its territory. As we have seen, the retreat by the Russians was more orderly, involving the sale of both Fort Ross (1841) and Alaska (1867). There has been much argument over how cheap the purchase really was, particularly since most resources apart from fur and gold were only accessible much later. But even in the short run the purchase further extended U.S. interest in the North Pacific. The Treaty of Washington, negotiated with the British in 1846, set the boundary with Canada.

Notwithstanding the Monroe Doctrine, the United States retained its interests in the Pacific, notably in Hawaii, and on the isthmus of Panama. A railway was constructed across the isthmus in 1855. Later a series of projects for canal construction culminated in eventual success in 1910. The hostile disease environment had proved a major obstacle, and the curbing of the threat of yellow fever was an important achievement. Completion of the project represented a significant step in improving transport links between the east and west coasts of the United States.

The short war with Spain in 1898 suddenly leapfrogged U.S. interests across the Pacific since it involved the establishment of U.S. control over the Philippines and the formal acquisition of Hawaii. Concern over the rise of Japan and an increase in its naval strength helped focus the latter interest. Although there was little conflict in the Pacific during the First World War, Japanese neutrality enabled that country to further increase its economic and naval strength, largely at the expense of the British. U.S. concern at the relative naval balance in the region increased still further. Hawaii, and in particular Pearl Harbor, became the base for a strengthened Pacific fleet.

During the steady growth of U.S. interest in the Pacific, the economy of the Western states, California in particular, had been growing very fast. The West, including the mountain states, grew from having only 2 percent of the total population in 1860 to 8 percent in 1910 and 15 percent in 1960. California by the 1970s accounted for 11 percent, but the share has leveled off since 1960. Consequently, in terms of population growth, the West, and California in particular, was for a very long period the fastest-growing region in the United States, with a continuous flow of migrants from other states attracted by the sun, high incomes, and good employment opportunities. In the early period incomes were greatly in excess of the national average and only converged on that average from the 1930s onward, never quite falling to that level. The relative share of national income contributed by the West was therefore well above its share in population.

However, it would be wrong to date the rise of the West, and particularly California, prematurely. The population of California was only 1.5 million in 1900 and still only 6.9 million in 1940. California eventually became by far the most densely populated area of European settlement in the Pacific, at 31 million by 1992, by which date the state had plunged into recession and some growth was being siphoned off to Arizona and New Mexico in the Southwest.

Other Areas of European Settlement

How far was the pattern of settlement of the United States, and its Pacific Coast in particular, typical of such settlement throughout the Pacific Rim? How far, for example, can we take economic development in California as a model of economic development in the areas of European settlement generally?

First, there are points in common. All shared in the strong market orientation, at least in respect to links with the international economy, notably with the "metropolis," whether this was located in Europe or shifted to the rapidly expanding Northeast of the United States. The degree of penetration of the domestic economy by the market differed much more significantly, with a general lag in Latin America.

The pattern of trade for all the areas of European settlement was initially similar. It involved the export of resource-intensive commodities in return for manufactures, both producer and consumer goods. Generally such a pattern is regarded as semicolonial. It is also associated with a significant import of capital and people from the metropolis. This distinctive pattern has prompted some historians to talk of a variant of capitalism, called settler or dominion capitalism, intermediate between the fully developed capitalism of the metropolis and the inchoate capitalism of the real periphery, the undeveloped world.

Settler societies are supposedly characterized by the diversion of a significant part of the surplus generated in the production and export of staples into higher incomes and consumption and thence into the diversification of the economy, particularly the development of a manufacturing sector. Again, the countries of new settlement shared both relatively high income levels and very much more diversified economies than their population size would lead us to expect.

Income levels in Australia, Canada, and New Zealand vied with those in the United States to head world rankings at the end of the nineteenth century. Moreover, the levels of income in the states of the Pacific Northwest and in Pacific Canada tended to be well above their countries' averages. Once again most of Latin America lagged seriously, including even Chile. The order of difference was at minimum two to one. Economic success was very much greater in the English-speaking parts of the Rim.

Initially a diversification of economic activity was promoted by a high level of natural protection, afforded by remoteness and high transport costs, from metropolitan imports. Behind this natural barrier, high income levels encouraged the production of a wide range of services and manufactures. Yet the profitable export of primary commodities was a two-edged sword in that it created both a divertible surplus but also a potential staple trap. The continuation of high exchange rates and high real wages threatened the competitiveness of manufactures and tradeable goods in general around the Rim once transport and communication improvements removed a large measure of the natural protection. Governments were not averse to substituting artificial protection—that is, tariffs and other restrictions on trade—for natural protection, even in Latin America.

Second, there are some points of significant difference between California and the other areas of European settlement. Most "new societies" were characterized by small domestic markets; indeed it is more accurate to talk of the tyranny of small markets than the tyranny of distance. Clearly California was an exception in that it could link up easily with the large and fast-growing market in the rest of the United States. Moreover, its potential in terms of population size and therefore its own market size was much greater than elsewhere. A large part of this greater potential may itself have been a consequence of proximity to a large market; both chicken and egg helped California. To some degree Canada could link up with the same market, but the international frontier did create a significant barrier to trade with the United States.

Australia, New Zealand, and Chile were by contrast small in population, remote from other large concentrations of population, and often separated by high levels of natural and/or artificial protection. As a consequence, the pace and degree of industrialization in these other new societies was much less impressive than in California. Their industrialization came to rely very much on the existence of tariffs, which were introduced in Victoria as early as the 1860s and within a short period also in New Zealand and Canada.

Another difference involved the role of government and community in the different areas. The problems of remoteness, resource deficiencies of various kinds, climatic instability, and small markets constituted a high-risk environment that encouraged a more active role for the government in the areas of European settlement outside the United States. Such a role as practiced in the Australian colonies was graphically, if rather inaccurately, described as colonial socialism.

Governments in the Australasian colonies and Canada deliberately adopted a developmental strategy based on a liberal policy of land distribution, assistance to migrants, and railway-building, either directly through public companies or by means of private enterprises enjoying a significant government subsidy through land grants. Once more Latin America stands out as particularly different because of the early distribution of the land to a small number of large landholders, which was a disincentive to the kind of migration that prevailed elsewhere.

California thus falls at one end of the spectrum of the mix between government and market. The timing of development in California accentuated the full playing out of a free market philosophy. At the other end of the spectrum were probably the highly governed Australian colonies. However, some combination of government action and market operation was vital to successful economic development. After all, both California and the Australian colonies were successful in terms of the income per head achieved, the former more so than the latter. It is a matter of opinion how other features, such as a more egalitarian distribution of income in Australia, are evaluated. The vulnerability of California to a possibly rapid deterioration of general welfare is also relevant.

7

Modern Japan and the "Little Dragons"

The Northeast Asian experience had changed what economics knew about development. European theories about protestantism and the rise of capitalism and industrialisation were now as satisfying as pre-Galilean astronomy.

—Ross Garnaut, *China's Growth in Northeast Asian Perspective* (1989)

East Asian Success

One of the greatest problems of economic history is how to explain the enormous upsurge of material productivity in East Asia during the past generation. As late as 1960 there were authors who saw how well Japan had recovered from its defeat in the Second World War but still did not believe that further significant development would take place or that elsewhere in the region it would take place at all. Many, many books and articles have subsequently tried to account for this East Asian "miracle." Perhaps miracles are always unexpected, but the sense in which the word is meant in this connection is "marvel," not something outside nature that cannot be explained.

Japan was the first great East Asian success. From very early in the twentieth century, the West recognized that here was an exception. A non-Western military force first beat a Western nation when the Ethiopians defeated Italy at the battle of Aduwa in 1896, but that was only a flash in the pan. The fact that the modernized Japanese military won the entire Russo-Japanese War of 1904–1905, sinking the Tsarist fleet in the process, announced that an Asian industrial power had arisen, for a long time the only non-Western one.

The extent of Japan's success, the enormous growth of its economy, especially after 1945 and more particularly after 1960, and its huge trade surplus with the

United States are what really concerned somewhat awestruck Western minds. In the 1980s the concern sometimes became almost hysterical. In the U.S. political arena "Japan-bashing" became a cheap way of trying to attract votes—cheaper, anyhow, than readjusting the U.S. economy to the new realities of the world. Western comprehension of the speed and vitality of economic growth in other East Asian countries, such as South Korea and Taiwan, dawned even more slowly than it did with respect to Japan.

The explanations commonly offered for East Asian growth emphasize either the role of the state or the productive merits of Confucian culture. A number of economists protest that if states have been effective this can only have been by chance, because states have to guess right about world markets or their planning (more accurately in East Asia, their steering) of the economy cannot work. The abject failure of central planning in the Soviet empire and the way in which China is starting to flourish by abandoning central control give a lot of support to the view that states are ineffective and the market ultimately rules. Despite loose talk of their invincibility, we know that even governments such as Japan's, with its influential steering agency, called MITI (the Ministry of International Trade and Industry), have made some bad bets. An economist would suspect that it is only a matter of time before any nonmarket agency guesses wrong. However, it is possible that the Japanese state has mostly guessed right since the war and that this does largely explain the country's success.

Economists are also inclined to deride the influence of culture. Where was culture, they ask, during all those centuries before 1945, when the whole Confucian region of East Asia could have done with a boost to its development? Nor, they point out, can an explanation based on culture account for regional differences in economic performance within the same general cultural area.

An even smaller group of scholars stresses the importance of institutions, as opposed to, or in addition to, the value system that elevates hard work, thrift, and a concern for education. The institutions involved are business firms. The Overseas Chinese form communities in many separate countries, but they are linked in business networks that arise from kinship and local affiliations. Their web of connections spanning East and Southeast Asia makes economic growth in the region inexplicable solely in terms of the policies of nation-states.

The difference between large Japanese corporations and the Overseas Chinese business is quite sharp. Whereas the Japanese used the central government to build up an economy of large firms (or perhaps one should say the ruling groups behind the central government used the Japanese), Overseas Chinese society used the family firm. To date both forms have been very effective.

In China itself, until the Maoist era (1949–1976), when central planning was embraced with a vengeance, governments were weak and corrupt, and the economy expanded mostly from below, as millions of small businesses multiplied. A plausible case has been put forward that coastal China experienced a commercial revolution during the nineteenth century. This activity, the work of private entrepreneurs, was peripheral to the state, literally in that the area involved was a strip along the coast, metaphorically in that it grew up on the edge of the Qing empire's control. There were two Chinas, the developing commercial coast and the agrarian interior, the latter holding the political power. When China became communist in 1949, the amoebalike replication of small firms continued only among the Overseas Chinese, wherever they had settled. That was mainly in Southeast Asia, but Hong Kong and Taiwan should be included.

The institutionalist approach needs something more. To comprehend the success of the Overseas Chinese business sector, the boom in world markets once trade barriers were lowered after the Second World War has to be taken into account. Access to the rich U.S. market was important. This access was also vital to the growth of Japan and South Korea, both of which received in addition U.S. expenditures designed to help contain China and Russia in the Cold War. Taiwan, South Korea, Hong Kong, and Singapore became the Little Dragons that followed Japan into high growth rates and industrialization.

None of the factors adduced to explain East Asian growth is independent, much less sufficient, whether government by dominant parties, world market trends, culture, or institutions. The patterns they form overlap one another, though not completely. For example, Taiwan has a structure of predominantly Chinese, family-owned firms, yet it benefited economically from the infrastructure constructed when it was a Japanese colony between 1910 and 1945. Korea had been a colony of industrializing Japan, too. Depending on how far we think Japanese development was derived from the West, Japan's colonies may conceivably be seen as secondary colonies of the Western world, acquiring its characteristic technology, such as railways, at one remove.

Before the long catalogue of factors affecting East and Southeast Asian development is ever complete, we are likely to respond to the historical detail by shrugging and saying, "That's the way it was." We can sympathize with a leading specialist on Japan, Chalmers Johnson, when he lists explanations for its postwar achievement and concludes that, to an extent, he agrees with them all. In order to think about the topic in an informed way, we need to absorb some recent history. We need to look at the record of economic change since the mid-nineteenth century in Japan and China and briefly consider more recent changes in the "Little Dragons."

The Early Industrialization of Japan

The political balance of Tokugawa Japan was fatally upset in the 1850s by the arrival of a U.S. fleet under Commodore Perry bearing demands that the country join the community of nations and open itself to world trade. The Russians,

French, and British were all contemplating similar moves. Since, in the eyes of influential Japanese, the alternative looked like the humiliation China had suffered after the Opium Wars, Japan agreed to open up. In succeeding years there were protests and some attacks on Westerners, but resistance to Western influences was far weaker than in China.

The conservative Tokugawa shogunate was overthrown in 1868 and the emperor restored to rule. This revolutionary act was called the Meiji Restoration. The "outer *daimyo*" were deeply implicated in it. The Meiji emperor was at once supported by a group of determined modernizers. Admittedly, the aim of this group was less to achieve economic growth for all the people than to strengthen Japan vis-à-vis the West, to avoid the confusion of late Qing China, and to react to the West along the lines of, "If you can't beat them, join them." The results were stunningly successful.

For the next fifty years Japan underwent exceptionally thorough and rapid economic development, quite astonishing considering the possibility in developing countries of a backlash from traditionalists; considering the financial as well as social costs of adopting many Western ways in the course of creating the infrastructure of an industrial country; and considering the fact that Japan had no role model—it was the first non-Western country to industrialize. In other non-Western areas, such as the Ottoman empire in Turkey, attempts to establish Western-style businesses with modern plants often failed quickly and abjectly. Not so, viewed overall, in Japan.

There may be a sense in which it is fair to compare Japanese industrialization only with the performance of other less-developed countries at the same period or after. Earlier, there had not been quite the same opportunity. By the late nineteenth century the technological equipment of the West was overwhelmingly superior and included many items that had not been invented at the time, say, of the Chinese emperor's famous rebuke to the British ambassador in 1799, when he said that the Celestial Kingdom produced everything it desired. Subsequent advances in transport and communications were particularly noticeable, and the real prices of manufactured goods were driven down and the goods standardized by machine production.

Still, the way Japan grasped industrialization was phenomenal. The will of the regime to catch up with the West was unparalleled among developing countries, and this drive was soon matched by an intense desire for change on the part of the urban public. Westernizing became a craze. One individual, Yukichi Fukuzawa, who had learned English from sailors, traveled in the United States and Europe in 1860–1862 and later sold *ten million* copies of a book commending Westernization. When copies of Elbert Hubbard's inspirational best-seller about personal reliability, *Message from Garcia*, were found in the tunics of Russians killed during the Russo-Japanese War of 1904–1905, the emperor ordered a huge edition to be printed in Japanese. Japan is a society that thinks exhortation works.

Japan's success stemmed in part from a better preparation for development than existed in other non-Western countries. It is hard to avoid a tinge of hindsight from this perspective. Societies and economies are complex systems, and many may quietly possess attributes or institutions that may flourish in fresh circumstances—may adapt to growth—and thus appear to have been more important in sparking growth than they really were. Despite such reservations, it appears as though the Tokugawa period inadvertently prepared the way by maintaining internal peace, which continued to be preserved by the Japanese government, not by a colonial power. This stability is not given to every society; as instanced by many African countries, colonizers may merely hold the ring between antagonistic forces, which fall into conflict after the colonists leave, making development very difficult. Japan had created a real as well as a mythical homogeneity of its people.

Under the Tokugawa there was by Western standards little law, yet society was orderly and contracts were enforceable. There were high levels of technical skill. Japan was a stylish, design-conscious society. By premodern or even modern less-developed country standards, it also had a high level of literacy.

None of these advantages absolutely guaranteed that development could actually be paid for, but here the country was both lucky and calculating. Rising agricultural productivity meant that peasant farmers were able to pay a high land tax, which enabled the Meiji government to accumulate capital. When Japan first entered world markets, it exported primary products. Most developing countries are obliged to do this at first; food and raw materials are what they mainly produce. Not much value is added or skill inculcated. The art lies in moving beyond the role of de facto resource colony.

Japan exported silk and tea. Fortunately, two other main suppliers of raw silk, France and Italy, were hit by silkworm disease. China's output was suffering from the aftermath of the Taiping Rebellion. The competition was virtually eliminated, and half of Japan's bill for importing the latest machinery and hiring a large number of technical experts from Great Britain, Germany, and the United States was met from the foreign exchange silk exports earned. Four thousand experts were brought in over about twenty years from the mid-1870s on.

Japan also built up a merchant marine, the sixth-largest in the world by 1913, which earned foreign exchange by carrying goods for other countries during the trade expansion before the First World War. Beyond these things, Japan received substantial reparations from China for alleged hurts and slights—in reality, because China lost the Sino-Japanese War in the 1890s and the Boxer Rebellion of 1906. After the war in the 1890s, Japan acquired Formosa (Taiwan) as a colony from China and in 1910 was also able to secure Korea. Predatory behavior thus paid. Monetary reparations paid a lot of bills. A pattern was established whereby Japan fought a series of wars for territory and resources, such as in the so-called Manchurian Incident of 1931, after which the puppet state of Manchukuo was set up on the Asian mainland. China was invaded in 1937, and the Greater East Asia Co-Prosperity Sphere was extended as far as Burma and New Guinea early in the Second World War.

Determined efforts enabled the country to escape China's fate. The "powers" did not colonize Japan. They did oblige Japan to keep tariffs minimal, preventing the building of infant industries behind protective barriers in the nation's own market. The country plunged into world trade naked, and its industries, forced to keep warm, had to produce at world market prices. It was sink or swim for exports and import substitutes, although until the 1890s trade was helped by a decline in the exchange value of the silver-based Japanese currency. Only in the period from 1906 to 1911, after Japan had made her presence felt by defeating Tsarist Russia and expressing new demands, was the West persuaded to relinquish special rights for its traders and acquiesce in the raising of Japanese import duties.

By that time Japan's manufacturing industries were firmly rooted. It is important to note that this transformation was not centrally planned after the fashion of command economies, although the government certainly did a great deal to modernize Japan. From 1868 to 1910 the state's share of total investment was between 40 and 50 percent. Government bore the costs of pilot plants in textiles, shipyards, and railways, but then sold them off. It did not establish nationalized industries. It did build hospitals, harbors, and schools, plus technical schools for medicine, navigation, commerce, and fisheries, along German and U.S. lines. The costly, wasteful showpiece investments common to later Third World developers were avoided.

Japan was clever at absorbing its samurai military caste into productive society. The samurai were bought out with government bonds that could be used as collateral to start businesses, thus solving with a single round of payments the problem that the Tokugawa had first tackled by making pensioners of the military caste. This measure in no way stopped Japan from recruiting professional military forces.

All told, the policies were sensible and pragmatic. They steered the economy and fostered it but never amounted to central planning of a socialist kind. Business was helped, but in overseas markets it had to make its own way at prevailing prices. The state saw itself mainly as the arena in which disputes could be dealt with and questions of resource allocation adjusted, if not solved.

An ardent sense of national interest was involved, not to say fabricated. Consumption was held down and private luxury minimized. Appeals to save more or consume less had some effect on Japanese society, an effect reinforced, as it still is, by the lack of generous social welfare payments or good state pensions. Even now income differentials are low. The CEOs (chief executive officers) of corporations are paid much less relative to shopfloor workers than are their Western, especially U.S., counterparts. Today the earnings gap in Japan between workers and the heads of automobile manufacturers is six times less than it is in the United States.

This salary distribution has always been said to have a soothing effect on industrial relations.

In the process of growth, on the other hand, the size of the home market is important, and if workers are not paid much they cannot buy, or even save, as much as they otherwise might. At any rate, the Meiji state was not tender to blue collar workers, suppressing labor militants. It did not discourage population growth, hoping thereby to keep the labor supply up and wages down. The lands it colonized had even lower standards of living and did not draw away Japanese migrants in the way many British colonies had.

An economic miracle thus took place between 1886 and 1911, a phase when Japan achieved the world's fastest growth rates for exports and successfully fielded an up-to-date army and navy against the hapless Chinese in 1894–1895 and the astonished Russians at Port Arthur in 1904–1905. The Japanese sank in the Straits of Tsu-shima every ship in the Russian fleet, which had sailed around the world from the Baltic Sea. Japan had thoroughly modernized its major industries. The government had funded the creation of railways, post offices, telegraph and telephone systems, and an electricity grid. All this was up-to-date and, of course, very expensive.

By the time of the First World War, then, Japan was established as a significant industrial power, the only non-Western example. During that war, the country was on the side of Great Britain, the United States, and their allies; Japan switched allegiances in the Second World War, siding with Nazi Germany. An instructive way of looking at the interwar period, when the direction changed, is to jump ahead and look back at alternative views of the causes of the Second World War as they pertain to Japan.

The first of these views is the standard Western one of Japanese perfidy, embodied in wartime propaganda such as the British pamphlet *Japan the Enemy* or scores of gung-ho Hollywood movies. In its portrayal of all things Japanese as hateful, this approach was abetted, it must be said, by such events as the sneak attack on Pearl Harbor and later suicidal *kamikaze* dive-bombing attacks; and, after the war, by Japan's long delay in making even a symbolic apology, its refusal to adopt school textbooks that teach the war period candidly, and its cavalier attitude toward the Asian women forced into its military brothels; and, once the country had become financially powerful again, by its rather open chauvinism, matching the chauvinisms of the West.

The story line by which the West accounts for Japan's wrongdoing has the officer class overwhelming civilian politicians in the 1930s, assassinating leaders who resisted militarism, and starting an aggressive expansion into the Asia Pacific region. The expansion becomes the imperialist extension of a weird medieval state under an emperor claimed to be a god. Japan's motives are thus presented as bizarrely political, welling up from deep, dark springs in the Japanese soul and Japanese political life. The means include the Rape of Nanking as Japan invaded

China, the impressment of Korean and other women into Japanese military brothels, the torture of prisoners, the Death Road, and other horrors. The result was a bitter, hard-fought war ending in the dropping of two atomic bombs on Japan in 1945, at Hiroshima and Nagasaki, and the unconditional surrender of the country.

The factual history here is correct, but there is a revisionist way of looking at the causes. In this version, the Japanese were acutely conscious of lacking secure overseas sources of food and raw materials for their growing population; felt encircled by Western colonies in Asia; were increasingly excluded by protectionist policies from markets in the West itself; and, interestingly (remember, this is between the wars), were already fearful of economic competition, as other Asian countries were becoming better able to supply at least their own manufactures. In addition, the speed of Japanese industrialization had left the country with an unprecedented dependence on widespread foreign trade. In principle, this trading strategy was safer than putting all the eggs in one basket. Unfortunately, all markets were hit hard by the international slump of the 1930s, and the Japanese felt particularly hurt and aggrieved.

Military expansion seemed a way to make sure of resources and markets. Furthermore, there were precedents in Japan's recent successful campaigns. Civilian members of the government scarcely doubted any more than the military did that war could pay. They were equally responsible for creating a nationalistic defense state with a planned military-scientific effort.

The low quality of Japan's manufactured goods between the wars can also be reinterpreted as an adaptation to the country's circumstances. It was standard in the West between the wars to dismiss the Japanese as cut-rate imitators, prone to rename their towns Sheffield or Birmingham so that they could stamp "Made in Sheffield" or "Made in Birmingham" on their wares. Many Japanese exports really were shoddy. But they were also cheap. They were aimed at the bottom tier of Western markets and especially at the low-income markets of mainland Asia. The West's fallacy was in thinking that because this was what the Japanese made, they could not produce anything else and were inherently uncreative.

That is a great mistake to make, about any people. It is especially mistaken about so technically adept and style-conscious a people as the Japanese. The very facility of the Japanese nevertheless seemed to reinforce the copycat story. In the sixteenth century the Japanese copied Portuguese muskets and solved a problem with the firing mechanism that no European armorer had overcome. At the end of the 1850s the first U.S. ambassador was asked to lend his horse and got it back at the end of the afternoon, by which time Japanese metalworkers had copied the iron horseshoes perfectly. Much of the manufacturing achievement after the Second World War was the product of "reverse engineering"—that is, of stripping down a Western product and building a better version of it from the bottom up.

But this insistence on imitation rather than creativity confused the factual history—what actually happened—with what could happen, and did happen, once incentives changed. It shows the dangers of thinking only like a historian and taking the facts for granted rather than thinking like an economist and believing that what is observed will probably alter when incentives change. An explanation of variations in Japanese scientific and technological creativity in terms of changing incentives is more satisfactory than one based on supposedly permanent racial or cultural characteristics.

Japan had established modern science within a single generation after 1868. Japanese filed many of their own patents and won many U.S. patents as early as the 1890s. A Japanese scientist won a Nobel Prize for atomic physics in 1935 (following which funding was switched to relatively routine military science). In the 1980s, after the enormous engineering and economic successes of the postwar years, a major effort was begun in pure science, which has made Japan the second largest publisher of scientific papers. The practical payoff has not been forgotten: 10 percent of the staffs of the biggest companies were engaged in R&D (research and development) by the end of the 1980s.

The Japanese Economic "Miracle" Since the Second World War

In 1945 Japan was occupied by the United States under General Douglas MacArthur. His administration included some New Dealers who had been unable to get their full program adopted in Franklin Roosevelt's presidency. They saw in conquered Japan a virgin field they could sow with reformist policies. On regaining independence in 1952, the Japanese rejected many of these ideas. They took the technology and aid offered when Japan was used as a forward base in the Korean War, but they did not accept, for example, U.S. measures to raise the status of women. However, one important reform measure with a lasting impact was a change in the tax system, which equalized incomes to an extent politically unacceptable in the United States itself.

The effects of the Second World War, which for the Japanese began early, with the invasion of China, lingered in Japan's war-damaged land. The youngest age groups who lived through the years of scarcity, those born in the 1930s, had internalized the ethos of hard work and low consumption already evident in early industrializing Japan. Fresh incentives are least able to erode habits learned in early childhood. Coupled with low welfare payments and low old-age pensions, this ethos has kept savings rates high.

It is easy to forget that, despite the extent of its industrialization, Japan was widely depicted as a developing country as late as the 1960s. The nation ran a deficit into that decade and in some years since. Oddly, given the abundance of consumer goods in modern Japan, a virtual siege mentality has been recreated by later events. The oil shocks were powerful frights. Despite an astounding reduction of 25 percent of energy inputs between 1979 and 1989, during which time industrial output *doubled,* the Gulf War of 1991 again reminded many Japanese that they depend on international order for markets, raw materials, and sources of energy.

Postwar Japan started out with the low labor costs of a developing country and the productivity of a developed one. Status and income differentials were reduced but not removed. The hierarchy in the factory was preserved to the extent that, although there were still incentives for managers, there was no wide "us-them" divide. Workers accepted the need for rigorous quality control. They did not block change, and it may be surmised that their relatively high levels of education and training helped them accept the need sometimes to shut down whole lines of production, as well as to carry out instant maintenance on the shopfloor, without causing demarcation disputes. Unlike typical Western workers, they became "team players." They were paid annual bonuses related to the performance of the company, and approximately one-third of them, in the larger corporations, received more-or-less secure lifetime tenure in their jobs.

Japanese education is distinctively biased toward science and engineering and manages to induce good results in average or below average pupils. Industrial training dates back to Meiji times; Mitsubishi had technical training establishments in shipbuilding before 1914 and carried them over when it entered the chemical industry. Japan probably leads the world in exploiting research results: R&D is done close to the production processes and with an ear open to the marketing men who communicate what buyers really want.

Leading industries, ones where technical change is in the air, attract able young people in other countries, too. Where Japan scores is in its ability to diffuse best-practice, bringing all companies up to the level of the industry leaders. Reverse engineering, industrial espionage, and the cheap ride that is obtainable from simply scrutinizing, or if need be buying, other people's patent specifications were all used to take Japan to the forefront.

It may not be too fanciful to see in this a tradition that has stretched forward from Tokugawa times, when government edicts spread instructions on the best way to carry out all sorts of technical tasks. In eighteenth-century Germany there was a similar tradition; Japan and Germany excel at best-practice diffusion. At any rate, Japan succeeded not by deregulating its economy but rather by calculatedly transferring good ideas about technology. The central government played an active role in this process, for example by setting production standards. But its main agency, MITI, did not plan production targets. It avoided the waste that comes from such bureaucratic rigidity, instead cajoling firms to behave in what the technocrats in Tokyo saw as the national interest, and allowing any that were really inefficient to go to the wall.

Immediately after the war, Japan perceived that the best markets were where incomes were highest: in the West. The reduction of barriers to trade made these markets more accessible, though Japan has continued to protect its home market. That market is relatively easy to protect since, in addition to tariffs, there are formidable costs to penetrating a cliquish society with tortuous ways of doing business and a difficult language.

After 1950 Japan first developed 'smokestack' industries, the old staple industries of textiles, steel-making, and shipbuilding. These were labor-intensive activities, and in Western countries the workers engaged in them were highly unionized and able to bargain for what, by Japanese standards, were high wages. Western, especially U.S., markets were targets for the Japanese. However, as Japan's own labor became more skilled and better paid and as lower-wage economies in East Asia began to crowd competitively into the export markets, Japan itself began to move around the Product Cycle. It started shifting to other types of industry, where more value was added and in which paying more for labor could be justified.

Different parts of the Japanese textile industry accordingly peaked at different times, according to their skill requirements. The country moved, as the United Kingdom had previously moved under the prodding of Japan's own competition, to expand sectors requiring more and more skilled labor. At each stage, the sectors adding less value and employing cheaper, less skilled workers were shed to competing countries, mainly elsewhere in the East Asian region. In other words, postwar Japanese growth was accompanied by systematic and flexible structural change, so that the composition of its industries was never still and the country continued to trade on its comparative advantage.

By 1977 smokestack industries were in decline around the world. Less educated, less skilled, blue collar work forces were shrinking. The impact of these changes was muffled for a while in Japan by the need for smaller, fuel-efficient cars after the oil shocks of the 1970s. This demand bolstered employment in the automobile industry, but eventually more of those jobs were moved to plants outside Japan employing foreign labor. Within Japan the emphasis shifted to still higher value-added products, first of all consumer electronics. These needed fewer resources per unit of product than automobiles and were thus doubly suitable for a resource-poor nation facing competition from countries with cheaper labor.

After about 1960, Japan's success in expanding its economy, export share, assets, and income was as spectacular as it was unanticipated. A better understanding of the nature of the country's industrialization between the wars might have reduced the element of surprise, though the postwar "miracle" did go well beyond the trend the war had interrupted. Subsequently, besides trying to spot what is special about the way individual Japanese corporations are organized and perform and making the first tentative efforts in the early 1990s to incorporate some of the lessons (especially regarding quality control) in U.S. company management, experts have devoted enormous attention to identifying what may be guiding the Japanese economy as a whole. This focus is especially strong in the United States, which has felt battered by Japanese competition and where resentment began to shoot upward in the late 1980s.

Since between them Japan and the United States produce about 40 percent of the world's total output of goods and services, a serious dispute between the two economic superpowers could be ruinous for everybody. Accordingly it matters a good deal just how Japan's growth did take place, though it matters rather more whether or not Western countries can either reconstruct their economies along similar lines, which seems unlikely, or be sufficiently inspired to find effective alternatives.

Clearly there is in East Asian companies a willingness to look further ahead than Western firms usually do. This is a surprising trait, given the upsets and riskiness of the area's history. In Japan's case longer planning horizons are connected with forms of corporate control going back to Meiji, in which banks are prominent on boards of management in a way they have not been in the United States since the 1920s. Banks can afford to take the long view. Shareholders, with their anxieties about earnings at the end of each financial year, count for little in Japan. Companies concern themselves with securing a large share of the market rather than with increasing next year's profit. They involve themselves closely with improving the quality of their products, trusting the engineer's view that quality will sell rather than the advertising agency's faith in ballyhoo. All these points reinforce one another in supporting long-term strategies, which have served Japan well to date.

The commonest assumption is that the Japanese state directed the entire operation. Given the transparent government ineptitude in most of the world, this view implies that the government of Japan, not to mention those in the other successful East Asian countries, possesses an exceptional magic. No doubt this magic was helped by advantages such as the "defense state" attitude of Japan, plus industrial and work-force organization that responded sensitively to suggestion, yet the role of the state is usually underlined. The government agency most often cited as responsible for steering Japan's economy is MITI. That ministry is thought of as efficiently cajoling, sometimes bullying, firms and whole industries either to develop new products or to close down plants in sectors seen as having little future.

According to this model, the government always steered the Japanese economy smartly around the Product Cycle, adopting the latest generation of goods and abandoning sectors in long-term decline. Yet the absence of true central planning of the kind that failed to perform in the socialist states, the lack of the fixing of prices or output targets, probably exposed the country to enough competitive discipline from world market prices to keep its industries on their toes. Japan had the advantage of government direction without its rigidity.

Without denying the current might of the Japanese economy, discussions of this kind can easily treat its successful performance (relative to Japan's own history or the Western economies) as equivalent to an optimal performance (the best use of Japan's total resources). Moreover, many of the innumerable books and articles on the subject seem to imply that Japan's growth is inexorable and will not slow down. They disregard three matters.

First, it is not clear what real discipline there is within an economy where bureaucrats and engineers decide what is to be produced. Clever men (in Japan it is men) have shown that they can make a mark if they are determined enough. Recovery from the military defeat of 1945 may have been the initial spur. The strategy is enormously effective—while it works. But what if the guesses go wrong? If frequent checks against market prices are not made, huge sums may be poured into activities that will not pay. All economies display multiple distortions as a result of political interventions designed to capture extra gains for some group or other. Japan has kept the costs relatively low—so far.

Second, MITI has by no means always guessed right. A prime example was its continued emphasis on the development of mainframe computers when the United States had moved on to personal computers, for which the world market proved to be eager. Moreover, even Japan is far from having an automatically rational national will; political processes can impede structural adjustments. Distribution, retailing, the automobile repair business, coal-mining, beef-raising, and rice-growing are all protected, inefficient activities. Producers' interests are permitted to dominate those of consumers. An engineering approach also runs the risk of the "prize marrow" fallacy, which refers to winning the prize at a fete for the *biggest,* or *technically* best, product, even if it costs more to produce than it will ever fetch and is accordingly not *economically* efficient.

Third, the assumption is that Japan's population will be willing to live and work as hard in the future as in the past and thus maintain existing growth rates. This, too, is unlikely, even in the medium term. Attitudes toward jobs and consumption are changing; the "new humans" born since about 1960 are less austere than were their parents or grandparents. Material consumption has soared, while no one predicted the boom in overseas tourism. Serious reading has declined among younger age groups in favor of comics. The labor market is changing. Foreign firms have introduced head-hunting, and young men are no longer so willing to remain for life with one company. The population is aging faster than anywhere in the world, which hints at a need to import foreign labor; indeed, this is already happening and may eventually disturb the social consensus as it has in Europe. There is also a move to retain women in the work force, which is likely to alter social behavior substantially.

Beyond even these hesitations about an equally ebullient future for the Japanese economy, changes are threatened in that Japanese multinational corporations have moved some manufacturing offshore, not only to countries in Southeast Asia and mainland China but also to the heartlands of Europe and North America. Goods imported into Japan by these companies are in competition with those of smaller companies that have kept their bases there. This competition must erode the solidarity of the business community and risk political conflict. National goals must lose some of their coherence, and the steering bureaucracy, notably MITI, will thus have less influence. If and when it comes, social change may be very rapid—consider the speed of the collapse of communist totalitarianism in Eastern Europe and the USSR. However, in the words of the wag, prediction is difficult, especially about the future. Western interpretations of East Asian economic history have been fickle. They may suffer from being "Orientalist"— that is, from taking on a coloring of Western worries or hopes, projecting them onto the mysterious East.

The Little Dragons and Modern East Asian Growth as a Whole

When we lift our gaze from Japan and try to account for the East Asian miracle as a whole, the task seems even more difficult. A satisfactory explanation must cover the postwar economic growth of South Korea, Taiwan, Hong Kong, and Singapore. Since geographically Singapore is Southeast Asian rather than East Asian, we will be drawn to consider the extension of the growth process to that part of the world. The industrial development of Thailand and Malaysia and the prospective, maybe imminent, acceleration of development in Indonesia requires us to treat the region as an extension of neighboring East Asia. (In terms of current growth, mainland China is another frontier for the advanced East Asia of Japan and the Little Dragons. One pattern overlays the next.)

For all its "Look East" policies, interest in Japan, and some Japanese involvement, Southeast Asia does not share the particular set of conditions more or less common to Japan and the Little Dragons. We say "more or less": Each explanation that accounts for several of the economies does not seem to account for quite all. As one example, the business culture of South Korea is more Japanese than Chinese, but even there the big corporations, *chaebol,* are often owner-operated, in the Chinese tradition, rather than management-run, as Japanese companies are; as another example, in Hong Kong the British colonial government has sheltered the economy but, unlike most governments in East Asia, has not taken on an active steering role.

Some of the explanations incorporate elements that are really part of what has to be explained, such as the growth of avid, consumerist domestic markets for goods within each East Asian economy. Others occasionally sound like "heads I win, tails you lose." For instance, great weight is placed on U.S. defense and aid expenditures, which certainly may be credited with injecting capital, transferring technology, and providing export markets at the height of the cold war in the 1950s and 1960s. But in the same breath, continued East Asian growth is explained as a response to the reduction of U.S. aid once the cold war began to wane. That is having it both ways. There *was* an urgent response to declining U.S. aid, just as Japan in particular sought markets further afield when a protectionist mood began to overcome the United States. But the response is what has to be explained, not the stimulus. East Asian countries might have sat on their hands instead. They might have proved hopelessly incompetent or corrupt and unable to respond, as many economies in the less developed world have done.

As it was, their response was vigorous. Their societies (in general), corporations, and governments have never let up since soon after the Second World War. Admittedly, East Asian economies then entered a period when many factors can be seen—mostly with hindsight—to have been in their favor. Southeast Asia will not have exactly those advantages. Let us look at the historically contingent factors first.

Recovery from the Second World War was under way from the end of the 1940s, in the case of South Korea from the end of the Korean War in the early 1950s. This was recovery from "hot" war but it was taking place in the context of persisting cold war between the communist Soviet Union and China on the one hand and, on the other hand, the West, led by the United States. Several Asian countries were beneficiaries. One or two became forward bases for the United States, which spent heavily to help them reconstruct.

Initial production was mainly for the domestic market within each country, although these markets were small because the populations were poor. The growth of exports gained from the liberalization of world trade following the General Agreement on Tariffs and Trade (GATT) in 1947 and the "Kennedy Round," which removed still more barriers in the 1960s.

Fresh opportunities thus opened up in the postwar years. But some of them, notably trade liberalization, opened up for most countries in the non-communist world. The question, then, is how to account for the special ardor with which the Little Dragons seized the chance. Important in this process was the destruction of old orders of society. Japanese or British colonial overlordship evaporated (except in Hong Kong, which remained a British colony). In Taiwan, which was taken over by the KMT (Kuomintang, the Chinese nationalist government in retreat from the victorious Communist armies in mainland China), the new rulers were not beholden to the local landlords. They shoved them aside in favor of reforms that put land directly into the hands of peasant farmers. This greater egalitarianism increased incentives to produce, unlike the landlord-dominated agricultures of Latin America or the Philippines.

A further reason for the responsiveness of the Little Dragons lay in the arrival in Taiwan and Hong Kong of entrepreneurs from the textile industries of Shanghai, also fleeing from the Communist takeover of 1949. Shanghai had become an industrial city in the nineteenth century and was infinitely more advanced than most of China. After communism deadened its business life, its history was continued after a peculiarly displaced fashion in the buildup of Taiwanese and Hong Kong industry. An irony is that in the 1980s Taiwanese and Hong Kong capital recolonized mainland China, so to speak, returning industrial jobs to several million laborers in Guangdong and Fujian provinces. Although this labor was cheaper than any remaining in the now-developed Little Dragons, the pay was many times better than was otherwise obtainable in mainland China.

South Korea and Taiwan were well placed by virtue of the investment made in them when they were colonies of Japan. Their infrastructure had been built up; more saliently, school participation and standards had been raised. Much is made of the pragmatic quality of East Asian education—all those engineers—but simply discovering that formal learning is possible is probably more important than the actual subjects studied, leading to much greater adaptability in a work force.

The overall effectiveness of economic policy in the Little Dragons since the Second World War is worthy of note. All the countries were given a sense of urgency by the threat from communist China, yet once again it is the quality and vigor of the response that really must be explained. Several governments listened to the advice of foreign or expatriate economists, in itself suggesting an intense rationality on their part, and as usual the recommendations tended to be antiprotectionist and in favor of export strategies. Entry into competitive world markets enjoins higher standards on producers, as anyone who has lived in a protected economy can testify. Little Dragon governments also started out with measures to make sure that capital was invested at home. When they founded businesses as government endeavors, they ran them only for a while and soon sold them to the private sector. Policy directions adjusted fairly fluently as conditions altered—but that, too, is something that needs to be explained rather than an explanation in itself.

Some of the successes in economic performance derived from fortunate circumstances of the time, and some can be lumped beneath the motto that "growth breeds growth"—or hidden behind it, since growth sometimes produces reaction (think of the collapse of Iranian modernization with the Khomeini revolution). At any rate, there was considerable "learning by doing" and a good deal of learning from or imitating regional competitors. Always there was the example of Japan. As far back as Meiji, the Japanese had been far more willing to copy the West than most elites in less developed countries have ever been; the Little Dragons could see that this was a continuing theme and that it paid.

The underlying Confucian culture of the region is a poor predictor of economic success. Most Confucian societies have failed to achieve real growth over long stretches of history. The special circumstances of the postwar period are what activated economic merits in East Asian value systems and brought them to the fore. The labor force was hardworking, literate, and eager to upgrade its education. In the wake of refugee exoduses from mainland China, it was in some countries initially a very young work force. The elite was meritocratic, hardworking, performance-oriented, and usually recruited via stern examinations—like concentration on exports, examinations are a real way to ensure standards. In their different ways, both expose society to competition. A special East Asian tinge was added in the form of concern with growth as a manifestation of a desirable social order.

Cultures change, however. East Asia may not be organized in the Western individualistic tradition, but the nature of its most important social groups has changed under the influence of growth itself. There has been a move away from ascriptive groups such as the family, to which one either belongs or doesn't, to achievement-oriented groups, which one enters by choice or on merit. This arrangement makes the matter of group membership more ambiguous than it may seem. In any case, emphasis on cultural explanations of economic growth can easily become implicit assertions that only Christianity and Confucianism foster the necessary values. That conclusion might consign the remainder of humanity to eternal poverty or handouts and should be thought about very carefully.

The factors put forward to explain the growth of the Little Dragons weave and interweave in a huge scholarly and journalistic literature. Some factors turn out to be reflections of others, caught in a different mirror. They overlap, and no plausible core seems to have been present in all cases. They are not sharp-edged enough, especially those relating to motivation, to permit us to test the following simple proposition: The country with the most suggested advantages should have had the highest growth rate.

Rather than emphasizing the way resources were mobilized in an active effort at industrialization, we may express the economic success of East Asia as follows: Release from depressive factors, such as the influence of greedy landlord groups, unleashed a powerful market response that was already latent in these societies because of their earlier experience.

The outcome was certainly far beyond the expectations of development economists and other commentators in the 1950s or even the 1960s. Japan and the countries that became the Little Dragons were considered too damaged by warfare and (with extreme irony) were often written off as too hampered by entrenched Confucian ideology to follow suit. Yet the four Little Dragons (including Singapore, with only three million people) are now among the world's top trading nations. South Korea is one of the two largest shipbuilders and a major producer of steel and manufacturer of automobiles. Taiwan has the world's second-biggest holding of foreign currency (second, be it noted, to Japan). Hong Kong has become one of the world's greatest financial centers. The growth rates of all four states have consistently outstripped those of most Western economies.

Southeast Asia: The Frontier of Developed East Asia

Southeast Asia stands rather apart, as if it does not truly belong to eastern Asia despite the fruitful presence of so many interlinked communities of Chinese and the rapid modern industrialization of first one, then another, of its constituent countries. Its achievement is not always acknowledged and has even been called "ersatz capitalism." Nevertheless, we may look on the region as an exciting laboratory, almost a zoo, containing amongst its economies a range of diverse specimens. Some of them are growing into Little Dragons themselves, others may do so soon, and one or two, such as undeveloped Papua New Guinea, are barely emerging from colonialism and in their remoter regions from the Stone Age. What may have been the last truly isolated human groups have been contacted in New Guinea within the past few years.

Taken as a macroregion, the "Lands Below the Winds" are untidy. Besides their general location, a tropical station in the monsoon belt, little exists to unite them except incomplete webs of similarities such as colonial histories, the presence of a number of Muslim regimes, and the communities of Overseas Chinese. Despite apparently high biological productivity signalled by lush tree cover, the region is one of peninsulas, islands, and river basins divided from one another by poorer uplands.

This was not the home of a unitary civilization but rather a zone of contact, overlap, and intrusion. Southeast Asia did not support one of the world's major populations. In 1400 the total population was only 21 million, in 1800, 44 million. Although such figures are always questionable, the implication would be that during those four centuries of human history the more-than-doubling of population actually meant that the region was going backward demographically relative to China or Europe, from what had been a promising start. In other words, some large Old World systems were expanding faster.

During this period the coastal areas supported significant trading cities and growing commerce. The role of women was prominent. Many urban women received some education and spoke several languages, functioning as merchants, even more than usual as rulers. Births were widely spaced, with seemingly less of the tendency in the direction of maximal biological reproduction displayed by some other Asian societies. But this role for women seems to have changed in the early modern period, possibly through increased domination by the world religions of Hinduism, Christianity, Confucianism (actually a philosophy), and Islam, which are all patriarchal. Certainly the status and social participation of women appears to have declined. The whole subject of female participation is so cloudy yet so interesting that it would merit a research effort directed at comparing Southeast Asia with other major regions of the world.

Early in the fifteenth century, a phase of economic growth seems to have been under way, mainly in coastal trading cities such as Malacca. This phase was fragile, and at the time certain other towns declined. Handicraft goods were made to order rather than kept in stock, which may suggest either a scarcity of capital or considerable uncertainty. Moreover, there was a relapse during the seventeenth century. Towns shrank, as they did in Europe and Japan, but whereas economic life in those parts of the world went on developing with the help of handicraft goods from the countryside, where costs were lower, this adjustment apparently failed to happen in Southeast Asia. The region did not move forward again until the second half of the nineteenth century.

Even though the Portuguese had captured Malacca as early as 1511, the setback in the early modern period was scarcely the direct result of Western imperialism, which over much of the region was marginal before about 1870. Colonial intrusions along the coasts did accentuate the political centralization of states, which was already going on because trade made the coastal rulers richer than those in the interior and because the coastal kings got first access to imported weapons. The continued expansion of Indian Ocean trade in the seventeenth and eighteenth centuries disadvantaged those who remained dependent on agricultural rents. This disparity between the coasts and interior was politically destabilizing. The Europeans, however, did not take over.

A possible explanation of the downturn is the "turning inward" of many Asian states. In Southeast Asia governments were typically weak, being organized around a single figure and lacking continuity if that person fell. The typical sequence was that an able person overcame rivals, came to the throne, and centralized the state. One or two generations later, military invasion or domestic revolt ousted a descendant, and the cycle started over again. The administration, such as it was, melted away. Another regime coalesced from the hangers-on of the new ruler. Southeast Asian states did not solve the problem of an orderly succession, the orderly transfer of power.

In this context, "turning inward," which otherwise sounds mystical, may have been partly a result of missionizing by the world religions and partly a result of the fact that political events happened to coincide in changing the rulers of a number of states at approximately the same period. There were cycles of royal power, for example, in Burma, Javanese Mataram (Indonesia), and Siam (Thailand). If the cycles coincided in several countries, the entire region might be weakened or become absorbed in internal struggles, as well as with changes in the realm of religious thought. It is not necessary to think that outside forces must have caused the whole of this loose synchronizing.

In general land was abundant, labor scarce. Wars were primarily slave raids designed more to get control of labor than of territory. One early Vietnamese ruler had his soldiers tattooed on the forehead: "army of the son of heaven." But the flights and confusion brought about by warfare depressed the harvest, leading to famines, and spread epidemic diseases. These secondary disasters may have depressed economic activity more than the fighting did.

The population of the region was low overall. States were formed apart from one another, establishing their cores where there was terrain suitable for growing rice. For example, South and North Vietnam emerged in the Mekong and Red River deltas under two separate ruling families. Such states were divided by disputed forest land inhabited by tribal peoples, lacking distinct political or property-rights boundaries. This ecological and political geography minimized fruitful contact, peaceful competition, and the diffusion of "best-practice" methods. There was thus neither an overarching state structure, as in China or Japan, nor a states-system, as in Europe. There was little need to offer public goods such as a good system of law courts in order to induce people to stay and not remove themselves to some neighboring kingdom where they may have hoped for a better deal, as happened in Europe.

Despite some elaborate codes, there was no really enforceable law. Political evolution had not reached the point at which the ruler himself could be expected to keep his (or, increasingly rarely, her) own laws. The test of innocence was still the ordeal, which amounted to torturing those potentially involved in a crime rather than making a serious attempt at identifying the criminal. Where states did not standardize weights and measures or coinage, transaction costs remained high. Well into the nineteenth century, until Western mints took orders or were set up in the region, currencies such as Siamese canoe money prevailed; roughly cast copper bars with no inscriptions or denominations whatsoever.

The European states were reluctant to involve themselves in the region, though Great Britain was drawn in when Burma tried in 1824 to expand toward British India, and France took over Cambodia when Vietnam and Thailand began fighting over it in 1870. Often the European aim was to safeguard real or imagined trade routes to China.

The Europeans were brought to prominence by a combination of their own expanding markets for tropical raw materials, the development of steamships, and the shorter trade routes consequent on the opening of the Suez Canal in 1869. European-operated plantations, especially for rubber, and mines, notably for tin, produced a stream of exports sufficient to cause the regional economy to grow between 1870 and 1913. The effect of the Europeans' presence can be seen in retrospect as a giant transfer of technology. It was European-sponsored development that brought in the main flow of Chinese immigrants as indentured laborers before 1870. Southeast Asian exports rose four or fivefold. By 1913 Thailand, Burma, and Indochina accounted for three-quarters of the world's rice exports. Between 1883 and 1913 the growth of per capita GNP, especially in Indochina, may have been as fast as in many industrial countries.

Meanwhile, there were responsive changes within a number of Southeast Asian countries. Thailand abolished property rights in the scarce factor, people—that is, it abolished forms of slavery. There was a political motive in doing so: to ingratiate the country with the Great Powers, given the antislavery consciousness of the time. The move was made less painful in that world rice prices were rising and the forced laborers of the corvée and the debt slaves were becoming dearer to feed. It was easier to cast them off to fend for themselves. Property rights began to be extended over the once-abundant factor, land, as it became relatively scarcer with the growth of population.

After the First World War, Southeast Asian economies began to perform much less well. At that time, world primary product prices fell in the interwar slump. After the Second World War, development economists looked back at this period as though it typified a perpetually dismal history of the region, as if the previous growth had never happened. This perception made it easier to blame Western imperialists for what was seen as the backwardness of the 1950s and to propound nonmarket solutions quite unlike the market expansion that in reality had caused the growth before 1913. The lack of knowledge about even so recent a period as the one ending with the First World War also obscured some of the region's true economic potential, which has become evident again during the last thirty years.

During the Second World War, the Japanese occupied the colonies of the Western powers as far afield as Burma and Indonesia. Although contemptuous of the Overseas Chinese and becoming more vicious as the war went on, the Japanese involved nationals from the Southeast Asian countries in local administration, training them, as the West had not, to run things themselves. When the independence struggles were won in a short space of years after 1945 and the Western powers had retreated once more, some of the independent nations of the region began to score considerable economic successes. Thailand, Malaysia, and most notably Singapore developed especially well considering the difficulties of finding political accommodations between their indigenous populations—Islamic in the case of Malaysia—and the Chinese business communities.

Despite Southeast Asia's measurable economic growth, its performance has been labeled *Ersatz Capitalism,* the title of a 1988 book by Japanese development economist Kunio Yoshihara. His grounds for thinking the economies shallowly rooted are that the enterprises tend to be concentrated less in manufacturing than in service activities such as distribution, in which the business networks of the Chinese have proved efficient; that the enterprises tend to be run by *compradors;* that they tend to rely on foreign technology; and that they tend to be characterized by rent-seeking (i.e., skimming off gains through political connections rather than adding value in production). Unlike East Asia, it is claimed, Southeast Asia does not compete vigorously in exporting manufactures.

These allegations are certainly exaggerated. There have been difficulties, to be sure. The countries of the region began to grow later than Japan, South Korea, or Taiwan. They suffer because they are less homogeneous societies. But rent-seeking is common enough everywhere; Japan contains more than a few massively

corrupt politicians. Most modern growth in any case involves technologies originating in the R&D departments of leading industries of a handful of developed
countries. Much of it has come to emphasize the service industries.

Some Southeast Asian countries are well developed, some just starting to
move, others still far behind. Gigantic Indonesia is only teetering on the brink of
major economic change; the great tropical forests in its outer islands are being
converted to agricultural land for settlers from densely populated Java moving in
a great, government-sponsored migration. Papua New Guinea's forests and minerals make it one of the three great untapped resource frontiers around the Pacific, the others being the Soviet Far East—part of the Rim that the eye always
glides over on a world map—and Antarctica. All of them are difficult to develop
for topographical and climatic reasons.

A fourth region, Siberia, was half-developed by the Soviets and because of its
rail link to the coast of the Russian Far East is already attracting the attention of
resource-hungry Japan and South Korea. Maybe the Amazon rain forest consti-
tutes a fifth frontier that will be drawn out of its comparative isolation on the
edge of the Brazilian economy into the economy of the Pacific Rim. The River
Amazon may flow into the Atlantic, but if a proposed road is built from its head-
waters back over the Peruvian Andes to link it up with the Pacific Coast, the natural resources of the region could be siphoned into Japan's orbit. If we think of the
developed world as bisected into Atlantic and Pacific spheres, they can be seen
competing for cheap resources at the margins between them.

Within Southeast Asia, old problems linger. A few hundred miles from the
supermodern airports at Singapore and Bangkok, there are open-access forests
with minority tribal peoples and possibly excessive logging, since property rights
in land still remain uncertain and investment in improving the land is thereby
discouraged. The uncertainty may even encourage clear-cutting by outside companies, turning old problems into new ones. Much of the tropical forest in the region is being very heavily logged, largely for the Japanese market, with little serious attention to sustaining the yield, let alone to preserving intact the original
forest ecosystem.

Despite all these things, the record of growth is creditable in several countries,
and the region is becoming more interconnected. Japanese investment has greatly
increased. Some of the countries have adopted "Look East" policies, testifying to
the attractions of the Japanese model. They have sought to extend their political
alliance, ASEAN (Association of Southeast Asian Nations), into a trade bloc. Although some countries, such as Burma and Cambodia, remain largely outside the
emergent community for reasons of ideology or imperfectly settled conflicts of
the most horrendous kind, the promise of development in Southeast Asia as a
whole is clear. Indeed, even Burma and Cambodia, with Yunnan province in
southern China, may be joining Vietnam, Laos, and Thailand in a new, informal
development zone.

We should notice, too, the subtle shift in expectations partly brought about by the prodigious successes in East Asia. We now expect change to take place from underdevelopment to industrialization within a single generation; some East Asian examples show that it can be done. To a substantial degree, so do two or three Southeast Asian cases. The changes in Southeast Asia during the 1970s and 1980s were rapid and profound, raising the possibility that dragons could emerge here, too.

8

Modern China

For China realisation of the need for change was far harder than for Japan.
—J.M.D. Pringle, *Chinese Struggles for Unity* (1939)

China Since the Mid-nineteenth Century

If we look as far back as the 1830s, China may seem to have been a better bet for industrialization than Japan. China had a much larger population, and Westerners have repeatedly seen this as an enticing market, sometimes to their ruin. (It has also been called a chimera, an illusion, the poverty of the population neutralizing its enormous size.) China also had mineral resources, which Japan proved not to have. Yet as history unfolded, the results were to be otherwise. In 1839 China was embroiled in the Opium Wars, only the first of many foreign incursions (including, ironically, those by Japan), demands for reparations, and seizures of bits of territory. Internally, severe problems in feeding the growing population at midcentury plunged the country into the long turmoil of the Taiping Rebellion.

The response by the Qing dynasty to the foreign challenge was weak and vacillating. It took the shock badly, even though the impact can scarcely have been greater than the Western intrusion was for Japan, which the Tokugawa shoguns had closed off to the world since the early seventeenth century. Yet not until 1901 did the Qing create a Board of Foreign Affairs. By that date Japan was already a military-industrial power.

This is not to say that there was no positive response, merely that the push by the Chinese central government was relatively feeble and inconsistent. Certainly armaments were modernized a little in the 1860s. During the next decade, students were sent overseas and some colleges were founded at home. New enterprises were established in food processing, transportation, and manufacturing;

some Western-style banks also were begun. Almost all these were concentrated in coastal China. Yet by 1912 only 363 mechanized factories were in existence, amidst a sea of thousands upon thousands of traditional small handicraft workshops. Fewer than 1 percent of all enterprises employed more than 500 hands. There was little positive spillover from the modern sector to the older sector. China is so big that although the modern machines did displace two million handicraft workers between 1879 and 1905, especially in handspinning, there was still a vast handicraft sector in 1949 and beyond.

China has repeatedly struggled with the question of whether or not to adopt Western technology, business methods, and international standards, ever since the first contacts. The problems of development were based at least as much on indecision as on "objective" economic difficulty. A scarcity of capital, for instance, was not a major limiting factor; mobilizing it was. The savings rate was high, a reflection perhaps of the high risks facing all individuals. There was enough capital for initial needs, but it tended to be locked up in land and precious objects. Merchant capital was the most liquid form available, and Chinese-owned businesses that did set up in the modern sector tended to be financed from this source.

Before the fall of the Qing dynasty in the 1911 revolution, industrialization was slowed by the way business was organized in the modern sector. Even today Western firms setting up in business in East or Southeast Asia are recommended to go into partnership with local agents. A reason for this advice may be the need for go-betweens in an environment where personal relationships matter and formal contracts are literally not worth the paper they are written on.

During Qing times, incorporating local administrators was a requirement, institutionalized in the joint responsibility system, in which foreign managers and local bureaucrats together ran the enterprises. Bureaucrats everywhere are personality types who are eager for power but loath to take real responsibility. Those under the Qing were particularly risk averse. There was corruption and nepotism. The Chinese state thus took a share of modern-sector business profits but would neither invest in industry (nor in modernizing agriculture), nor yet again leave foreign managers alone. Although the net impact of foreign economic intervention was positive, in these circumstances it was not sufficient to galvanize an enormous economy that was heavily dependent on traditional agriculture. Change came a little faster after China's defeat by Japan in 1895 but still remained sluggish. By Japanese standards it remained weak even after the fall of the Qing in 1911.

Once again, as for Japan in the same period, there are standard and revisionist interpretations of the economic experience. Conventionally, these years are seen as ones with the inept Nationalist government (the KMT) incapable of controlling the rise of warlord regimes in parts of its territory, unable to suppress the rise of a communist movement, and ultimately unable to resist Japanese occupation of much of the country. Many KMT policies existed on paper only, notoriously the clean-up campaign, with its injunction to pick up orange peels at a time when the bodies of abandoned children were stacked in alleyways for disposal on garbage dumps. Given the setting of conflict, it is usually accepted without hesitation that economic progress was painfully slow. The Chinese ruling class is seen as a set of rent-seekers, not profit-makers. Government offices were for sale, and the highest bidders happily went in for extortion in order to recoup the price they had paid. Militarily, the KMT was on the back foot. In 1938 it was obliged to move its capital far inland to Chungking, a virtually medieval city where there had not been so much as a telephone until 1931.

The task of modernizing China would have been awesomely challenging even had the circumstances been better. Far too few specialists had been trained in modern methods of administration, production, or simple installation and maintenance. Traveling in Nationalist China in the 1930s, C. P. Fitzgerald found a hotel room with an electric light but no switch: The staff was amazed that anyone would ever want to have such a boon turned off. Great Britain and Japan controlled much of the modern sector, the railways, coal mines, and ironworks. In 1936, for example, the British carried 40 percent of all waterborne traffic. The imperial government had scarcely prepared the country for the economic development that was hoped for in the euphoria of the 1911 revolution.

Despite this factually correct picture of China's incapacities and miseries, more than one revisionist nevertheless detects positive movement. The current revisionist opinion is that the 1920s and 1930s actually saw real growth. In the terms of the leading "optimist," Thomas Rawski, average personal consumption went up at an annual rate of 0.5 percent between 1914–1918 and 1931–1936. There are two parts to his argument. The former involves the technical exercise of assembling the statistical data on which the conclusion rests; these data are highly suggestive without, perhaps, being quite convincing. The latter involves attempts to undermine the "pessimistic" case.

Rawski attributes many of the genuine signs of distress during the two decades to the frictions of transition; in other words, he regards them as the inevitable but passing costs of achieving growth in a backward country. There were bound to be losers as well as winners. Growth in average real income per head took place, but income distribution became less equal—the rich got richer and the poor got *relatively* poorer. International research generalized in the "Kuznets' Curve" suggests that this experience is usual in the early stages of growth. Additionally, the world depression of the 1930s imposed costs on China through the contraction of overseas markets.

Other straws blow in the revisionist wind. The growth of trade unions between 1936 and 1946, for instance, need not be seen as a sign that labor was being oppressed but rather as an indication that it was becoming strong enough to organize countervailing power. The working day was reduced to ten hours; child labor decreased; the gap between male and female wage rates narrowed. And although it is usual (and morally proper) to lament the unpleasantly Dickensian conditions in many factories, the simple fact that some of the factories made soap actually indicates that there were consumer gains—winners as well as losers—the type of second-order effect economists are trained to notice. During the depths of the depression, too, although the price of grain fell, so did the price of land. Thus, for the peasantry, costs as well as receipts went down. The fall in land prices and rents was "sticky." They fell more slowly than grain prices, so there was plenty of room for conflict between landlord and peasant. This trend should not be permitted to obscure the gradual reduction in costs.

The most obvious pessimistic counter to all these observations is the evidence of so much conflict and warlordism during republican times. Rawski insists, on the contrary, that the warlords were much less damaging to the economy than the sound and fury of political history would imply. The wars cost only a few percent of total output and caused very few deaths compared with the total population. Once a man had seized control of an area, his interest lay no longer in robbing or damaging it but rather in building up its productive potential and taking a steady yield of taxes. Warlords soon learned not to confiscate goods from the merchants since these were the people most likely to help the economy recover. Some warlords actually drew up plans for the development of their territories, and one was farsighted enough to send students overseas.

If Rawski and the other revisionists prove to be correct overall, the achievements of communist China during the Maoist period (1949–1976) will not seem so striking. The baseline of development from which the Maoists started will have been higher than was thought. The Maoist period was in any case marred by twists and turns in policy and by an ideologically contrived famine that caused 30 million deaths. This has been described by a Beijing scholar as "the worst catastrophe in human history." It was the result of collectivizing agriculture, a policy that had already been shown to be disastrous by the mass famine deaths in the Stalinist Soviet Union. For all that, if the longer-term gains in life expectancy during Maoist times were factored in (which can be done by calculating the income equivalents of the years gained), the period would almost certainly outclass the republican period in economic achievement. There seems to have been no comparable demographic gain between the wars.

When the Communists came to power they faced unimaginable difficulties. First, there were the problems of scraping together the resources to develop a less developed country, on the scale of the biggest country in the world. These were the problems that stemmed from relying on a backward farming system using archaic methods, a poor infrastructure, notably in the area of transportation, and all the many interlocking problems of ignorance, disease, and poverty that make becoming less poor so hard.

Second, there were difficulties hanging over from China's own history—the smallness and already antiquated nature of the modern sector and the fewness of the centralized, authoritarian elite, who alone knew how things worked. On the other hand, China's past had given it advantages compared, say, with Africa: There was an educated bureaucracy, lots of commercial experience, and prior acquaintance with complicated institutions.

Third, there were problems created by the bias of communist ideology and the fact that this ideology was, considered realistically, subject to whatever interpretation the man at the top happened to put on it at a given moment. In other words, although claiming a monopoly on truth, Chinese communism was riven with factional fighting and did not stick to any one line of policy. Mao was a commanding but insecure dictator.

The bias of policy included wasteful hatreds of all kinds. These might be defended by some as understandable but damagingly neurotic responses to the earlier sufferings of China and of the Party's violent struggle for power. There was a hatred of all the middle class (except of course those who were high in the Party)—never mind that the bourgeoisie alone was the repository of advanced skills. Slogans such as "Better Red than Expert" did not brook well for management training. Mass imprisonment and murder of arbitrarily named "class enemies," bizarre research projects (one involved trying to turn the faintly phosphorent luminosity from a fungus on goldfish into a substitute for "capitalist" batteries), and obligatory farm work for students for as long as six years all meant a horrendous waste of desperately needed skilled people. During the Cultural Revolution, Mao unleashed bands of thuggish students to humiliate, torture, maim, and kill those who, frankly stated, were their elders and betters. This was no way to run a railroad.

Actual economic policies were wasteful, too. They were biased against the market. They favored central planning, with an excessive emphasis on Soviet-style heavy industry; arbitrary production targets; impossible efforts to coordinate all the myriad transactions throughout the economy; and rigid fixing of prices, which destroyed their usefulness as a means of indicating how to allocate resources. The policies led to ruinous fads, such as the establishment of a wave of little steel mills in backyards. Above all, they involved collectivizing agriculture, with no exit permitted, which removed the incentive to work hard and led to the Great Famine of 1958–1961. After this disaster there were some relaxations in this sphere, trumpeted as fresh sacred truths revealed to the leader. (Previous policy errors and general instability were never, never admitted to have been his fault or the fault of the Party, not in China and not by the large band of starry-eyed fans of Mao in the West.)

Hatred of foreigners tended to isolate China, making the country lean toward wasteful attempts at self-sufficiency and miss out on the benefits of trade. Hatred was made to include the Soviets once China fell out with the USSR, its sole important ally and source of development aid.

By 1952 the state already controlled 80 percent of heavy industry, 90 percent of foreign trade, and most prices. China had moved to embrace state capitalism on the Soviet model, with five-year production plans. What followed was a strenuous effort at modernizing the country, at first targeting the development of heavy industry. For a long time it was believed that these command-economy policies were working, despite China's isolationism, the minimizing of foreign trade, and the break with the Soviet Union.

Certainly it was accepted at the highest levels in the West that economic growth rates were substantially higher in China than India, which invited comparison as another large agricultural Asian country achieving independence at much the same time (1947) as the Communist takeover of China and likewise regulating its economy, though without the same enforcement of central planning. More considered investigation suggests that many Chinese official statistics were unreliable and that the growth rates of the two countries were much the same during the 1950s, 1960s, and early 1970s. The repressiveness, central planning, and alterations in policy had been costly in China: Better Red than Expert.

After Mao's death, reformers came uppermost and made some rapid changes in a very different direction. In 1978 China gave up appeals to undertake mass "voluntary" work (an inefficient but not completely ineffective means of raising productivity, and certainly a cheap one); colleges were opened to train factory managers; Chinese students were permitted to travel overseas to study; agriculture was decollectivized; peasants were given control over their land (short of private ownership); and market incentives were introduced.

The response was immediate and massive. Farm output rose by 8 percent per annum between 1979 and 1983, compared with an estimated 3 percent from 1953 to 1978. China actually became a grain exporter. Between 1978 and 1984 the real income of the peasantry doubled. The base from which this growth took place was admittedly very low indeed, but a doubling in six years is a remarkable tribute to the power of material incentives. The initial response by peasant families was to consume their earnings, improving their standard of living in simple and direct ways—for instance, by putting glass in their window openings. This sparked a demand for petty consumer goods, and industries in the countryside boomed to supply them. Rural industries helped to provide employment for labor no longer needed in farming and thus reduced the enormous problem of the unemployed in the countryside, though Chinese officialdom still admitted to a total of 80 million unemployed by 1990. Strenuous efforts to prevent these people from migrating to the cities in the usual Third World fashion were becoming increasingly ineffective.

The cause of productivity growth was not simply the marketization of agriculture after 1978. It was mere fortune that the weather was good in the early 1980s.

Beyond that, overheads had already been provided: The commune system had provided electrification and large irrigation works; the state had built large fertilizer factories. Price incentives to peasant farmers could not, by themselves, have produced the observed results, and it is now probable that the government cannot afford to keep up the previous level of investment in the infrastructure. One reason is that peasants are now receiving as income money the state formerly collected as taxes and invested in public works; another is that higher farm prices cut directly into the state's budget, since it subsidizes the food bought by urban consumers. Reduced public expenditures are also evident at the local level, where extensive surveys show that the cadres, the Party officials, although freely admitting the previous lack of incentives, still believe that in the newly rich villages there is inadequate provision for welfare needs and communal facilities.

During the 1980s equally astonishing changes took place in the industrial sector. China's state industries are chronically inefficient and are in effect subsidized by taxes levied on the new private sector. The inefficient way in which they are managed is compounded by other inefficiencies in the public sector, such as frequent power cuts. But in the private sector, the growth was startling. By the early 1990s the coastal provinces were achieving very rapid growth rates, helped, but by no means entirely organized, by Overseas Chinese entrepreneurs from Taiwan and Hong Kong. Whole villages specializing in manufacturing textiles or shoes had moved from Taiwan to Fujian. Hong Kong businessmen were said to be employing anything from one and a half to three million workers in Guangdong province, numbers nevertheless dwarfed by the labor force in export industries set up by natives of the coastal provinces who rediscovered their entrepreneurial skills almost overnight.

The frontier of East Asian manufacturing thus now utilizes the cheap labor of mainland China. From a world in which China played little part in world trade and had an unproductive economy run by central planners, and from the world of the cold war and the dispute between the People's Republic of China (PRC) and Taiwan, with mutual shelling on a daily basis, much of the coastal mainland has been incorporated into the world economy. This was the outstanding achievement of the 1980s. It was more striking than the earlier "miracles" of Japan and the Little Dragons because it took place in a country that had been totally opposed to free market activity, to the involvement of capitalists, and above all to foreign capitalists interested in competing on the world market.

This astonishing turnabout raised expectations for political as well as economic freedoms. In 1989, students who wanted democracy in China challenged the system in a mass demonstration in Tiananmen Square in Beijing. The conservative element in the system responded on June 4 by sweeping the square clear and running tanks over those who resisted, jailing student leaders for nebulous crimes. There was a brief attempt to roll back the economic reforms. Since then, central government rhetoric has insisted that there must be no "bourgeois liberalism" in China, meaning that the old Party members and their nominees must remain unchallenged in office. The propaganda was redoubled after the collapse of the USSR; the Party is frightened that it will nourish its own reformer, a Chinese Gorbachev. Meanwhile, liberalization has quickly resumed in the economic sphere.

What are we to expect? History has not come to an end. The future is particularly difficult to forecast with a centralized system in which real politics depend on largely hidden struggles among elite families and factions, all masquerading behind a love of the common man and all willing to imprison or murder anyone who appears to threaten them.

One possibility, then, is successful repression by the more reactionary members of the old guard in Beijing. We must remember that after 1949 these people had effectively closed down the stock exchange and bustling trade of Shanghai, turning a world-class trading port of great value to China into a shadow of its former self. Antimarket ideology, when it is based on observing the sufferings of those who cannot cope with an unreliable free market for labor, can thus be powerful as well as dogmatic. Yet market-based industrialization took such a renewed hold in some parts of southern China in the 1980s that it is no longer easy to envision its wholesale suppression. Somewhat more likely, though perhaps still not very likely, would be a splitting of China between the growing coastal areas and the more purely agricultural interior. Bustling Guangdong has little in common now with, for example, Szechuan, an inland province that possessed not a single railway in 1949 and still has only two rail links with the outside world. We can only speculate about such possibilities, but China is a much less unitary country than it appears: It is a collection of regions experiencing divergent rates of economic and social change, held together more by politics than by economics.

China is poor and lacks personal freedoms. Of nine countries (apart from oil producers) rated in the worst category for rights and liberties by Freedom House (an international monitoring agency), seven were also in the lowest income category during the 1980s. China was one of them. Yet the growth of island and peninsular Asia has spread to the mainland and is strongly affecting the 310 million people who live in seven coastal provinces, radically transforming the lives of many of them. This is outstandingly the case in Guangdong, which lies in the hinterland of one of the original Little Dragons, Hong Kong. Major political accidents apart, growth *is* likely to be sustainable there. The political will for change is evident at the provincial level and backed by underlying economic efforts. Over 80 percent of prices are now set by the market rather than the state, yet the provincial government has managed to find the money for heavy investment in the infrastructure and communications system. Bottlenecks that may occur in that sector elsewhere in Asia, conceivably in Thailand, are less likely in Guangdong. East Asia's fifth Dragon may turn out to be Guangdong rather than Thailand or Malaysia—not that either of those lands has been doing badly.

More promising still is an outcome that has continued to shape itself ever since Tiananmen, despite the political reaction in Beijing. This is a slow spread of economic change from the coastal zone, the result of trade and population flows within China. This spread would generalize the material progress. Perhaps the population will be content with material rather than political rewards. At the moment there are many, many women workers making toys, clothing, footwear, watches, and cameras in the sweatshops of Guangdong who are simply grateful to have left the countryside and to be earning several times what they earned at "stoop labor" in the rice paddies, even though what they earn is still several times less than industrial workers in more developed countries. People unused to even the mildest prosperity, let alone the concept of individual freedoms, may for a long time settle for mere prosperity. China may survive by continuing to reform its economy without officially reforming its polity.

The economic reforms thus continued under their own steam after Tiananmen, despite the repression. In the early 1990s the call from one side in China was that the reforms should be accelerated without upsetting the existing power structure—indeed, that reforms might better preserve socialist privilege than would a return to a command economy. In short, capitalism was to produce the goods, and socialism, which everywhere in the world had conspicuously failed to do so, was to reap the rewards—much as Karl Marx said. Marx did not expect the problems of technological change and high production to be solved outside the powerful competitive mechanisms of the capitalist system.

How may China then change? Already political leaders in the developed provinces protect their businessmen from the interventions of Beijing. As wages rise, education is gained, and occupations become more skilled, we may eventually expect within the system more demands for political representation and the freedoms without which creativity, including technological creativity, is unlikely to flourish. China's rulers in history were not utterly insensitive to the need to sway in the people's breeze. They were afraid of losing the perceived right to rule, the so-called Mandate of Heaven. The hope for China must be that its leaders will evolve into true politicians, seeing that their own interest lies in making it possible for ordinary Chinese to acquire not only the goods but also the opportunities that people everywhere show they want.

9

The Cities

The city has been the focus of human development for some six thousand years. Indeed the word city comes from the same root as "civilization"—a Western-centered derivation but one not inappropriate to the experience of the rest of the world. Cities everywhere ... have played both a symbolic and an enabling or presiding role as pinnacles of human achievement and as centers of innovation.

—Rhoads Murphey, *The Fading of the Maoist Vision:*
City and Country in China's Development (1980)

Transnational Urbanization

The preceding chapters have considered the nature and causes of economic development in individual states or in groups of states with similar characteristics. However, some important processes are transnational. For instance, the Chinese living outside China do not live in any one state: historically, they have moved to one of several regions, pushed by political or racial strife and pulled to often distant places that offer new opportunities. In agriculture, for certain crops and farming systems such as rice growing, there are common technologies and problems that have nothing to do with the political boundaries of nation-states. Most important of all is the process of urbanization, which affects the bulk of the Pacific Rim's, and the world's, population.

It has been argued that the main impetus to economic development comes from towns and cities, in which the main dynamic forces of technical progress are concentrated. Rural areas only respond to initiatives originating from within urban areas. A case has also been made that the main constraint restricting the pace of economic growth is a limit imposed on the rate of urbanization by the high cost of the associated infrastructure. The combination of these arguments places the city at the center of any explanation of the process of economic development.

There are many large cities around the Pacific Rim, some of them megalopolises, huge urban centers of global economic and cultural significance (see Map 9.1). Every economically successful region in the Pacific Rim has as its cornerstone a dynamic city with the ability to create jobs and exports. Tokyo (with a number of surrounding cities), Los Angeles, San Francisco, Hong Kong, Guangzhou, Shanghai, Wuhan, Seoul, Taipei, and Singapore are the current economic stars of the Rim. They are major centers of manufacturing, commerce, and finance. They have developed cheap and efficient methods of producing goods and providing services, and in doing so they have stimulated economic growth in their surrounding regions. These cities have characteristics of great economic importance in common with all the prosperous cities of the world.

There is a cycle to the process of economic growth in cities. Cities that start as low-cost producers, using cheap labor and land to make simple imitations of other cities' products, will in time face problems of rising costs and competition. Without new waves of product diversification and technological change, a mature city may become uncompetitive and suffer from an out-migration of capital and skilled labor. The "city cycle" is a general characteristic of city growth and of economic development in general. Any city going through the cycle faces problems and challenges that are to some extent separable from those of the individual nation-state in which that city is located.

In the 1960s Arnold Toynbee predicted that humankind's principal problem, once the threat of nuclear war had been eliminated, would be rapid urbanization as a result of an increasing rate of population growth. "This problem of world-wide urbanization is now rushing to meet us," he wrote. The cold war is now at an end, but the effects of rapid population growth still loom over the global economy and environment. The United Nations predicts a world population of over ten billion by the end of the twenty-first century—more than double current numbers. With increasing mechanization and rising productivity in agriculture, it is inevitable that the world will have a greater number of very large cities. The condition of cities will go a long way toward determining the economic opportunities and quality of life available to humankind.

The study of cities in a vast region like the Pacific Rim must consider a range of urban experience. The cities of the Rim include those of developed regions (in the American West and Australasia), the Third World (such as Mexico City and Jakarta), and the developed part of the former Third World (like Hong Kong and Singapore). Although the majority of the population (usually around 60 to 80 percent) in most Pacific Rim countries lives in cities, there are countries where a large nonurban population remains. Over half the Rim's population in 1980 lived in China, Indonesia, or Thailand, where around 80 percent of the total popula-

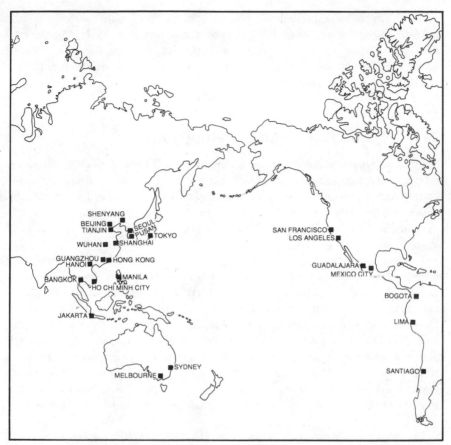

MAP 9.1   *Major Cities of the Pacific Rim*

tion depended on villages, fields, or jungle for its livelihood. The Rim has some of the world's most efficient and pleasant cities, as well as some of the most ghastly.

This diversity is instructive. The various cities of the Rim are coping with the problems caused by population growth. Cities have characteristics that contribute to economic expansion, and the creation of new jobs encourages faster rates of in-migration. Usually this migration exceeds the supply of available jobs, so that many new arrivals must wait for further economic growth before they obtain work. As a result, cities often develop large areas of poor housing that are crowded and unhealthy. In tackling this problem, a city is constrained not simply by the current state of its economy but also by its history. Anyone who lives in or does business with a city is affected by its past development, especially by early decisions as to planning and land use.

In this chapter we explore the development of the Pacific Rim's major cities and how this history influences today's cities. We also consider the likely effects of current city-building trends. The conclusion is partly optimistic, partly pessimistic: History shows that safe and efficient cities *can* be built and maintained, but the ability to do so is not distributed evenly.

The City and Economic Development

Some cities are political and administrative centers. Others are of cultural, educational, or religious significance. However, most cities are places of industrial and commercial activity, which tend to be located there for sound economic reasons. Cities can stimulate economic growth because they usually have three advantages over smaller, less densely populated settlements: economies of location, scale, and agglomeration.

A settlement located at the intersection of major trade routes, at some point where a change in the mode of transport is required (where goods have to be transferred from, say, land to water transport), will be well placed to attract investment in transport facilities and commercial activity. If the settlement is close to resource deposits or rich farmland, the advantages of location are strengthened. San Francisco is a prime example. Wuhan, located on the Yangtze River, is 600 miles inland, but the river is still wide and deep enough for large ocean-going ships. Smaller boats from further up the Yangtze transfer their cargo here. Wuhan is where the river trade intersects with the main Beijing-Guangzhou railway. Raw materials for heavy industry are close by, and Wuhan is one of China's major industrial centers.

Big cities provide producers with a large market and cheap labor force. These elements will often justify large-scale investment in plant and equipment, which will reduce per unit production costs. Furthermore, it is cheaper to build the infrastructure needed if there is a large and concentrated number of users and taxpayers. Because of economies of scale, cities are more likely to provide adequate schools, hospitals, and sanitation than are smaller settlements.

Economies of agglomeration refer to the economic benefits derived from the clustering of people with specialized training. The availability of skilled workers, and of producers' inputs and spare parts, makes it easier for urban industries to adapt and improve the design, methods, and materials of production. Items that cities have formerly imported may be copied and successfully produced locally. In turn, these new products may be exported to other cities. In a book called *Cities and the Wealth of Nations,* Jane Jacobs has argued that this competitive, imitative technological change is possible only in dynamic cities. Cities that fail periodically to create new waves of import replacement inevitably lose ground to other cities and suffer the problems of poverty and stagnation. Import-replacing cities stimulate the economies of their surrounding regions by creating new markets for food and raw materials, which encourages increased productivity in agriculture, and by the growth of jobs and investment (in infrastructure and in nonurban jobs such as food processing). Jacobs sees the growth of dynamic cities as indispensable to economic development.

Jacobs's argument is hard to test. It is difficult to say with precision whether city growth is a cause of economic growth or an effect of it. The literature exploring the issue further is scanty. The best-known contribution is E. A. Wrigley's study of the growth of London between 1650 and 1750. Wrigley concludes that London's demand for food and other products raised agricultural productivity and released some land workers from food production, thereby permitting the expansion of proto-industry—simple cottage crafts and manufacturing. The rapid growth of Edo (Tokyo) during the seventeenth century had a similar effect on the Japanese economy. There is clear evidence that urban growth stimulated agricultural change in the U.S. West and Australasia during the nineteenth century.

Even if city growth is judged to be an outcome of more general growth processes throughout the economy, cities still provide a locus for technological change and for much of society's capital stock. The building and servicing of cities gives further impetus to economic activity. Although the discrete contribution of cities to economic growth remains problematic, it is certain that economically developing regions also have growing cities. In the modern Third World, urban growth is generally most rapid in the countries with the strongest economies; economic growth and urbanization are roughly coterminous. Societies that experience economic growth have to confront the problems inherent in city growth.

There is a basic contradiction about cities and city life. Because the essence of cities is people clustering and moving around a given location for mutual economic and cultural benefit, every "good" aspect of city life is at least partly offset by negative features. Thus Shanghai hums with economic activity and opportunities for material advancement, but the city is very crowded as a result (*so* crowded, in fact, that the city government has established a Male Sexual Function Rehabilitation Engineering Committee to deal with some of the problems associated with an extreme lack of privacy). On the other hand, "liveable" places such as Hobart and Auckland offer affordable and pleasant housing, but jobs are not abundant.

The case of Los Angeles illustrates some of the inherent problems of city growth. If the counties of Los Angeles, Orange, Riverside, San Bernardino, and Ventura were a separate country, its economy (with a gross output of $336 billion in 1989) would be larger than that of China. Through its transition from an agricultural center to heavy industrial city and then to a diversified service and high technology manufacturing economy, Los Angeles has sustained an ability to create new jobs and exports. By the 1980s it could challenge New York for the title of the United States's premier city, though in recent years unemployment rates have been above the national average because of defense cutbacks and downturns in other sectors.

Los Angeles is dominated by a sprawl of single-family detached houses and dispersed workplaces. Since the 1920s the spread of suburbs has outrun a once-excellent public transport system. Most people need a car to get to work, shops, and schools and face long journey times on crowded freeways. The problems of the underclass and its chronic poverty, exacerbated by political fragmentation (the metropolitan area is a patchwork of independent cities, the poorest of which lack the tax base needed to provide effective amenities), boiled over during the riots of 1965 and 1992.

California is physically located on major seismic faults. Like Japan, a substantial part of its wealth is clustered in areas that are vulnerable to major earthquakes. If a major earthquake, which has been expected for some time, cripples Los Angeles, it has been said that the event would "enter the history books as the greatest domestic disaster since the Civil War." In short, the concentration of the factors of production precisely here is in some respects advantageous and in others disadvantageous.

The Urbanization of the Pacific Rim

During the thirteenth century the Venetian merchant Marco Polo claimed to have spent years traveling through Asia. In China, he found at Kinsai (Hangzhou) "without doubt the finest and most splendid city in the world." Kinsai covered a large area but was still crowded: Away from the wide, main streets were areas jam-packed with houses, shops, workshops, and other buildings. Polo estimated that the city had a circumference of about 100 miles. He has been accused of exaggeration in this and other matters, but contemporary Chinese sources here bear him out. An account written in 1235 states that the city extended for more than twelve miles to the north, west, and south. "Even if one walks for a couple of days, busy streets and crowded houses are still in sight." Modern scholars put the city's thirteenth-century population at around 2.5 million. The largest European city, Paris, had a population of only 160,000 in 1250.

Asia has had giant cities for over a thousand years. Korea's ancient capital, Kyongju, may have had a population of one million at its eighth-century peak. During the T'ang dynasty, the Chinese capital Chang'an (Xian) had a population of around one million within its walls and another million without. During the Song dynasty the growth of great cities such as Hangzhou was linked to the increasing commercialization and monetization of the economy. Data quantifying the increased level of urbanization in the Chinese economy are not yet available. However, city descriptions and evidence of the scale of commercial activity (for instance, in the late thirteenth century enough rice was sold each day in Hangzhou to feed an average of six to seven million people) do support the hypothesis that this was a highly urbanized economy. Mark Elvin suggests that in 1300 China was more urbanized than it was in 1900, when only 4 percent of the population lived in cities of at least 100,000 inhabitants.

In 1500 all but three of the world's twenty largest cities were located in Asia, the Middle East, or Africa (see Map 9.2). Of the eight large cities in Asia, six were in China. There was a major alteration to this distribution over the next few centuries. By 1850, thirteen of the world's twenty biggest cities were in Europe or across the Atlantic Ocean. With the rise of Europe and the Atlantic economy, the center of gravity of world urbanization shifted away from Asia and the Pacific.

From the late eighteenth century through the nineteenth century, Europe experienced massive, unprecedented population growth as a result of a demographic "modernization cycle." Hitherto, both birth and death rates had been at high levels. The modernization cycle began as death rates fell with the control of many diseases and improvements in nutrition while high birth rates were maintained. From 1750 to 1900 Europe's population almost trebled, from 140 million to 390 million.

This rapid population growth created in most European countries a problem of surplus rural labor. The population of rural areas grew much faster than job opportunities in agriculture, especially in northwest Europe, where competition from overseas became severe. The growth of industry and commerce in towns, along with emigration to regions across the Atlantic and beyond, helped to mop up some of the excess numbers. Capital, labor, and technology were transferred to provide European industry with needed primary products and bigger markets for industrial goods. The nineteenth century saw the emergence and consolidation of a world economy, centered on an increasingly urbanized and industrialized Europe, with an expanding flow of international, multilateral trade. The search for raw materials, markets, and investment opportunities brought about a new phase of European imperial interest in the Pacific Rim.

After the Opium War between China and Britain, the Treaty of Nanking (1842) gave foreigners special privileges in China. Hong Kong was ceded and established as a British colony, and a number of port towns (eventually about 100) were made freely open to foreigners. In these "treaty ports" foreigners were subject to the laws of their own countries rather than Chinese law, and Western commercial and financial interests flourished. Substantial industrial development was created by the transfer of Western capital and technology. Shanghai became the largest treaty port, growing spectacularly from 149,000 inhabitants in 1865 to over three million by 1930. The success of Shanghai and the other Westernized ports was humiliating for the Chinese, especially when foreign residents correctly stated that the treaty ports were "oases of light in a waste of darkness and stagnation."

In the century preceding the First World War, European states competed to acquire, administer, and develop new territories for strategic and economic gain. In

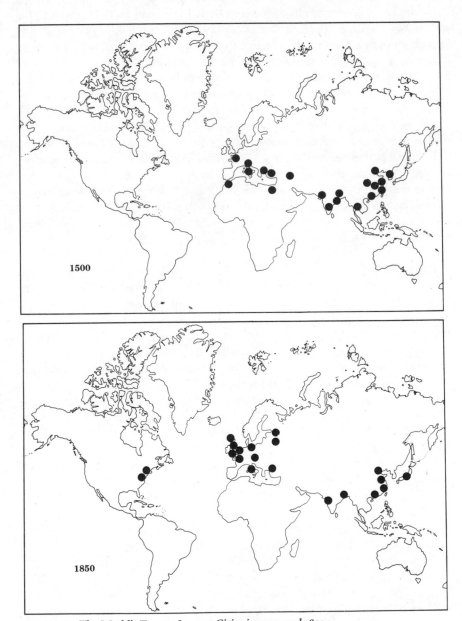

MAP 9.2   *The World's Twenty Largest Cities in 1500 and 1850*

addition to Hong Kong, Britain acquired Singapore (1819), Malacca (1824), Malaya (1875–1895), Sarawak (1888), and Brunei (1891). The Dutch increased their control over Java and set up colonies in Sumatra, Borneo, and the Moluccas. The French began their conquest of Indochina in 1859. The United States established Pacific bases at Hawaii and in the Philippines in 1898. Siam (Thailand) remained independent but still became a leading rice exporter with the aid of British capital, ideas, and technology. As these regions were integrated into the international economy, a number of port towns grew strongly: Hong Kong, Saigon (Ho Chi Minh City), Singapore, Batavia (Jakarta), Manila, and Bangkok had an average population of 90,000 in 1850; by 1930 the figure had risen to 566,000, a rate of growth of 6.6 percent per annum. Urbanization was also rapid in Japan with the successful development of manufacturing after the Meiji Restoration.

From around 1880, Latin America became a specialized supply region as the rate of European and U.S. investment in the region increased. Railway building and direct investment stimulated the export of commodities such as minerals (from Chile and Peru), nitrates (from Chile), oil (from Mexico), coffee (from Colombia), and fruit (from Central America and Ecuador). This greater emphasis on production for the export market gave cities new work, and from 1850 to 1930 the average population of Mexico City, Lima, and Santiago rose from 140,000 to 755,000, an average increase of 5.5 percent per annum.

The spread of European influence to other parts of the Pacific Rim in the second half of the nineteenth century stimulated the growth of new cities. After the U.S. Civil War railroads were extended quickly across the Great Plains to the Pacific. The Canadian railways, which opened up the prairies, also reached the Pacific Coast. Settlement spread around the arable parts of Australia and New Zealand. There was rapid population growth, and the development of highly productive farming, grazing, and mining regions supplied food and raw materials to the industrial areas of Europe and North America. On this new frontier of European settlement, a batch of towns was founded and grew at great speed, some becoming major metropolises. By 1930, four of these cities—Los Angeles, Sydney, San Francisco, and Melbourne—each topped the one million population mark.

As Map 9.3 shows, by 1925 all but a handful of the world's big cities were in Europe or the United States. New York was the largest, with London not far behind. The Ruhrgebiet, Manchester, Birmingham, and Glasgow symbolized Europe's industrial power, whereas in the United States industrialization was responsible for the growth of Chicago and Detroit into large, prosperous cities. Of the world's twenty largest cities, only Tokyo and Osaka had grown independently of the stimulus of the Atlantic economy.

In the developed world the demographic modernization cycle came to an end during the 1930s. Rates of population growth flattened out because of lower birth rates (caused by improved education, family planning, and higher consumer ex-

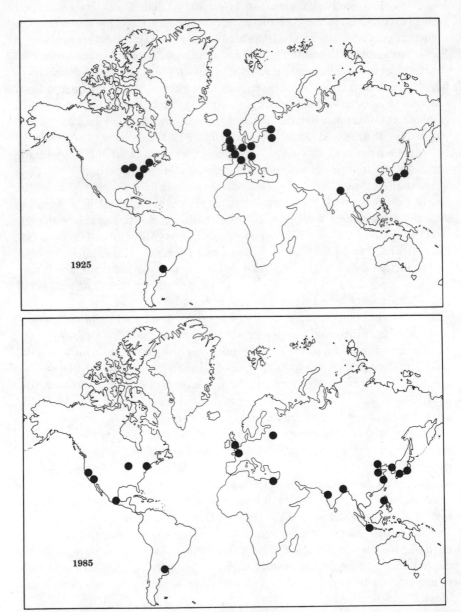

MAP 9.3   *The World's Twenty Largest Cities in 1925 and 1985*

pectations). Since the Second World War population growth in Europe and Japan has been very slow compared with that of the nineteenth and early twentieth century, approaching zero in recent years. However, in developing countries the cycle was just about to begin. Third World death rates have since fallen sharply while high birth rates have continued. Many killer diseases have disappeared, and improved agricultural technology has reduced (but not eradicated) the incidence of famine. In many countries (notably parts of Southeast Asia, such as Indonesia and the Philippines) population is growing at a very rapid rate.

From 1950 to 1980 the total population of Pacific Rim countries grew from nearly 1.3 billion to 2.2 billion, an average rate of growth of 2.5 percent per annum (see Table 9.1). In Japan, the former Soviet Union, and North America, population growth rates have been slower than the Pacific Rim average. Population growth in China and Australasia has been at the Pacific Rim average (the former has restrained population growth by family planning policies, the latter has encouraged it through assisted immigration). Population growth has been most rapid in Central America, South America, and Southeast Asia.

During these years of demographic expansion, the urban population of the Pacific Rim grew at 4.9 percent per annum. On the one hand, cities in the most prosperous and economically successful parts of the Rim have thrived. In Japan, many cities switched successfully after the Second World War from light industries such as textiles to heavy industries, petrochemicals, and synthetic fibers. As a result, the 300-mile-long area from Tokyo to Kobe, which includes Yokohama, Nagoya, Kyoto, and Osaka, congealed into a giant megalopolis with a current population of over 40 million. Hong Kong emerged as a financial and manufacturing powerhouse. From 1945 to 1985 the number of Korean and Taiwanese cities of more than 200,000 inhabitants rose from nine to thirty-five.

The United States's involvement in the Second World War created a huge demand for mining, manufacturing, and assembly plants, aerospace and electronics industries, and large military installations close to the Pacific. Federal government investment transformed the U.S. West into a giant boomtown. and cities in California and Southwestern towns such as Phoenix, Houston, and Dallas reaped the benefit. These regions had cheap sites for industry, offices, and housing, good transport links with the rest of the country (especially after the interstate highway building of the 1950s), and climates either naturally pleasant or made tolerable by the development of air conditioning. In the most successful of these cities, governments pursued pro-growth booster policies to attract industry and commerce. New car-dependent suburbs at the edge of cities generated employment growth in offices, factories, and shopping malls.

Yet the most remarkable urban growth has taken place in the Rim's less developed regions. From 1950 to 1980 the urban population of Central America grew at an annual average of 9.5 percent, South America at 8.3 percent, and Southeast

TABLE 9.1   Pacific Rim Regions: Rates of Total and Urban Population Growth (percent per annum), 1950–1980

	Total	Urban
East Asia	2.5	5.9
Japan	1.3	3.7
China	2.7	5.7
Southeast Asia	3.4	7.5
Australasia	2.7	3.8
USSR	1.6	4.6
North America	1.7	2.5
Central America	5.1	9.5
South America	3.9	8.3
PACIFIC RIM	2.5	4.9

SOURCE: United Nations, *Estimates and Projections of Urban, Rural and City Populations, 1950–2025: The 1982 Assessment* (New York: United Nations, 1985), Table A–7.

Asia at 7.5 percent. In 1930 there were only four cities in Latin America with more than 200,000 inhabitants; by 1985 the number had increased to sixty-eight. In Southeast Asia the number of cities of this size rose from three to seventy. In the 1960s and 1970s Seoul, Mexico City, Manila, Lima, and Jakarta all grew at rates exceeding 5 percent per annum. Further down the urban hierarchy, growth rates of between 8 and 15 percent per annum were recorded in a host of Latin American and Southeast Asian cities.

The total population of the Pacific Rim grew by 75 percent between 1950 and 1980, the urban population by 147 percent. The population of small towns, villages, farms, and other nonurban places rose by only 47 percent. There has been a transfer of labor from the rural to the urban sector through migration, but for the most part it has been natural population increase—high birth rates and low death rates—which has caused the rising urban population of developing countries. In developed countries the natural rate of urban increase is close to zero, and cities must rely on internal or overseas in-migration to increase their populations.

The slowdown in the growth of developed-world cities and the rapid growth of Pacific Rim cities has once again altered the spatial pattern of world urbanization. The Pacific Rim has returned to prominence. By 1985 most of the world's large and rapidly growing cities were located on the Rim (see Map 9.3). Four of the world's five biggest cities are Pacific Rim ones. Yet the Rim's modern urban system is far less dominated by China than was the case in the premodern period: Japan, South Korea, the Philippines, Indonesia, the United States, and Mexico, as well as China, now all have at least one representative in the world's top twenty cities.

Problems

In the poorest parts of the Pacific Rim—in Latin America and much of Southeast Asia—the cities and their built environment, or physical fabric, have generally not coped well with growing numbers. The word "city" evokes images of vast, over-crowded shantytowns, basic or nonexistent sanitation, severe pollution, and traffic congestion. City growth and its associated problems are often regarded as the terrible price developing countries must pay for economic development.

Disquiet about city growth and its consequences is not confined to the Third World. The sprawl of single-family suburban housing, a signature of cities in the U.S. West and Australasia, is creating mounting economic and environmental costs. These low-density cities inevitably depend primarily on private transport for the movement of people and goods, because public transport is inevitably less cost-efficient and flexible in dispersed, multicentered cities. This suburban sprawl did not begin with the automobile. Towns such as Los Angeles, Vancouver, and Melbourne, founded in the nineteenth century, were dominated by low-density suburbs from the start. They formed part of a "new urban frontier" of Anglo-Saxon cities along the Pacific. High, fairly evenly distributed incomes encouraged heavy spending on housing, and efficient public transport systems encouraged building in distant suburbs. Cars and freeways later allowed low-density development to continue.

Low residential densities and a dependence on cars are also characteristic of the new places of work that have been built outside older cities, chiefly in North America. Joel Garreau calls these new concentrations of office and retailing jobs "edge cities": They are built on the edge of town on what was recently farmland, and they have an edge (i.e., an advantage) over conventional cities in that it is cheaper and more profitable to develop them than it is to redevelop already built-up areas. "Edge cities" are the main location of new office and retail space in North America, and Garreau predicts that this trend will continue worldwide.

The cities that are built this way are heavy and inefficient consumers of scarce resources. In 1980 average per capita gasoline consumption in Los Angeles, San Francisco, Sydney, and Melbourne was 7.8 times that of high-density Tokyo, Singapore, and Hong Kong. Per capita road space in the former group of cities was 5.9 times that of the latter. In the low-density cities 76 percent of the journeys to work were by car, compared with only 15 percent in the high-density cities.

At first sight, cities such as Melbourne and Manila appear to be polar opposites. Manila's population grew at an average of 3.3 percent per annum during the first half of the 1980s, Melbourne's at only 0.9 percent per annum. Manila is an archetypal Third World city, with obvious poverty and a ramshackle physical fabric; Melbourne is characterized by a sprawl of housing that is relatively salubrious. Even so, in both types of city there is concern about the capacity of the physical fabric to cope with future population increases. There is a general assumption that slower rates of population growth will make for more efficient and less polluted cities. Accordingly, many analysts favor policies to slow down the expansion of cities, especially in Southeast Asia and Latin America. There is also pressure in many developed-world countries to limit overseas immigration, which in these regions is the main factor in city growth. Advocates of further immigration restriction in the United States, Canada, and Australia often cite the inability of cities to absorb extra numbers.

It has been argued that Third World city growth has not taken place as a result of economic development. Rather, it is said, cities have grown through their own high rates of natural increase and because of policies such as protective tariffs, tax incentives, and overvalued exchange rates, which have been designed to build up urban industrial capacity. Peasants have migrated to the cities either because they were pushed from the countryside by natural disasters or political and military strife or because they were pulled to the towns by the prospect, however slim, of in time securing decent-paying work. Because city growth requires heavy investment in housing and infrastructure, which can usually be provided cheaply in rural areas, it has been argued that the redistribution of labor from country to city creates diseconomies of scale. Where cities grow for noneconomic, chiefly political reasons and as a result are large and excessively costly to run, the situation has been called *overurbanization.* Overurbanization is held responsible for surplus and underemployed urban labor forces and the consequent poor housing, sanitation, and other ills.

The concept of overurbanization is finding favor with many who view the rapid growth of Third World cities with alarm. They see interventionist policies to check the runaway growth of cities as essential to economic and environmental well-being. During the 1960s and 1970s many Asian national and city governments tried to limit the growth of their largest cities, without much success. Through restrictions and incentives, these governments attempted to keep workers and industries in rural areas rather than in large cities. By the 1990s governments in a number of Asian countries had adopted a policy of "urban diffusion," which sought to encourage the growth of smaller cites by channeling public investment in infrastructure and private investment in manufacturing away from the big cities.

China's efforts to limit the growth of large cities and promote industrial development in rural areas are much admired in certain quarters. These policies, born of China's traditional distrust of cities and high regard for peasant and village life, seek to restrict migration to the cities and foster the creation of local, small-scale industrial enterprises. A feature of the Maoist era was the transfer of young urban workers and graduates to the countryside to perform "purifying" manual labor side-by-side with peasants. Yet the limited success of China's Maoist rural industrial programs and the dire physical condition of its cities (built and equipped to spartan standards and shockingly polluted) are a poor advertisement for such antiurban, interventionist policies.

Some economists have taken issue with the concept of overurbanization and policies to restrict city size. They have argued that city growth provides the resources needed to tackle urban problems. Rapid urban growth provides economies (rather than diseconomies) of scale, which make large "lumpy" investment in needed infrastructure more feasible. Furthermore, as cities grow, land and housing prices and other costs rise, which can inhibit further expansion by cutting average disposable incomes and capital accumulation. These price signals cause a market adjustment that slows city growth by discouraging in-migration or forcing industry to pay higher wages to attract labor. The model developed by Allen Kelley and Jeffrey Williamson predicts that by the end of the 1990s Third World urban growth rates will have slowed down markedly because of these limits to growth, as well as falling birth rates associated with the end of the demographic modernization cycle.

Restricting the growth of city populations is not a good way to improve the urban environment. Such policies may well do more harm than good by driving away the population of working age and leaving cities with a lower tax base. The growth of city economies, and thus of their population, usually causes immediate problems but also creates the resources needed to deal with those problems.

Cities on the Cheap

In this debate there is an assumption that slower rates of population growth will automatically make urban problems more manageable. Kelley and Williamson write that when urban growth is checked, "fewer complaints will be heard from the urban planners, and reports of urban environmental decay will lose some of their popular interest." For Kelley and Williamson, it is endogenous limits to city efficiency that will in time work to check urban growth. Less optimistic analysts argue that interventionist policies will be needed to correct the distortions in Third World economies that make for high urban growth rates.

Modern urban problems have by and large been diagnosed without much notice being taken of the economic history of cities. It is usually argued that history tells us little in the case of Third World cities because their rates of growth and the severity of their problems are unprecedented. Certainly there are some aspects of modern Third World city growth (such as low death rates and high rates of natural increase) that differ from the historical pattern. But high rates of urban population growth—currently around 4–5 percent per annum in the Third World—are by no means a new phenomenon. In the premodern period the overall trend was for towns to grow relatively slowly, but there are many instances of rapid urban growth resulting from political factors, particularly the establishment of new capital cities. Between 1265 and 1270, when Peking was established as the capital of the Mongol dynasty, its population grew at an average of 30 percent per annum. When Hideyoshi unified Japan and established Osaka as his capital in 1583, the city's population, which stood at 60,000 in 1580, rose to 400,000 by 1600, a rate of increase of 28 percent per annum. Edo (Tokyo) was transformed from a group of fishing villages in 1590 to a city of over one million inhabitants by 1700. If we assume that Edo's population was initially 10,000 (a generous estimate), then during the seventeenth century the city grew at an average rate of 90 percent per annum.

Peking, Osaka, and Edo coped reasonably well with these high growth rates: They were well policed and administered, adequately paved and drained, and generally cleaner than their European counterparts. Edo built a remarkable system to supply water. It may be argued that, in creating reasonably safe and serviceable urban environments, premodern Asian cities faced *greater* difficulties than those of the modern Third World. By modern standards, premodern communications and building technology were far more limited, building materials were weaker and less durable, and sanitation and fire-fighting technology were poorer.

Furthermore, the problems of modern cities such as Melbourne—currently growing at less than 1 percent per annum—have nothing obvious to do with an excessive rate of population growth. In the 1920s Los Angeles grew at 11 percent per annum, yet it avoided the creation of major slums and provided most new arrivals with the kind of high-standard housing to which they aspired.

When cities cannot cope with extra numbers without experiencing housing and environmental problems, the problem is not with the *rate* of urbanization but rather the *capacity* of the urban apparatus to cope with the extra numbers. To live or invest in a city and benefit from the economies of location, scale, and agglomeration it provides, individuals and businesses must bear a range of costs associated with the building, equipping, and servicing of that city. These congestion costs include the capital, land, and labor required for housing and infrastructure, the need for adequate commuter arrangements, the task of dealing with problems of pollution and waste disposal, and the risk and incidence of major losses of labor and capital stock in times of natural disaster and warfare.

Congestion costs rise whenever individuals use scarce resources in a way that reduces the supply and quantity of resources available to others, thereby creating externalities such as crowding and pollution. Because the market cannot put a price on fresh air, clean water, and road space to ensure that users pay for all of the resulting costs, there is an incentive to overuse these resources. Such behavior may be cheap for the individual but will impose a heavy burden on the rest of society.

Individuals can only remain in a city if their share of congestion costs (measured by house rents, commuting costs, and taxation) does not exceed their share of the economic wealth generated by that city (measured by its total income). For businesses, higher congestion costs mean more expensive factors of production (in high-cost cities, land will be expensive and wage premiums may be needed to attract labor). High costs may put a city at a serious competitive disadvantage. Thus, any city may be expected to build the type of physical fabric that minimizes congestion costs in relation to its economic advantages.

There is no standard pattern to the way in which congestion costs are reduced. It depends on a number of institutional and economic variables. Initial planning decisions affect some of these variables, such as site features and topography, proximity to water supplies, and patterns of land use and ownership. Other important factors include population density, ethnic stratification, spatial patterns of residence and workplace, building and sanitation technology, political structure, and the public sector's priorities, tax base, and administrative competence. The mix of variables differs from case to case, so that low-cost housing may be compacted near the center in one city but sprawl out at the edge in another. One city may have adequate paving and sanitation but flimsy and small housing; another's housing stock may be fairly well built but crowded and poorly served by infrastructure. There are endless fine details distinguish the physical fabric of one city from another. What most cities have in common is a need to cut congestion costs and create a system that is cheap to build and run. Yet a strategy that is at first relatively inexpensive may over time create further problems, leading to a *rise* in congestion costs. Cheap, closely spaced housing will reduce the amount of resources needed to shelter a city's population and allow large numbers of people to live near sources of employment. However, with further population growth this housing stock may become overcrowded, with inflated rent levels, amplified problems of sanitation, and greater vulnerability to natural disasters. When people try to avoid these problems by living at the city's edge, their actions exert upward pressure on congestion costs. Extra land and building materials are required for individual housing; moreover, society faces higher bills for the provision and maintenance of infrastructure and lengthier average commuting times as the city expands outward.

Such increases in congestion costs are the key limit to urban growth in Kelley and Williamson's model. If these costs rise faster than a city's ability to generate new wealth, one may assume that, given total rationality and perfect information, people will be less willing to live in or move to cities. In reality, when a city's economic advantages have weakened or its congestion costs have risen (or both), its inhabitants have tended to respond with strategies to minimize congestion costs. By accepting bedrock housing standards in poorly serviced slums or in cheap, self-built shelter, the poor and unskilled can reduce the costs of city living and hang on to some hope of improved well-being. Thus, when the costs of urban living rise, slower population growth and improved living conditions will not always be the result. In many cases the "limits to growth" have simply made growing cities more crowded and dirty.

Cities with environmental and housing problems are those that have needed to lower their congestion costs. A city that can house and service large numbers at minimal expense can provide those who wish to improve their economic lot with affordable shelter, at the same time releasing resources for job-creating investment in commerce and manufacturing. By building a low-cost physical fabric, cities with few economic advantages can improve their chances of generating economic development. The result is faster, but messier, economic growth. These are "ugly" cities built on the cheap, places that for all their horridness still provide a toehold for those who wait in line for decent-paying jobs.

Today's Solution, Tomorrow's Problem

There was a town of only limited significance until the early nineteenth century that subsequently grew quickly into a major city. As migrants, many of them impecunious, poured into the city, landlords met the need for cheap shelter by economizing on housing space and amenities. The typical house was narrow and dark, built in brick, often with its back adjoining that of another row of houses. To help pay the rent, tenants cut costs by subletting parts of their houses to other families. Latrines, though formally required by building regulations to be provided in each house, were rare. Water supplies and drainage were poor; the place stank.

This town might have been any of several dozen in Europe or North America in the mid- to late nineteenth century. Chicago or Baltimore, perhaps. Prague, or Hamburg. Mention that the city's unhealthy environment was investigated by a social reformer named Chadwick and the student of British towns will immediately identify Manchester or Liverpool. As it happens, the city is Hong Kong. As it happens, the critic of Hong Kong's sanitation was not the celebrated Sir Edwin Chadwick but his son Osbert, appointed by the British government in 1882 to report on the unhealthiness of the city. As much as any of the above-named towns, Hong Kong exemplified the cost-cutting and resultant problems of the "ugly city."

Asian cities have traditionally been crowded places, with tiny houses, shops, and factories packed shoulder to shoulder and narrow streets swarming with people. It has often been suggested that the high density of Asian cities reflects a cultural preference for this way of living. In 1878 the *Hong Kong Government Gazette* described the city's crowding and subletting of houses as "the outcome of a lengthened experience among the Chinese of living in large and crowded cities, and are as deep rooted as most of their social customs." However, there are reasons for the willingness of Asians to live in crowded urban housing that go beyond possible historical experience or cultural preference. In places where there is a shortage of building land, such as Hong Kong and Singapore, crowding is understandable. But even the Asian cities with room to spread out have been closely spaced. As noted previously, although thirteenth-century Hangzhou covered a very large area, its houses and shops were often built overhanging streets or waterways. Sometimes alleys were blocked completely by illegally extended buildings. This physical profile evolved because residents preferred to forgo living space in return for proximity to the city's business and employment opportunities. Economic advantage outweighed the disadvantage of crowding.

Furthermore, houses in Asian cities were usually only single-storied, and hardly ever more than two stories high, because of the risk of earthquakes. The dense housing was built mainly of wood and bamboo, as such houses bend and sway in an earthquake (whereas brick ones are prone to collapse), but with cooking and heating done on simple open braziers the risk of fire was very high. Over 800 major fires have been recorded in Tokyo since 1602, 13 of them caused by earthquakes. Few non-Western cities have had their fire history documented as fully as Tokyo. Anecdotal evidence—numerous references to "frequent" and "devastating" fires—indicates that conflagration was a very common problem in Asian cities. For instance, William Rowe notes that in late nineteenth-century Hankow (part of Wuhan), fire was a chronic problem. There were hundreds of fires each year, including blazes in 1887 and 1892 that each lasted for three days, "and the need to rebuild large burnt-out sections of town was routinely anticipated."

With space at a premium, there was an inflation of rents when the population of Asian cities increased during the late nineteenth and early twentieth centuries. High rents forced some people, especially new immigrants, into cheaper housing outside the city limits, but there was a strong tendency to offset rising housing costs by accepting less room. By running up some new internal walls, landlords could turn a building that had housed two families into one capable of housing four or more families. Crowding was a rational response to the high cost of living in fast-growing cities.

A further way of cutting costs was through the provision of only basic sanitation. Most Japanese and Chinese cities were free of the problem of human excrement flooding the streets (it was collected carefully by householders and sold, very profitably, to farmers as fertilizer). But street-paving and drainage were generally of very poor quality: Tokyo's city government simply dumped and spread loads of sharp stone and gravel, letting vehicles and pedestrians' feet do the work of compacting the new road. Drains were open and often blocked with litter. Shanghai had no organized system of street cleaning, only open middens on most street corners, and the city's waterways were grossly polluted. Dead babies were put out in the garbage in Shanghai's alleyways. Hong Kong streets in the 1930s had tins in which people could dispose of dead rats. Building regulations requiring drains and water closets in houses were ignored. Thousands of coal-burning fires created a shroud of smoke and falling soot. Between 1821 and 1932, Shanghai averaged an outbreak of cholera every twenty-eight months. There was a serious outbreak of plague in Canton (Guangzhou) and Hong Kong in 1894 that killed 10,000 people, whereupon steamships leaving those cities spread the disease around the world. The plague killed an average of a thousand Hong Kong residents each year until 1907.

Ironically, some of these seedy cities of the nineteenth and early twentieth century now rank with the world's most efficient cities. Hong Kong and Singapore are often cited as workable urban communities. In both places, solutions to problems of housing and commuting have been found in excellent public housing and mass transit systems. The cities' air, streets, and waterways have been cleaned up (though it must be said that Hong Kong's Victor Harbor remains unsatisfactorily polluted). This improvement has been so rapid and substantial that it is worth considering the reasons for it.

When a city chooses a low-cost method of dealing with a particular problem, it is likely that the costs of the strategy will rise over time. For instance, a city government that cannot afford to build a sewer system may instead pay scavengers to remove the contents of latrines and clean the streets. However, over time, the relative costs of these two alternatives will usually change. Scavenging is labor-intensive, with few economies of scale; sewerage is capital-intensive, with substantial economies of scale. Thus, as population density rises, the former will become more costly, the latter cheaper. Furthermore, scavenging is an imperfect form of sanitation, and as a city becomes more crowded the incidence of disease will increase.

As incomes and expectations rise, however, a city may be able to afford the investment needed to clean up and improve its physical fabric. Rising incomes are a necessary but not a sufficient condition for urban improvement. There is also the matter of political constraints. Where government is stable and effective and has the will and tax base to tackle urban improvement, there is likely to be adequate provision of public goods. Where large areas of urban land are publicly owned and sold or used by the government for housing and infrastructure, and where land ownership is subject to correct pricing policies, the sites needed for city-building are likely to be affordable and used effectively. Externalities can be contained by government intervention in the pricing of urban resources, meaning that people who overuse resources will face taxes and penalties that increase the private cost of their behavior to a level close to the social cost. When governments get this pricing right, they create disincentives to pollute or to make inefficient use of scarce resources. In cities where average incomes are rising and government administration is competent, the costs of collecting payments and policing regulations will become a less serious constraint on urban improvement.

The cases of Hong Kong and Singapore show that where the public sector makes urban improvement a priority, its actions are most effective in high-density cities. It is more difficult to use land efficiently and price the use of resources correctly in cities where housing and jobs are scattered over a wide area. The more compact the city, the easier it is to collect payments and enforce regulations. There are economies of scale for efficient land use (such as public transport and multistory housing), whereas inefficient land use (such as vacant land, low-rise housing, and large areas of roads and parking lots) creates serious problems. Hong Kong developers have been known to demolish an apartment block within one month of its construction to make way for a more profitable office block.

By the mid-1950s a belt of squatter camps obstructed the expansion of Hong Kong. The publicly owned land the camps occupied was needed for industry and permanent housing, and the crowded nature of the settlements made them vulnerable to fire and epidemics. In 1953 the largest squatter camp, Shek Kip Mei, was destroyed by fire, and over 50,000 people were left homeless. Rather than allowing the camp to be rebuilt as before, the government seized the opportunity to begin a major clearance of squatter districts, relocating displaced people in multistory public housing. Gradually, the city's housing problem was solved in a way that provided affordable shelter and still freed up land for other uses.

In Singapore, taxation of large and small polluters has been effective, through measures including the auctioning of permits to manufacturers who wish to use chlorofluorocarbons, the sale of permits to car drivers using the city's roads, and the banning of chewing gum. Not many people will draw much comfort from the above example: Few governments can introduce policies the way Singapore does, without regard for electoral popularity. In democratic societies policies such as road pricing, hardly a vote-winner, may never be proposed. This observation leads one to ask: What role does political structure play in the process of urban improvement?

Most city governments are under pressure to attract investment and in so doing to allow investors to cut costs. Guadalajara, Mexico, is in many ways one of the best-run cities along the Pacific Rim, with adequate public housing and effective urban services. But in 1992 the city's sewers exploded, with major loss of life and capital, when the waste products drained into them by chemical and other industries ignited. The city government had allowed these practices, fearing that if it had not turned a blind eye the industries would relocate in a city that did.

Until fairly recently Japanese cities were under similar pressure. With cities competing to attract industry, businesses could simply disregard pollution control ordinances. By the mid-1970s most of Japan's waterways were tainted with industrial waste, untreated sewage, and agricultural chemicals. The air was thick with smog and smokestack emissions. Residents of the city of Yokkaichi were vulnerable to "Yokkaichi asthma"—mercury poisoning caused by pollution from nearby petrochemical plants. Happily, the situation in Japan has improved. Polluting industries are now taxed heavily, and the revenue is used to finance pollution control. The change has occurred partly because of rising incomes and partly because of the altered structure of the economy (smokestack industries are now less important). A groundswell of support for a cleaner environment is now a feature of Japanese politics. Ordinary citizens have helped to bring about change through democratic processes. The example shows that correct environmental policies can be devised and enforced without the coercion of tough, nondemocratic regimes.

With modern technology and effective government, high-density cities can be efficient and safe places in which to live and work. But well into the twentieth cen-

tury, high population densities normally made for unpleasant and dangerous urban environments. When, in the late eighteenth century, London's merchant elite
chose to live away from the city center in villas located in healthier and more private surroundings at the city's edge, they started a fashion that was copied in
other English towns, then in North America and Australasia. Suburbs, once the
location of noxious trades and poor housing, became the desired place to live.
The cities of the New Urban Frontier, dominated by low-density suburbs, were
built as a reaction to the crowded cities of Europe and eastern North America.
Thus, homebuyers in Los Angeles extolled "the value of sunshine, of space and of
individual homes as against crowded housing and tenements without proper provision for light, air, yards, lawns, trees, shrubs, flowers, and individual home
units."

In most cities average incomes were such that only a privileged minority could
afford suburban housing and the expensive, time-consuming commuting required. On the other hand, the booming economies of the New Frontier cities
provided the high incomes needed to turn this expensive dream into reality for
the majority of the population. The rapid rates of migration that caused these cities' populations to swell gave further impetus to economic prosperity. Migrants
were generally skilled and well off, not peasants or low-income laborers. One
needed capital to afford the long and expensive journey to the U.S. West or Australasia, and when these migrants arrived their spending added to the aggregate
demand for goods and services. The cities' public transport systems were extensive and geared to opening up new suburbs. In short, the forces making for suburban development were present in full measure, and the result was the creation
of sprawling cities with a high standard of housing and infrastructure provision.

By the start of the First World War, the New Frontier cities had laid out vast ex-
panses of suburban housing ("the vaster the better" declared one booster from
Los Angeles) served by public transport. These cities had been built at great expense during an age of considerable prosperity. This form of city-building was at
first relatively cheap, but as population growth continued it became more and
more difficult to construct and service a city in which most of the population had
enough space for a suburban house and lawn.

Consider the example of Los Angeles. It was founded in 1781, one of a large
number of pueblos (agricultural villages) established by the Spanish government
in its American territories. The Pueblo of Los Angeles was at a freshwater site fifteen miles inland from the Pacific. A century later it was the hub of five railroads,
three of which ran to the Pacific, another through the San Bernardino Valley.
These railroads linked a number of sparsely populated settlements, such as Pasa-
dena, Long Beach, Pomona, and Santa Monica, set amidst orange groves and
market gardens. One of the world's largest networks of electric streetcars (over
1,000 miles of track was operating by the 1920s) fanned out into the region's developing suburbs and confirmed its low density.

Streetcars enabled Los Angeles to develop extensive suburbs, but when cities spread outward in this way it becomes more difficult for public transport systems to operate effectively. In the 1920s life in Los Angeles came to center increasingly around the automobile. During the decade Los Angeles's population increased by 115 percent, and car ownership rose by a remarkable 415 percent. By 1930 there were 1.5 residents to every car. The city widened its downtown streets and built a huge mesh of six-lane roads, called boulevards, to accommodate the extra traffic flow. People with downtown jobs drove to work. Cars were used for shopping trips. Workers used their cars to get to the factories and oil refineries that had sprung up around the metropolitan area. Cheap, mass-produced cars and a lavish road network placed even far-flung suburban subdivisions within reasonable commuting distance.

The days of the streetcar companies were numbered. With the region's commuters scattered far and wide, streetcar lines were never profitable per se. The typical route was long and sparsely populated, and streetcar companies could only operate if they were paid a subsidy by the owners of the real estate they served or if they invested directly in suburban development and ran streetcars as a loss leader to boost land sales. Before the First World War the streetcars raced along at speeds of up to 55 mph, but as the population density along the routes increased, the need for more stops reduced the average speed. The streetcars became more crowded. When the lines converged downtown, intolerable traffic congestion resulted. Companies never accumulated sufficient capital to invest in new rolling stock or build faster underground or elevated tracks.

Once commuters drifted away from public transport and began using their own cars, the rise in traffic created electoral pressure to increase road capacity. The electorate's preferred solution to the traffic problem—public investment in new, high-capacity roads without stoplights or intersections—was hardly surprising, given that the cost of a system of "freeways" was only half that of a new rapid-transit system. Most Los Angelinos simply did not want anything resembling the hideous elevated railroad of the Chicago Loop. Without public subsidy the financially troubled streetcar companies collapsed, and buses emerged as the main form of public transport. Once the mass transit system and its downtown hub became marginalized, problems of further congestion inevitably led to demands for more road and parking space, making the city more car-dependent.

In the other New Frontier cities there was a similar, inexorable trend away from public transport. There was a determined campaign after the First World War to ease Sydney's street congestion by tearing up the tramway system (Sydney's first tram route was removed in 1939, and its last tram ran in 1961). New highways and bridges made commuting easier but soon added to the level of crowding and delays. When the two transbay bridges in San Francisco were opened in the 1930s, there was an immediate increase in traffic in the city center. Plans were soon drawn up for a "basic cure," a system of freeways bypassing the city center to ease traffic congestion.

These low-density cities covered too much ground for their public transport systems to operate effectively. People came to rely on their cars, especially for suburb-to-suburb commuting, and were less likely to use public transit or to support public subsidies to make good its losses. However, simply providing the resources needed to make car driving more convenient is a trap: Once cars become a city's dominant form of transportation, public transit is never more than an increasingly unprofitable adjunct. As new roads provide better access to peripheral suburbs, the extra traffic creates bottlenecks, requiring extra investment in road capacity. Major expenditures for new rapid-transit systems cannot provide a workable solution to any low-density city's transport problems: Such projects have either been rejected as too expensive (as in Seattle during the mid-1960s) or proved inadequate (as was the case with San Francisco's Bay Area Rapid Transit, or BART, network). In his book *Great Planning Disasters,* Peter Hall writes that BART "has almost completely failed to end the typical Californian's long love affair with his car." What were once seen as solutions to urban problems—suburban housing, cars, freeways, and wider roads—have now in themselves become urban problems.

In Latin America and much of Southeast Asia, low-density urban development is also the norm. But the suburbs there bear little resemblance to those of the New Urban Frontier. In cities such as Mexico City, Lima, Manila, and Jakarta, at least a third of the population has built its own shelter in settlements where living conditions approximate those of a rural village. In some settlements, housing is serviceable, streets are paved, and drains and water supplies are adequate. In general, though, the physical fabric is of only basic standard. Building sites have either been obtained illegally, by squatting on unoccupied, usually government-owned, land, or have been bought from landowners who have subdivided their land but have not obtained planning permission to do so. The squatters live in hope that the state will give them legal title to their house sites and provide basic infrastructure; in the "pirate" subdivisions people purchase legal title to the land, but there is usually no infrastructure.

There is a vigorous debate over what to do about these self-built settlements. City governments have traditionally regarded them as "cancers," and urban planners usually consider them obstacles to good civic design. In the 1960s many settlements were accordingly bulldozed and their inhabitants forced to go elsewhere. This attitude is conveyed by Jan Morris's account of Lima in 1963:

> Straggling up towards the summit ... squats a slum so bestial, so filthy, so congested, so empty of light, fun, colour, health or comfort, so littered with excrement and garbage, so swarming with barefoot children, so reeking with pitiful squalor that just the breath of it, borne on the fresh sea wind, makes you retch into your handkerchief.

However, there is a growing body of opinion that would regard the above description as gratuitously unflattering. The leading supporter of self-help as a solution to the Third World urban housing problem is a British architect, John Turner, who from the mid-1950s on worked in Lima advising communities who wished to establish *barriadas* (shantytowns). Although many observers saw the *barriadas* and their equivalents in other cities as vile slums, Turner and like-minded people saw them as places of hope, where private and public investment would eventually raise the standard of housing and amenities. Some settlements have now been established for several decades, and the occupiers have extended their houses and upgraded them with tiled roofs and glazed windows.

Self-built settlements are one way the urban poor can reduce their housing costs. In many Third World cities where conventional housing is scarce and expensive, self-building is tolerated and even encouraged by governments. This is a cheap solution, perhaps the only feasible one in the circumstances. The worry is that an uncontrolled spread of settlement will make it impossible to provide cost-effective infrastructure later. This has happened in Jakarta and Manila. Each sprawls for over 1,500 square miles—more than three times the area of Los Angeles—and is mostly unsewered and lacking safe drinking water. In 1991 an outbreak of cholera in Lima spread to other Peruvian cities and to Ecuador, Colombia, and Brazil, providing strong evidence of the inadequacy of shantytown sanitation.

The past weighs heavily on cities' present problems and characteristics, and many cities have been unable to carry out the policies needed to establish a set of institutions conducive to urban improvement. Manila, for instance, has failed to levy or collect property taxes to encourage landowners to use urban land for productive purposes (rather than withholding it for speculative gain) or to sort out which level of government (city or national) should pay to have the network of canals and open drains unblocked.

The cities best equipped to provide effective services and improve the quality of their environment are those that for historical reasons have managed to contain urban sprawl. Bogota, for instance, was sited in the midst of rich farmland, and squatting on alienated land was forcibly checked by the state. This policy encouraged consolidated land use: in 1985 Bogota's population density was nearly eight times that of Lima. Cities such as Shanghai, Shenyang, and Tianjin—where the population is densely housed and people can still conveniently walk, cycle, or take public transport to work—have the opportunity of developing a safe and functional physical fabric if they get their policies right. Currently their physical fabric leaves much to be desired, but so did Hong Kong's and Singapore's forty years ago. The Rim's low-density cities will find it more difficult to cope with population growth: Their inefficient land use and dependence on cars is literally set in concrete.

10

The Pacific Economy: Summing Up

Stretching from rich Japan to poor China to rural New Zealand and across to the west coast of America, the Pacific is a disparate region divided by history, religion, language, culture, government and levels of wealth and development. It has been united only by growing opportunities to make money.

—The Economist, November 11, 1989

The Core Relationship

The Second World War accelerated the process of economic integration in the Pacific. There were two symbolic turning points: The Japanese attack on Pearl Harbor in December 1941 brought the United States into the war, and the fall of Singapore to the Japanese in February 1942 severely damaged European prestige and stimulated a second wave of decolonization, which freed the nations of Southeast Asia soon after the war.

The United States lost and recaptured the Philippines. U.S. armies played a significant part in rolling back the Japanese military. Indeed, the Allied victory in the Pacific was largely a U.S. victory. The U.S. occupation of Japan involved the United States in the Asia Pacific region in a way never previously experienced. The nation played a significant role in the reconstruction of Japan, extending considerable aid under the Dodge Plan, the Asian equivalent of the Marshall Plan for aid to Europe.

Shortly after the Second World War the Communists took over in China, extending thereby the cold war to Asia and the Pacific. The United States provided help to the Chinese Nationalist regime in Taiwan, and the Dodge Plan was a mechanism by which it encouraged the reconstruction and revival of the Japanese economy as a capitalist bulwark against the further spread of communism in Asia. The Korean War (1950–1953) led to even more direct U.S. involvement in Asian affairs and created a further recipient of U.S. aid, South Korea.

The rapid revival of East Asia during the 1950s and 1960s surprised many. After briefly pursuing a policy of import substitution behind protective tariffs, the East Asian governments adopted a policy of promoting exports of manufactured goods. The first industrialization phase involved strong export-led growth with the emphasis on labor-intensive manufactures. In the second phase, partly as a reaction to a rise in real wages, there was a shift to higher-skilled and capital-intensive production for export; labor-intensive production moved to some other Asian economies that were still at earlier stages of development. The third phase was marked by an even more decisive shift to high technology production. During this phase there was an increase in the relative importance of domestic demand–led growth. Only Japan has so far passed fully through all these stages. Others, such as the four Little Dragons, are firmly ensconced in the second phase.

The resource-poor economies of East Asia deliberately sought out sources of the raw materials necessary for the labor-intensive and more traditional capital-intensive phases of manufacture. Such raw materials were available in the more recently settled societies of the Pacific Rim (i.e., those of the Americas and Australia), whose economies were flexible enough to adapt to meet the rising demands. There is no doubt that increasing levels of income and population would have also stimulated a demand for imported foodstuffs had the agricultural sectors of East Asia not continued to be heavily protected. The demand for raw materials will continue only as long as the economies in the early phase of development are themselves resource-poor, as, for example, Thailand, Indonesia, and Malaysia are currently. However, the demand for foodstuffs may increase if there is a freeing of imports.

Much of the early economic development of postwar East Asia relied on the openness of the U.S. market, to which a significant proportion of the manufacturing exports was dispatched. There was a potential complementarity in the trading relationship between the English-speaking nations on the Rim, particularly the United States, and East Asia. The good resource endowment and high wages of the United States allowed it to exchange resource-intensive and high technology commodities for East Asian manufactures, initially of the labor-intensive variety. An increasingly competitive manufacturing sector in East Asia came to threaten the existence of the traditional labor-intensive sectors of the United States, such as textiles, footwear, and clothing. These were eventually protected by informal quotas. Next, the traditional capital-intensive sectors linked to steel and engineering, particularly the automobile industry and basic electronics, were threatened. The main U.S. industrial belt of the Northeast and Midwest became the Rust Belt. U.S. trade deficits were the order of the day.

In its industrial heyday the United States had been a significant exporter of capital. This capital outflow now reversed itself: Offsetting the current account deficit depended on an import of capital. The willingness of Japanese institutions to hold U.S. government bonds made this importation possible. The United States's deteriorating trading position was reinforced at least until the mid-1980s by an overvalued dollar, a legacy of its reserve currency role. When the U.S. economy was strong, many countries and institutions were willing to hold their monetary reserves in dollars, thus raising the demand for them and keeping their value above what trade alone dictated.

A common reaction to these economic difficulties was a strident call within the United States for protection. Informal agreements with East Asian nations, particularly Japan, moderated the harshest effects of potential competition and thereby abated the strongest demands for protection. During all this, California retained a healthy industrial sector based on an advanced research and development infrastructure. Silicon Valley, the early center of microchip production and a leader in the information technology revolution, kept the state's economy booming at least until Japanese competition also began in high technology products.

The economic relationship between Japan and the United States has been the core relationship integrating the Pacific, insofar as it has been integrated. This relationship rests on the traditional concept of comparative advantage, the specialization in commodities that intensively use the factor of production with which a country is best endowed. It is paradoxical that the United States's main exports to Asia by value have been such resource-intensive commodities as grain, timber, coal, and soybeans. High technology exports such as computers, aircraft, and nuclear power stations have accounted for only about one-tenth of U.S. exports to Asia. In return, the United States has imported manufactures and capital from resource-poor but labor-rich and increasingly capital-rich East Asia. Despite all the talk about strategic trade theory, existing patterns of trade for the most part still reflect resource endowments: It is very difficult for government policy to "create" comparative advantage, although the trade in manufactured commodities and services produced in both regions is increasing in relative importance.

Other relationships in the Pacific have echoed this core relationship. The relationship between the United States and the Little Dragons has imitated that between the United States and Japan. The relationship between Canada or Australia on one side and Japan or the Little Dragons on the other has tended to fit the same pattern, although the exact commodities traded may differ. Australia has exported coal, iron ore, bauxite, and wool, amongst a quite varied list of primary commodities. The English-speaking areas of new settlement have all taken advantage of resource abundance to develop this trading relationship but have also tapped into the new sources of savings appearing in East Asia since their own internal savings ratios have fallen so dramatically.

The Pacific Century

The growing importance of the core relationship has persuaded many that the world is entering the Pacific Century, although the starting date is never exactly specified. For a generation now, they have been convinced that the Pacific Rim would become to the twenty-first century what the Atlantic Basin was to the eighteenth and nineteenth centuries. The vision of a world economy centered on trade between the Americas and Asia rather than between the Americas and Europe has indeed been mooted since the late nineteenth century. After the United States annexed the Philippines in 1898, President Theodore Roosevelt predicted that the "Atlantic era ... must soon exhaust the resources at its command," and that "the Pacific era, destined to be the greatest of all, is just at its dawn." In 1912 Henry Huntington, a Los Angeles railroad and real estate magnate, stated that "Los Angeles is destined to become the most important city in the country, if not the world. Its front door opens on to the Pacific, the ocean of the future. The Atlantic is the ocean of the past." Several statements of this kind are to be found in old speeches and articles, though Melbourne authors Wood and McBride expressed skepticism in 1946. They did not expect southern and eastern Asia to become predominant in world affairs and claimed it would be rash to say so.

Since the 1970s the continuing economic success of East Asia and the far west of North America has rejuvenated the idea of the Pacific Century. If it comes to pass, the economies of the region will be concerned overwhelmingly with trans-Pacific trade. The major players will become richer in the process, creating further trade opportunities and capital movements that will provide a stimulus to the region's poor economies. Many in developed regions such as Australasia and British Columbia, which grew wealthy in the nineteenth century as efficient suppliers of resources to the Atlantic economy but have since struggled to maintain a diversified economic base, see position on the Pacific Rim and proximity to its markets as guaranteeing a resolution of their economic problems.

Moreover, in most Pacific Rim nations ordinary residents are likely to have noticed, in the media or in everyday observation, mounting evidence of links with other Pacific Rim countries. For instance, Hispanics and Asians accounted for 85 percent of California's population growth in the 1980s. At the 1980 census, 76 percent of California's population was white; by the early twenty-first century there may be no clear racial majority. *The Economist* has observed that "many Asian family businesses are now really Pacific-rim ones: the patriarch lives in Hong Kong or Taipei; some of the factories are in Malaysia or Thailand; but the research and development, the marketing and (often) the brightest children are in California, Seattle or Vancouver."

The cultural developments have been vigorous. California, Southeast Asia, and many of the Pacific islands have rapidly become major tourist destinations. Japanese corporations have made conspicuous investments, buying out Columbia

Pictures and Universal Studios in Hollywood, for example. Furthermore, the Japanese are planning to finance and build a series of major construction schemes called the Global Infrastructure Project. This concept includes a canal across the Isthmus of Kra in Thailand, hydroelectric plants in Latin America, two tunnels from Hong Kong to mainland China, and a new road between Asia and Europe ("the Silk Highway"). New high tech cities, or "technopolises," have been built in Japan, and plans have been made to build one also in Australia. U.S. (specifically, Los Angelino) culture is almost ubiquitous. Throughout the Pacific Rim, Hollywood movies are watched, U.S. music is listened to, and baseball is played. For many people these trends are not always welcome or comforting, but they point to a degree of integration of the Pacific Rim's component parts by a pop culture. It is difficult to imagine this phenomenon being reversed.

Nevertheless, the concept of the Pacific Century has proved unpersuasive to many observers. To begin with, most of the examples in the preceding paragraphs could be matched by others showing that the region has strong links with much of the non-Pacific world. Although the United States remains Asia's major trading partner (the value of Asian-U.S. trade in 1987 was almost three times that of Asian-European trade), Asia's commercial links with Europe are strengthening. Nor is the United States abandoning trade with Europe: The value of this commerce grew by 5 percent per annum (in constant dollars) from 1967 to 1987. During the same period, Asian trade with Europe grew at 16 percent per annum. The Global Infrastructure Project, as the name suggests, is not confined to the Pacific Rim; it includes dams and irrigation works for Africa and the Middle East. Japan is also involved financially in the English Channel Tunnel project.

There are two sides to this coin. Economic integration and the widening of factor markets imply both greater economic competition and greater economic vulnerability. The whole world economy, including its Pacific part, pulsates increasingly together. In addition, the relative rise of Japan is associated with the relative decline of the United States.

Within the Pacific, as elsewhere, there has been a proliferation of both economic and political groupings. The most prominent of these are the Association of Southeast Asian Nations (ASEAN), a political alliance that has expressed its intention to become a free trade area over a period of ten years, and the North American Free Trade Agreement (NAFTA), as yet in its very early stages. Both represent tentative steps in the direction of more formal political and economic integration. Of greater potential coverage (because it has a wider membership) is the Asia Pacific Economic Cooperation (APEC), established in 1989. Still only a forum for discussion, it has no formal organization. There are still some significant absentees, such as Russia and the Latin American countries.

Clearly the translation of informal economic integration into a more complete political or economic union is unlikely given the lack of cultural unity or common interests among Pacific Rim nations and the significant advantage of an open world economy for most states within the region. Much effort has been expended in making the Uruguay round of GATT negotiations a success, but this outcome appears less and less likely, and a genuinely free trade world remains a distant prospect. Yet pressure groups within GATT, such as the Cairns group of agricultural exporting countries, have a presence both within the Pacific region and outside it, implying that even a breakdown of GATT would not propel the region into total isolation.

Despite the universal pop culture, fundamental dissimilarities between Pacific Rim countries remain. These may be reduced but not effaced. California culture may sell worldwide, but it influences, rather than swamps, most local cultures. Many Japanese may be fascinated by Western culture, but Japanese traditions persist, and the society remains largely closed to outsiders. Japan does not allow permanent immigration. Some notable cases of successful economic growth have been achieved under nondemocratic regimes quite different from those of Atlantic descent. In Taiwan, Singapore, and South Korea, economic reforms have been pushed through by authoritarian governments, which sets these countries apart politically from the Rim's democratic nations and reduces the chances of peaceful integration.

Although it is always difficult to assess which tendencies reported in the media are temporary and which are likely to last, the idea of a Pacific Century is an exercise in futurology. The trends of recent history—rates of economic growth and changes in trade flows—have been extrapolated freely. This is an unsound procedure. In the mid-nineteenth century few people would have predicted much of an economic future for Japan or Southern California. *No one* would have expected a dusty, seedy town such as Los Angeles ever to amount to much. A century later, Japan and the Little Dragons seemed to many observers far less likely to achieve economic success than India or postcolonial Africa. Economic geography may be quite volatile, especially over periods of a couple of generations.

In this book we have *not* argued that the Pacific Rim is or shows clear signs of becoming an integrated economic region. We do *not* make, or support, predictions of a Pacific Century. The Pacific Rim is of interest to us because of its diversity. The immense contrasts within the region make it excellent for a comparative study of the process of economic growth and the associated problems, admittedly the more so because of the speed and scale of East Asia's rise.

Our broad, if rapid, survey may help to promote a little skepticism about the common models of historical development, based as they are almost wholly on Western experience. Comparative history is a way of sorting the clues, distinguishing trends of lasting, general significance from short-run, local phenomena. The bird's-eye view offered here reveals tendencies and relationships that are less obvious in close-up "national" histories.

In traditional economic history, *intensive* economic growth is held to have begun abruptly in one place: in eighteenth-century Britain during the Industrial

Revolution. Growth was thus a product of European initiative and values, in particular the Protestantism of northwest Europe. In recent decades our conception of world economic history has increased greatly, and a purely Eurocentric view of economic success no longer seems appropriate. We now understand that in the premodern era economic growth was achieved from time to time in a number of places, many of them on the Pacific Rim. The notable examples are in China during the Song dynasty (and earlier, in all probability) and in Tokugawa Japan. The splendid performance of East Asian economies since around 1960 has completely undermined any lingering notion that European values are a prerequisite for economic growth.

Some writers have attempted to blur the economic independence of East Asia by arguing that the values of Confucianism (thrift, family loyalty, education, hard work, pride in one's work, and punctuality) are broadly similar to those of the Protestant work ethic. But the idea that, deep down, the Japanese and other East Asians are just like Europeans lacks credibility. Earlier in the twentieth century, the conservatism of Confucian culture was often held categorically responsible for Asia's lack of economic success at that particular time. History shows that cultural values are eventually malleable: Market-based behavior can be learned and adopted given the right incentives (or lack of disincentives). Although the cultural tradition of a particular country usually does affect its business climate (witness, for instance, the unique Japanese methods of negotiation and labor management), there are undoubtably more general factors that remove the obstacles to economic growth and are shared by *all* successful cases regardless of the particular cultural complexion.

The central impediments to economic growth are not culture or values, affect behavior though these do, but political incentives and disincentives. A political system that encourages market-based behavior by appropriate taxation and the provision of public goods is a common feature of historical instances of economic growth. Weak or corrupt rulers who overtax or underinvest (or both) create serious disincentives for merchants and peasants, which are usually sufficient to smother the prospects of *intensive* economic growth.

When changes take place in the political set-up to create incentives or remove disincentives, the opportunity for economic growth arises, even in hitherto undeveloped regions. Political changes may also act in a negative way to dissipate the conditions that have encouraged growth, even if that growth has been a normal condition for centuries. This sort of change has led to a number of major shifts in the locus of world economic activity: China's slow decline as an economic power, the rise of Europe and the Atlantic economy, and the rapid, sustained growth of California and East Asia.

According to this view of world history, what the nations of the Pacific Rim have in common is the *potential* for *intensive* economic growth. Whether that potential is realized depends always on a number of constraints, mainly political factors but also to some extent the riskiness of the physical environment. Obviously, the obstacles are tougher in some regions than in others. Political structures are usually slow to change, and in some regions the impact of poverty and political weakness is compounded by a high level of vulnerability to natural disasters.

Future prospects for the different nations depend to a significant degree on their ability to remove key obstacles and prevent the emergence of fresh ones. Such possibilities are discussed in the final chapter.

11
Prospects

It is not a luxury for an investment manager to study the history of the countries in which he or she invests. It is a vital and inherent part of the analytical task of assessing risk and assessing performance potential.

—Robert Lloyd George, *The East-West Pendulum* (1992)

What can we learn about the future prospects of the Pacific Rim from the history recounted in this book? The first lesson is that we cannot simply extrapolate into the future short-term trends from the recent past. History is neither linear nor circular. Accelerating technical change or political upheaval can quickly transform key economic relationships. The trick is to recognize long-term trends and indeed the intermittent reversals of those trends. No existing theory of *very* long-term economic development—of how economic growth begins and is sustained—is particularly satisfactory. Economic history does not allow us to make an exact prediction of the future, but it does have forecasting value in that it can illustrate both those long-term trends that give some insight into the prospects of particular regions and the political and economic constraints on particular changes in trends.

It is much more difficult to predict the rare breaks of trend, such as the unprecedented rise of the East Asian economies, than to provide an investment manager with the general historical awareness needed to build up a risk and reward profile of individual countries. Without that background, however, the manager will be totally rather than only partially disoriented. Trends and reversals are often concealed by the "noise" of short-term fluctuations and are themselves made up of a variety of cycles, some economic, some political, always combining at different points in their unfolding. Good economic history interprets the past in terms of both trends and cycles, distinguishing one from the other.

In considering the prospects for the region, it is essential to consider the relationship between geopolitics and economic systems and in particular not to fall into the trap of believing that markets alone either can or have determined economic success, perhaps especially in East Asia. A major test of the importance of markets alone will be the future of a reformed Latin America. The entire concept of a Pacific Century depends upon the quiet sidelining of the experience of such major Pacific regions.

The recent changes of signal note have included the waning of U.S. hegemony, leaving the world with no clear leader at a time of widespread recession. Again it is important to realize that new developments, especially advances in communication technology and the spread of webs of multinational business, reduce the likelihood that this leaderless world will plunge into a new Great Depression.

Another outstanding recent change has been the collapse of Soviet and Eastern European communism, contrasting with the surprising arrival of decentralized politics in China, which has permitted rapid economic growth in the southern Chinese provinces. The interweaving of political and economic reform in Russia and China makes for an interesting contrast, helping us to understand better the nature of the interaction between politics and economics in the process of development. In any event, changes of regime or of policy in these two giants have ended the cold war and have promised to remake the whole pattern of economic and political power, particularly on the Pacific Rim.

China rather than Japan may prove to be the largest single economy in the Asia Pacific region—provided, of course, that it can permanently resolve its internal and cyclical political tensions. The core relationship may no longer be between Japan and the United States; we propose to hazard the guess that it may be between Japan and China, with the English-speaking parts of the Pacific Rim less central than they have been for a century or two.

We may be living, therefore, in the very midst of a major reversal that makes forecasting very difficult. We need to consider the implications of this possibility at greater length.

Until very recently the economic and political world was dominated by three characteristic features; first, U.S. economic hegemony, confirmed by the Second World War, which raised U.S. output by 50 percent while leaving other leading economies prostrate; second, the cold war, which began almost immediately after the Second World War and encompassed the world, including the Pacific; and third, the reconstitution of the gold exchange standard under the Bretton Woods system, with fixed exchange rates and reduced barriers to trade. The effect of these characteristics was to reverse the interwar isolationism of the United States and involve it in a global role. At the same time it accelerated the linking of the main world commodity and capital markets.

As indicated, each of these features has now disappeared. U.S. hegemony may still exist in the military field, but the revival of the European countries and of Japan has exposed the United States to strong economic and technical competition. "Imperial overreach" by the United States is only one aspect of a complex picture. The era of hegemonic stability when the United States dominated the world economy and its main institutions, such as the IMF and World Bank, has ended.

The collapse of communism in Eastern Europe has been much more dramatic, quite the most unexpected and unanticipated event of the recent past. Between 1989 and 1991 every communist regime in Eastern Europe fell, and the Soviet Union itself fragmented into its fifteen constituent republics. This collapse has made Europe much more inward-looking and has removed the external threat to capitalism (unless, perhaps, this is eventually to come from a militant Islam). The ending of the cold war has also undermined the rationale of the alliance system that previously bound Western Europe and Japan to the United States. Francis Fukuyama's assertion of the "end of history" in the alleged blanket domination of the world by the Western type of democratic and free trade economy is the last gasp of a cold war rhetoric that has repeatedly oversimplified the nature of economic and political systems.

The collapse of the fixed exchange rate occurred earlier, beginning in 1971 with the United States's movement "off gold." The dollar had already become vulnerable as a reserve currency as the U.S. share of world output and trade declined. The decline was and is relative, not absolute. The United States still maintains a world lead in terms of GDP per head expressed in internal prices or in purchasing power parities. However, there are a number of other nations converging on this level of GDP per head, including Japan, Singapore, and Hong Kong among the Asia Pacific economies. The convergence was accelerated by the poor response of U.S. governments, and the Western world in general, to the oil price hikes of 1973 and 1979.

The main changes in the world today are subsumed under the heading "globalization." The technical revolution in communications has been an unprecedented stimulus to the formation of global markets. It has given such a stimulus to the development of the capital market that the amount of investment funds circulating the international economy vastly exceeds those required to finance international trade. As a consequence, floating exchange rates do not necessarily remove imbalances on trading accounts; there is no automatic equilibrating mechanism.

The role of multinational enterprises further limits the economic sovereignty of individual nations. Because multinationals can move where they will, they deliberately choose to operate within each of the incipient, rival economic blocs in order to minimize losses from possible beggar-my-neighbor policies. In this way they subvert the protectionist intent of individual governments. Both these factors encourage the pursuit of openness between blocs and compatible economic policies.

Clearly these changes in the world economy have significant implications for the Pacific. The core relationship is itself changing. There may be a relative delinking of East Asia from the English-speaking economies. Already there is a pronounced rise in the relative importance of intraregional trade—that is, trade between nations within the Asian area. A greater regional autonomy of growth may result from a number of factors, and the concept of the Pacific Rim as an integrated unit may weaken accordingly.

First, changes in technology have tended to decouple industrial growth from raw material inputs, which are no longer as important as they were. A massive growth in high tech manufacture and the provision of services in the most advanced economies, such as Japan, will accelerate this decoupling by promoting growth with proportionately fewer inputs.

Second, the new economies brought within the dynamic Asian regional grouping are much better endowed than the old ones with foodstuffs and raw materials. These resources can therefore be more frequently obtained from within the region than from the English-speaking world.

Within the Asian region itself, the key relationship is likely to be that between China and Japan. Is it potentially a complementary or a competitive relationship? The possible autonomy of the region rests on the maintenance of a stable relationship between these two nations. China is undoubtedly on the economic move, but will it continue to grow at such a breakneck pace and in the same way?

In this book we have raised two issues concerning economic achievement in China. The first relates to the nature of the interaction between politics and economics in large empires of the Chinese type. The second relates to the cyclical behavior characteristic of political systems in China.

We have argued for the primacy of politics over economics. Markets cannot impose themselves on political systems, regardless of their nature. Political action can rapidly extinguish economic growth by centralizing decisionmaking better left to free market operation. At best the act of suppression engenders considerable risk and uncertainty, even if it does not fully succeed.

The current rapid growth of the southern provinces in China has resulted from a de facto devolution of decisionmaking, unexpected in a communist state. Not only are the provinces of Guangdong and Fujian left to their own devices, with decisionmaking devolved even further to the local level, but outsiders from Hong Kong and Taiwan are allowed access to provide the positive stimulus of significant entrepreneurial and capital inputs. Does such a development threaten the political integrity of China? Will a cyclical recentralization occur with dampening consequences for economic development in the South?

An interesting comparison can be made with Russia, where political reforms have run ahead of economic reforms, with the obvious results of political anarchy and a contracting economy. The centralized autocracy—a unifying feature of Russian history—has gone, with nothing to replace it. The old certainties have disappeared. Economic decisionmaking in such a context has become a risky business. On the Pacific edge, for example, it is unclear who has the authority to make decisions, or even whether the Russian Far East will split off from the Russian Republic in the future. (Incidentally, stabilization in this area would provide Asia with a plentiful source of raw materials for industrialization.)

In China, economic reform preceded political reform: The sudden injection of a much stronger measure of market activity certainly promoted economic growth. Some of the acceleration resulted from the high level of competence shown by decisionmakers in the timing and sequence of reforms. However, a general acceptance of the need at least to pay lip-service to the central authority, plus the turning of a blind central eye to decentralization, has created a favorable political framework for economic growth. Perhaps the momentum of economic change in the South is now such as to prevent the reversal of the process—that is, a de facto recentralization of political authority. The question remains: Can the political system accommodate such developments, or is the very dynamism of the economic system destabilizing? The absorption of Hong Kong by China in 1997 will be an acid test. The eventual reunification of the three Chinas offers the prospect of the crystallization of a new China as a much looser federation. China, outside Tibet and Sinkiang, is much more homogeneous culturally than Russia and can probably live with a variety of economic policies that might tear a diverse country into jealous sections.

Continued economic success within China would create the possibility of all sorts of complementarity with the Japanese economy. Rising incomes offer the prospect of the substitution by Japan and the Little Dragons of the Chinese market for the U.S. market. The "myth of the large market" would become reality. Moreover, China has a potential range of foodstuffs and raw materials that could substitute for Australian exports to Japan. Japanese investment and know-how would help promote the exploitation of China's natural resources.

The same kind of relationship exists in embryo between Japan and Southeast Asia. Should China fail to sustain its economic growth, Southeast Asia might play something of the role outlined for China above, though on a lesser scale. Already trade between East and Southeast Asia is expanding rapidly on the basis of both the old comparative advantage and the new comparative advantage "created" by innovation in product.

Events in Latin America have also been looked at in the East Asian mirror—too much so. The conventional economic wisdom interprets East Asian success and the failure of Eastern Europe as a vindication of the free market. In this view, economic policies freeing up the market in other Pacific regions will extend the core relationship as a mechanism of both economic dynamism and economic integration. Our interpretation of Pacific history shows the oversimplification lurking in this view. The particular experience of Latin America can act as a touchstone for such an interpretation.

As yet, Latin America has not participated significantly in the core relationship, partly as a result of history, partly because of choice. The region's general failure to secure a full economic breakthrough has been blamed on its association with a world economy that was capitalistic and exploitative. Theories of dependency and informal empire encouraged the adoption of policies of economic autarky or, as they are more often called, import substitution. Most Latin American nations erected protective barriers against outside competition and were ruled by governments that directly promoted domestic economic activity. Strong coalitions supporting such policies emerged, consisting of workers, public servants, manufacturers, professionals, and shopkeepers. Political strife became extreme between the populist parties supported by these groups and the more traditional groups of landowners, exporters, and the financial sector. Winner-take-all politics was exacerbated by army intervention and frequent coups d'état. Latin America persisted until the late 1980s in this program of import substitution, which limited its integration into the Asia Pacific region. If the unhappy Philippines is included because of its heritage as a Spanish colony, Latin America currently stands as the least promising major part of the Pacific Rim. Russia and the countries of Latin America are in this sense the forgotten economies of the Pacific debate.

The case of Latin America is particularly interesting as a test of purely market panaceas. Many times in their history, Latin American countries have confounded predictions of imminent economic success. Such predictions are reappearing today amid a wave of euphoria about prospects based on a change of government policy from a program of import substitution to one of export promotion. Market regulations will be dismantled, it is forecast, and the government will withdraw from the field of economic activity. The rationale for such a transition rests on a particular interpretation of East Asian success.

A case for optimism might rest on the alleged existence of a vast pool of latent energy awaiting release by such deregulatory action. To take but one example: Hernando de Soto has argued that as much as half of the Peruvian economy is at present "informal"—that is, operating outside the formal legal system. If so much entrepreneurial talent can force itself to the surface through all the regulatory layers in modern Peru, what growth might take place with the removal of the obstructions? Although Latin American society and institutions may remold themselves to sustain rapid growth—and it would not be inconsistent with our interpretation for growth to react back in this way—a big load of history weighs against such a possibility in this instance.

There are two difficulties with this optimism. First, the view ignores the major differences of political context and contingent circumstance between East Asia and Latin America. It assumes away particular historical experiences. Any rounded account of East Asian success needs to consider the economic guidance or steering (but emphatically *not* planning) by relevant governments; the postwar existence of open world markets, especially in the United States; the stimulus of the cold war and the associated flow of financial and other aid; the specific colonial background of individual nations; and the degree of concern for education and improvement in human capital. These policies and contingent circumstances have favored economic growth in East Asia, but they are not present in Latin America today. Equally worthy of attention, as we remarked, is the winner-take-all politics so rampant in Latin America, making for a dramatic level of political instability. If disincentives are removed, the door will be open for countries in Latin America to grow. We would expect them to do so at a slower rate than Japan and the Little Dragons did and the southern Chinese provinces are doing.

Second, there have already been two abrupt changes of economic performance in Latin America since the Second World War. From 1945 to 1980 real per capita incomes in Latin America grew at an average annual rate of close to 3 percent. Agricultural productivity and life expectancy increased, and there was a downward trend in birth rates, family size, infant mortality, and illiteracy. Yet these accomplishments have generally drawn only stinted praise from observers of the region. There are less savory aspects of life in Latin America that divert attention from the good news: political and military strife, such as death squads and the disappearance of political opponents and dissenters, and other elements of a generally dismal human rights record. In the 1980s the picture became even bleaker: Latin America went through one of its periodic debt crises, being unable to service its debts to Western banks. Investment virtually ceased, inflation ran wild, and the region's average real GDP per capita fell by 11 percent. Reversals of performance are common features of Latin American history.

The fragility of political systems and difficulties in pursuing a consistent policy in Russia and Latin America should induce caution in predicting any acceleration of the rate of economic advance based only on their adoption of market-promoting policies or resemblance to the historically special case of East Asia. It would be difficult for either area to do worse than it did in the 1980s, but this is still possible. However, the general picture in the Pacific area does suggest some convergence of economic growth rates, or at least the disappearance of the extreme disparities of the 1980s.

There is a natural process by which the rich and successful lose their economic dynamism. In the absence of a major depression, there is no reason why the English-speaking countries should not show a continuing improvement in economic welfare—but, on present showing, only at an unimpressive rate. In the scenario drawn above, these countries could become, relatively speaking, peripheral to the economic life of the Asia Pacific. In this sense the Pacific would have turned full circle, not only in the movement of technical hegemony away from the United States but also in the nature of its integration. The recent interlude of economic integration through the core relationship will have ended. Japan and China have an ancient relationship: a twenty-first-century version of it may come to dominate the region, for better or for worse.

Further Reading

Introductory Materials

A useful introduction to the geography of the Pacific is Gordon L. Wood and Patricia Ross McBride, *The Pacific Basin: A Human and Economic Geography*, 2nd ed. (Melbourne: Oxford University Press, 1946). Information on the region's vulnerability to natural disasters has been drawn from M. Bath, "Earthquakes, Large, Destructive," in S. K. Runcorn (ed.), *Dictionary of Geophysics*, Vol. 1 (Oxford: Pergamon Press, 1967), pp. 417–424, and Stephen H. Schneider, "The World's Crazy Weather," in *1984 Britannica Book of the Year* (Chicago: Encyclopedia Britannica, 1984).

A splendid account of the debate as to the origins of modern humans is Brian M. Fagan, *The Journey from Eden: The Peopling of Our World* (London: Thames and Hudson, 1990). Alan Thorne and Robert Raymond, *Man on the Rim: The Peopling of the Pacific* (Sydney: Angus & Robertson, 1989), is an excellent introduction and overview of patterns of migration, settlement, and plant and animal domestication in the region. See also Johan Goudsblom, "The Domestication of Fire as a Civilizing Process," *Theory, Culture & Society* 4 (1987), pp. 457–476, and N. G. Butlin, "The Paleoeconomic History of Aboriginal Migration," *Australian Economic History Review* 29 (1989), pp. 3–57.

On hunter-gatherer societies, see William H. McNeill, *Plagues and Peoples* (Harmondsworth: Penguin Books, 1976), Chapter 1; Geoffrey Blainey, *Triumph of the Nomads: A History of Ancient Australia* (Melbourne: Sun Books, 1975); and Colin White, *Mastering Risk: Environment, Markets and Politics in Australian Economic History* (Melbourne: Oxford University Press, 1992), Chapter 1.

Population data in this chapter have been calculated from Colin McEvedy and Richard Jones, *Atlas of World Population History* (Harmondsworth: Penguin Books, 1978).

The rise of military regimes in agrarian societies is analyzed in Johan Goudsblom, "The Formation of Military-Agrarian Regimes," in Johan Goudsblom, E. L. Jones, and Stephen Mennell, *Human History and Social Processes* (Exeter: University of Exeter Press, 1989), pp. 79–92. For an overview of the history of early Chinese regimes, see Mark Elvin, *The Pattern of the Chinese Past: A Social and Economic Interpretation* (Stanford: Stanford University Press, 1973). See also Kenneth R. Hall, *Maritime Trade and State Development in Early Southeast Asia* (Sydney: George Allen & Unwin, 1985). The crucial role of politics in promoting or retarding *intensive* economic growth is explored in E. L. Jones, *Growth Recurring: Economic Change in World History* (Oxford: Clarendon Press, 1988).

Early East Asia

China

On early Chinese civilization, see Ping-ti Ho, *The Cradle of the East: An Inquiry into the Indigenous Origins of Technique and Ideas of Neolithic and Early Historic China, 5000–1000 B.C.* (London: University of Chicago Press, 1976), and Leon E. Stover, *The Cultural Ecology of Chinese Civilization: Peasants and Elites in the Last of the Agrarian States* (New York: Mentor Books, 1974). For other long views of the Chinese, see Deng Gang, *Development Versus Stagnation: Technological Continuity and Agricultural Progress in Pre-modern China* (Westport, CT: Greenwood Press, forthcoming 1993); Mark Elvin, *The Pattern of the Chinese Past* (London: Eyre Methuen, 1973); C. P. Fitzgerald, *The Chinese View of Their Place in the World* (London: Oxford University Press, 1969); and, for a full history, Jonathan Spence, *The Search for Modern China* (London: Hutchinson, 1990).

For the Song "economic revolution," see Gary G. Hamilton and Chi-kong Lai, "Consumerism Without Capitalism: Consumption and Brand Names in Late Imperial China," in Henry J. Rutz and Benjamin S. Orlove (eds.), *The Social Economy of Consumption* (Lanham, MD: University Press of America, 1989), pp. 253–279, and E. L. Jones, *Growth Recurring: Economic Change in World History* (Oxford: Clarendon Press, 1988).

On the apparent stagnation between Song times and the late Qing period, see Kang Chao, *Man and Land in Chinese History: An Economic Analysis* (Stanford: Stanford University Press, 1986), and E. L. Jones, *The European Miracle: Economies, Environments and Geopolitics in the History of Europe and Asia,* 2nd ed. (Cambridge: Cambridge University Press, 1987). See also Jones, "The Real Question about China: Why Was the Song Economic Achievement not Repeated?" *Australian Economic History Review* xxx (1990), pp. 5–22.

Japan

In English there is little material of a broad kind on early Japanese economic history, but see W. Wayne Farris, *Population, Disease and Land in Early Japan, 645–900* (Cambridge, MA: Harvard University Press, 1985); Thorne and Raymond, *Man on the Rim*; and J. W. Hall, et al., *Japan Before Tokugawa: Political Consolidation and Economic Growth, 1500–1650* (Princeton, NJ: Princeton University Press, 1981).

For a general history of the Tokugawa period, see Conrad Totman, *Japan Before Perry: A Short History* (Berkeley: University of California Press, 1981). A sketch of the economic changes appears in Jones, *Growth Recurring.*

The European Intrusion

On pre-Columbian America see the following: First, useful introductions include John H. Rowe, "Inca Culture at the Time of the Spanish Conquest," in Julian H. Steward (ed.), *Handbook of South American Indians: The Andean Civilization* (Washington, DC: Smithsonian Institution, 1946); John V. Murra, *The Economic Organization of the Inca State* (Greenwich, CT: Jai Press, 1980); Frances Berdan, *The Aztecs of Central America: An Imperial Society* (New York: Holt, Rinehart and Winston, 1982). See also Nigel Davies, *The Aztec Empire: The Toltec Resurgence* (Norman: University of Oklahoma Press, 1987); John Hyslop, *Inca Settlement Planning* (Austin: University of Texas Press, 1990); and Robert K. Logan, *The*

Alphabet Effect: The Impact of the Phonetic Alphabet on the Development of Western Civilization (New York: William Morrow and Co., 1986).

There is no systematic overview of the European impact upon the Pacific region, but there are some first-rate treatments of specialized areas. For example, there is a brief review of the technical interchange in A. R. Hall, "Epilogue: The Rise of the West," in Charles Singer et al. (eds.), *A History of Technology*, Vol. 3 (London: Oxford University Press, 1957). There is also an excellent study of the ecological impact by A. W. Crosby, *Biological Imperialism: The Biological Expansion of Europe 900–1900* (Cambridge: Cambridge University Press, 1986). The best attempt at a general history is O.H.K. Spate, *The Pacific Since Magellan*, in three volumes: Volume 1, *The Spanish Lake;* Volume 2, *Monopolists and Freebooters;* and Volume 3, *Paradise Lost and Found* (Minneapolis: University of Minnesota Press, 1979, 1983, and 1988). Rather shorter and more limited in scope is J. A. Lower, *Ocean of Destiny: A Concise History of the North Pacific, 1500–1978* (Vancouver: University of British Columbia Press, 1978). The first integration of the Pacific by a regular shipping link is discussed in W. L. Schurz, *The Manila Galleon* (New York: E. P. Dutton, 1959). There is a discussion concerning the forward movement of the frontier of Russian settlement into North America and its later retreat in Colin White, *Russia and America: The Roots of Economic Divergence* (London: Croom Helm, 1987).

The polar positions in the debate concerning the influences molding "new societies" are stated in L. Hartz, *The Founding of New Societies: Studies in the History of the United States, Latin America, South Africa, Canada and Australia* (New York: Harcourt, Brace and World, 1964), and F. J. Turner, *The Frontier in American History* (New York: Holt, Rinehart and Winston, 1962 reprint). Schools of thought have evolved around these positions. Well worth reading as variants on these viewpoints are R. C. Harris, "The Simplification of Europe Overseas," *Annals of the Association of American Geographers* 67 (1977), pp. 469–483, and T. G. Jordan and M. Kaups, *The American Backwoods Frontier: An Ethnic and Ecological Interpretation* (Baltimore and London: Johns Hopkins University Press, 1989).

On the nature of the new settler societies and their economies, see Donald Denoon, *Settler Capitalism: The Dynamics of Dependent Development in the Southern Hemisphere* (Oxford: Clarendon Press, 1983), and Warwick Armstrong, "The Origins of Dominion Capitalism," in W. E. Willmott (ed.), *New Zealand and the World: Essays in Honour of Wolfgang Rosenberg* (Canterbury: University of Canterbury, 1980), pp. 28–44.

On more specialized topics, the following have been useful. The inequality of the early exchange between Europe and Asia is discussed in A. Attman, *The Bullion Flow Between Europe and the East 1000–1750* (Gothenburg: Institute of Economic History, 1981). On the relative size of the silver flows across the Atlantic and Pacific see D. O. Flynn, "Comparing the Tokugawa Shogunate with Hapsburg Spain: Two Silver-Based Empires in a Global Setting," in J. D. Tracy (ed.), *The Political Economy of Merchant Empires* (Cambridge: Cambridge University Press, 1991). The distinction between colonies of permanent settlement or temporary sojourn is developed in A. Grenfell Price, *The Western Invasion of the Pacific and its Continents* (Oxford: Clarendon Press, 1963).

The general context of long-run economic development in the West is well described in Angus Maddison, *Dynamic Forces in Capitalist Development: A Long-Run Comparative View* (Oxford: Oxford University Press, 1991). A sound and attractively presented history of economic events in the twentieth century is Sidney Pollard (ed.), *Wealth and Poverty* (Bromley, Kent: Harrap, 1990).

The American Century

Many of the ideas only touched upon in this chapter are discussed at much greater length in Colin White, *Russia and America: The Roots of Economic Divergence* (London: Croom Helm, 1987). Notable among these are the concepts of dense government and risk management. This book also extends to the thirteen colonies that later made up the United States the notion of a competitive multicell system of the type described in Jones, *The European Miracle*.

There is a multitude of textbooks on the economic rise of the United States. Probably the best is Jonathan Hughes, *American Economic History* (Glenview, IL: Scott, Foresman and Company, 1987). The same author has also written an excellent introduction to "mixed enterprise" in North America: *The Government Habit: Economic Controls from Colonial Times to the Present* (New York: Basic Books, 1977). The particular experience of the United States is placed in a wide context by Paul Kennedy, *The Rise and Fall of the Great Powers* (New York: Random House, 1989).

A good comparison of early experience in the two Americas is J. Lang, *Conquest and Commerce: Spain and England in the Americas* (New York: Academic Press, 1975). An interpretation of Latin American history consistent with that adopted in this book is developed in C. Veliz, *The Centralist Tradition of Latin America* (Princeton, NJ: Princeton University Press, 1980). In the same vein there is a brilliant exposition of current economic problems in Peru that can stand as representative of all Latin America: H. de Soto, *The Other Path: The Invisible Revolution in the Third World* (New York: Harper and Row, 1989).

The classic works on the United States's technical dynamism and organizational innovativeness are Nathan Rosenberg, *Technology and American Economic Growth* (New York: Harper and Row, 1972), and Alfred Chandler, *The Visible Hand: The Managerial Revolution in American Business* (Cambridge, MA: Harvard University Press, 1977). The degree of economic achievement at different points in U.S. history is shown by Alice Hanson Jones, *Wealth of a Nation To Be: the American Colonies on the Eve of the Revolution* (New York: Columbia University Press, 1980), and Arthur Lewis, *Growth and Fluctuations* (London: Allen and Unwin, 1978). The importance of economic resources in the economic success of the United States is stressed in Gavin Wright, "The Origins of American Industrial Success, 1879–1940," *American Economic Review* 80 (1990). On the importance of energy inputs see D. Greenberg, "Energy Flows in a Changing Economy, 1815–80," in J. R. Frese and J. Judd (eds.), *An Emerging Independent American Economy 1815–75* (Tarrytown, NY: Sleepy Hollow Press, 1980), and J. A. James and J. S. Skinner, "The Resolution of the Labour-Scarcity Paradox," *Journal of Economic History* 45 (1985), pp. 513–540. The more recent loss of economic dynamism by the United States is discussed in Lester Thurow, *Head to Head: The Coming Battle Among Japan, Europe and America* (New York: William Morrow and Co., 1992).

More specialized treatments are also abundant. For a good introduction to the particular characteristics of the South, see Carl N. Degler, *Place Over Time: The Continuity of Southern Distinctiveness* (Baton Rouge and London: Louisiana State University Press, 1977). There is still no general economic history of California or the U.S. West that can be recommended. For an introduction to this region see James J. Rawls (ed.), *New Directions in Californian History: A Book of Readings* (New York: McGraw-Hill, 1988). The impact of water scarcity in the West is discussed in Donald Worster, "Hydraulic Society in California: An Ecological Interpretation," *Agricultural History* 56 (1982), pp. 503–515, and Marc Reisner, *Cadillac Desert: The American West and its Disappearing Water* (New York: Penguin Books, 1986). On the Owens Valley see Robert A. Sauder, "The Agricultural Colonization of a Great Basin Frontier: Economic Organization and Environmental Alteration in Owens Valley, California, 1860–1925," *Agricultural History* 64 (1990), pp. 78–101. The significance of transport is the main focus of James Vance, *Capturing the Horizon: The Historical Geography of Transportation Since the Transportation Revolution of the Sixteenth Century* (New York: Harper and Row, 1980). For the early history of Los Angeles see Robert M. Fogelson, *The Fragmented Metropolis: Los Angeles, 1850–1930* (Cambridge: Harvard University Press, 1967).

There are good introductions to U.S. involvement in the Pacific. See J. A. Lower, *Ocean of Destiny: A Concise History of the North Pacific, 1500–1978* (Vancouver: University of British Columbia Press, 1978), and Arthur P. Dudden, *The American Pacific From the Old China Trade to the Present* (New York and Oxford: Oxford University Press, 1992).

For the contrasting case of Australia, see Colin White, *Mastering Risk: Environment, Markets and Politics in Australian Economic History* (Melbourne: Oxford University Press, 1992), and Lionel Frost, "Government and Economic Development: The Case of Irrigation in Victoria," *Australian Economic History Review* 32 (1992), pp. 47–65.

Modern East Asia

Besides innumerable histories of the component areas and some of the region as a whole, there was already in the interwar period a sizeable body of work on the Japanese "menace" and the likely fate of China. During the last thirty years or so this Western concern has mutated into a virtual industry offering explanations of the rise of East Asia. Americans concerned with Japan are the central students of this topic, although it has become of such significance that it has now been tackled by people from many countries and all the social sciences. The current industry is both journalistic and academic. In the former case it is much affected by the exigencies of the moment and, although academic writings are less swayed by these, they remain without much agreement on how to explain East Asia's economic success. The following references barely scratch the surface of the mountain—or rather, volcano—of books and articles, but most of them contain useful further references, and many of their authors have written other valuable studies. The works cited have been chosen for their insights into important aspects and processes of economic history rather than to represent all schools of thought, let alone provide full narrative coverage. Any public library may be expected to contain standard histories and popular accounts of the region.

East Asia and the Asia Pacific Region as a Whole

Alexander Besher, *The Pacific Rim Almanac* (New York: Harper Collins, 1991) is quirky but compendious. Gerald Segal, *Rethinking the Pacific* (Oxford: Clarendon Press, 1990) is more solid and skeptical. An older study is E. Stuart Kirby, *Economic Development in East Asia* (London: Allen & Unwin, 1967). Among the myriad works trying to account for the subsequent rise of the region's economy, one by Ziya Onis stands out ("Review Article: The Logic of the Developmental State," *Comparative Politics* 24[1991], pp. 109–126; see also Steve Chan, "Catching Up and Keeping Up: Explaining Capitalist East Asia's Industrial Competitiveness," *Journal of East Asian Affairs* V (1991), pp. 79–103; East Asia Analytical Unit, Department of Foreign Affairs and Trade, *Australia and North East Asia in the 1990s: Accelerating Change* (Canberra: Australian Government Publishing Service, 1992); and James Riedel,

"Economic Development in East Asia: Doing What Comes Naturally?" in Helen Hughes (ed.), *Achieving Industrialization in East Asia* (Cambridge: Cambridge University Press, 1988). Riedel's market-oriented interpretation may be contrasted with the institutionalist works by Chalmers Johnson noted in the sections on Japan and the Little Dragons.

China

On the nineteenth and early twentieth centuries, sample Yen-p'ing Hao, *The Commercial Revolution in Nineteenth-Century China: The Rise of Sino-Western Mercantile Capitalism* (Berkeley: University of California Press, 1986), and David Faure, *The Rural Economy of Pre-Liberation China: Trade Expansion and Peasant Livelihood in Jiangsu and Guangdong, 1870–1937* (Hong Kong: Oxford University Press, 1989). For the warlord period, see Lucien Bianco (translated by Muriel Bell), *Origins of the Chinese Revolution, 1915–1949* (Stanford: Stanford University Press, 1971); C. P. Fitzgerald, *Why China? Recollections of China 1923–1950* (Carlton, Vic.: Melbourne University Press), which must stand for all the travelers and "China hands"; and, for the revisionist view, Thomas G. Rawski, *Economic Growth in Prewar China* (Berkeley: University of California Press, 1989).

On the Maoist and some of the subsequent Communist period, see J. Y. Lin, "Collectivization and China's Agricultural Crisis in 1958–1961," *Journal of Political Economy* 98 (1990), pp. 1228–1252; Rhoads Murphey, *The Fading of the Maoist Vision: City and Country in China's Development* (New York: Methuen, 1980); Tiziano Terzani, *Behind the Forbidden Door: China Inside Out* (London: Unwin Hyman, 1987); and, for a discussion of the statistics and comparison with India (the economic performance of which Western fellow travelers used to compare unfavorably with that of China), see Wilfred Malenbaum, "Review Article: A Gloomy Portrayal of Development Achievements and Prospects: China and India," *Economic Development and Cultural Change* 38 (1990), pp. 391–406. Regional discrepancies are calculated in Kai Yuen Tsui, "China's Regional Inequality, 1952–1985," *Journal of Comparative Economics* 15 (1991), pp. 1–21, and regional prospects are discussed by Robert Delf, "Saying No to Peking," *Far Eastern Economic Review* (April 4, 1991). For the environmental costs of communism, see Vaclav Smil, *The Bad Earth: Environmental Degradation in China* (London: Zed Press, 1984).

On the period since 1979, when market incentives have been reintroduced increasingly into China, see Victor Nee and Sijn Su, "Institutional Change and Economic Growth: The View from the Village," *Journal of Asian Studies* 49 (1990), pp. 3–25. Obviously the mood within China and about China changed greatly after the government massacre of pro-democracy students in Tiananmen Square on June 4, 1989, but the guide by Frances Wood (*A Companion to China* [London: Weidenfeld and Nicolson 1988]) remains fresh and commonsensical. On the potential market in China, see, on one hand, the skepticism of Lynn Chu, "The Chimera of the Chinese Market," *The Atlantic Monthly* (October 1990), pp. 56–68, and on the other the evidence of enormous growth and likely prospects in *Southern China in Transition: The New Regionalism and Australia*, a report put out by the East Asia Analytical Unit, Department of Foreign Affairs and Trade, Canberra (1992). On China and its larger region, see J. Wong, "Integration of China into the Asian-Pacific Region," *The World Economy* 11 (1988), pp. 327–354.

Japan

For the implications of early history see R. S Milward, *Japan: The Past in the Present* (Tenterden, Kent: Paul Norbury, 1979). For the Meiji and subsequent background, see William W. Lockwood, *The Economic Development of Japan: Growth and Structural Change 1868–1938* (Princeton, NJ: Princeton University Press, 1968); S. Sugiyama, *Japan's Industrialization in the World Economy, 1859–1899: Export Trade and Overseas Competition* (London: Athlone Press, 1988); and Kunio Yoshihara, *Japanese Economic Development*, 2nd ed. (Tokyo: Oxford University Press, 1986).

On the evolution of the postwar Japanese economy, see Chalmers Johnson, *MITI and the Japanese Miracle: The Growth of Industrial Policy, 1925–1975* (Stanford, CA: Stanford University Press, 1982), and William Chapman, *Inventing Japan: The Making of Postwar Civilization* (New York: Prentice-Hall, 1991). On the performance of that economy, an inside businessman's view is Akio Morita, *Made in Japan: Akio Morita and Sony* (London: Collins, 1987), and a notably well-informed outsider's view is that of businessman Mark A. Zimmerman, *Dealing With the Japanese* (London: Unwin Paperbacks, 1988). A succinct interpretation by a U.S. economist is Alan S. Blinder, "More Like Them?" *The American Prospect* 8 (1992), pp. 51–62, and a profound analysis of the political basis of Japanese life is Karel Van Wolferen, *The Enigma of Japanese Power: People and Politics in a Stateless Nation* (London: Macmillan, 1989).

For modern and possible future changes in Japan's economy, see Peter Drucker, "Japan's Choices," *Foreign Affairs* 65 (1987), pp. 923–1041; S. Hayden Lesbirel, "Structural Adjustment in Japan: Terminating 'Old King Coal,'" *Asian Survey* XXXI (1991), pp. 1079–1094; and Ronald Dore, "An Outsider's View," in Kozo Yamamura (ed.), *Japan's Economic Structure: Should it Change?* (Seattle: Society for Japanese Studies, University of Washington, 1990), pp. 359–378. Ron Dore is not really an outsider—he is the doyen of Japanese studies, and everything he has written on the topic is worth reading, as is the remainder of Kozo Yamamura's book, not to mention Yamamura's other numerous works on Japanese economic history.

Among recent works about the supposed Japanese threat to the U.S. economy, see the blockbuster by David Halberstam, *The Reckoning* (New York: Avon Books, 1987), which compares the fortunes of Nissan and misfortunes of Ford. In addition, see George Friedman and Meredith Lebard, *The Coming War with Japan* (New York: St. Martin's Press, 1991), which is more informative than its catchpenny title might suggest; and, among the inevitable counterscare literature, Bill Emmott, *The Sun Also Sets: The Limits to Japan's Economic Power* (New York: Simon and Schuster, 1989).

The Little Dragons: Taiwan, South Korea, Hong Kong, and Singapore

A convenient starting point is Ezra F. Vogel, *The Four Little Dragons: The Spread of Industrialization in East Asia* (Cambridge, MA: Harvard University Press, 1991). See also Alice H. Amsden, *Asia's Next Giant: South Korea and Late Industrialisation* (New York: Oxford University Press, 1989); Bruce Cumings, "The Origins and Development of the Northeast Asian Political Economy: Industrial Sectors, Product Cycles, and Political Consequences," *International Organization* 38 (1984), pp. 1–40; Chalmers Johnson, "South Korean Democratization: The Role of Economic Development," *The Pacific Review* 2 (1989), pp. 1–10; and Tibor Scitovsky, "Economic Development in Taiwan and South Korea: 1965–1981," *Food Research Institute Studies* XIX (1985), pp. 215–264. For Hong Kong and Singapore, start with Theodore and Frances Geiger, *Tales of Two City-States: The Development Progress of Hong Kong and Singapore* (Washington, DC: National Planning Association, 1973), and W. G. Huff,

"Patterns in the Economic Development of Singapore," *Journal of Developing Areas* 21 (1987), pp. 305–326. For major recent appraisals, see two reports published in 1992 by the prolific East Asia Analytical Unit, Department of Foreign Affairs and Trade, Canberra: *Korea to the Year 2000: Implications for Australia,* and *Australia's Business Challenge: South-East Asia in the 1990s,* which both have implications for more than merely Australia's prospects.

Southeast Asia

A range of periods to the present is covered in the following: Chris Dixon, *South East Asia in the World-Economy* (Cambridge: Cambridge University Press, 1991); E. L. Jones, "A Framework for the History of Growth in Southeast Asia," *Australian Economic History Review* XXXI (1991), pp. 5–19; W. A. Lewis, *Growth and Fluctuations 1870–1913* (London: Allen & Unwin, 1978); and Kunio Yoshihara, *The Rise of Ersatz Capitalism in South-East Asia* (Singapore: Oxford University Press, 1988). The extent to which the region has changed in fundamental ways is revealed by Charles Hirschman and Philip Guest, "The Emerging Demographic Transition of South-east Asia," *Population & Development Review* 16 (1990), pp. 121–152.

Interesting work on Thailand is being done by David Feeny. See especially his *The Political Economy of Productivity: Thai Agricultural Development, 1880–1975* (Vancouver: University of British Columbia Press, 1982). On Indonesia, the classic is Clifford Geertz, *Agricultural Involution: The Processes of Ecological Change in Indonesia* (Berkeley: University of California Press, 1963); from here, skip ahead to the collection of papers by Anne Booth, et al. (eds.), *Indonesian Economic History in the Dutch Colonial Era* (New Haven, CT: Yale University Southeast Asia Studies Monograph Series 35, 1990).

The "Overseas Chinese" have been instrumental in bringing about economic change in many of the countries of Southeast Asia: see C. P. Fitzgerald, *The Third China: The Chinese Communities in South-East Asia* (Melbourne: F. W. Cheshire, 1965); S. G. Redding, *The Spirit of Chinese Capitalism* (Berlin: Walter de Gruyter, 1990); and, for a fascinating account of the reciprocal transformation of an overseas Chinese family by Thai society, see Botan (translated by Susan Fulop Morell), *Letters from Thailand* (Bangkok: Duang Kamol Book House, 1977).

The Cities

For a useful general introduction to the characteristics and problems of large cities that pays due attention to Pacific Rim cases, see Emrys Jones, *Metropolis* (Oxford: Oxford University Press, 1990). See also Richard Lawton (ed.), *The Rise and Fall of Great Cities: Aspects of Urbanization in the Western World* (London: Belhaven Press, 1989).

Data on urbanization and total population in this chapter have been drawn from Tertius Chandler, *Four Thousand Years of Urban Growth: An Historical Census* (Lewiston/Queenston: St. David's University Press, 1987); Victor Showers, *World Facts and Figures* (New York: John Wiley and Sons, 1979); and United Nations, *Estimates and Projections of Urban, Rural and City Populations, 1950–2025: The 1982 Assessment* (New York: United Nations, 1985).

On cities and economic development, see Jane Jacobs, *Cities and the Wealth of Nations* (Harmondsworth: Penguin Books, 1984); W. A. Lewis, *The Evolution of the International Economic Order* (Princeton: Princeton University Press, 1977); E. A. Wrigley, "A Simple

Model of London's Importance in Changing English Society and Economy, 1650–1750," in his *People, Cities and Wealth: The Transformation of Traditional Society* (Oxford: Basil Blackwell, 1987); Samuel H. Preston, "Urban Growth in Developing Countries: A Demographic Reappraisal," in Joseph Gugler (ed.), *The Urbanization of the Third World* (Oxford: Oxford University Press, 1988); and Lionel Frost, "Anglo-Saxon Cities on the Pacific Rim," in T. C. Barker and A. Sutcliffe (eds.), *Megalopolis: The Giant City in History* (London: Macmillan, in press).

For a summary of the overurbanization debate, see Lionel Frost, "Cities and Economic Development: Some Lessons From the Economic History of the Pacific Rim," in G. D. Snooks (ed.), *Longrun Analysis in Economics* (London: Routledge, in press), and Allen C. Kelley and Jeffrey G. Williamson, *What Drives Third World City Growth? A Dynamic General Equilibrium Approach* (Princeton: Princeton University Press, 1984).

An excellent starting point for the study of Chinese urbanization is Murphey, *The Fading of the Maoist Vision*. See also Elvin, *The Pattern of the Chinese Past;* Kang Chao, *Man and Land in Chinese History: An Economic Analysis* (Stanford: Stanford University Press, 1986); William T. Rowe, *Hankow: Conflict and Community in a Chinese City, 1796–1895* (Stanford: Stanford University Press, 1989); Kerrie L. Macpherson, *A Wilderness of Marshes: The Origins of Public Health in Shanghai, 1843–1893* (Hong Kong: Oxford University Press, 1987); Victor F.S. Sit (ed.), *Chinese Cities: The Growth of the Metropolis Since 1949* (Hong Kong: Oxford University Press, 1988); William A. Byrd and Lin Qingsong, *China's Rural Industry: Structure, Development, and Reform* (Oxford: Oxford University Press, 1990); E. G. Pryor, *Housing in Hong Kong,* 2nd ed. (Hong Kong: Oxford University Press, 1983); and Yue-man Yeung, "Cities That Work: Hong Kong and Singapore," in Roland J. Fuchs, Gavin W. Jones, and Ernesto M. Pernia (eds.), *Urbanization and Urban Policies in Pacific Asia* (Boulder: Westview Press, 1987). On Japanese cities, see Norie Huddle, Michael Reich, and Nahum Stiskin, *Island of Dreams: Environmental Crisis in Japan* (Tokyo: Autumn Press, 1975).

On cities in the U.S. West and Australasia, see David Hamer, *New Towns in the New World: Images and Perceptions of the Nineteenth-Century Urban Frontier* (New York: Columbia University Press, 1990); Lionel Frost, *The New Urban Frontier: Urbanization and City-Building in Australasia and the American West* (Sydney: New South Wales University Press, 1991); Gerald D. Nash, *The American West Transformed: The Impact of the Second World War* (Bloomington: Indiana University Press, 1985); Bradford Luckingham, *The Urban Southwest: A Profile History of Albuquerque–El Paso–Phoenix–Tucson* (El Paso: Texas Western Press, 1982); and Mel Scott, *The San Francisco Bay Area: A Metropolis in Perspective,* 2nd ed. (Berkeley and Los Angeles: University of California Press, 1985).

For the student of the modern city, three fascinating books are recommended: Robert Fishman, *Bourgeois Utopias: The Rise and Fall of Suburbia* (New York: Basic Books, 1987); Joel Garreau, *Edge City: Life on the New Frontier* (New York: Doubleday, 1991); and Peter W.G. Newman and Jeffrey R. Kenworthy, *Cities and Automobile Dependence: A Sourcebook* (Aldershot: Gower, 1989).

There is an excellent literature on the history of Los Angeles. Perhaps the best starting point is Scott L. Bottles, *Los Angeles and the Automobile: The Making of the Modern City* (Berkeley and Los Angeles: University of California Press, 1987), which has an up-to-date bibliography. Anyone who has an interest in Los Angeles ought to read Reyner Banham, *Los Angeles: The Architecture of Four Ecologies* (London: Allen Lane, 1971), and Robert M. Fogelson's classic, *The Fragmented Metropolis.*

On the problem of earthquakes in California and Japan, see Michael Rogers, "When the Earthquake Hits L.A.," *Rolling Stone* 359 (November 4, 1982), pp. 57–60; and "Waiting For the Big One," *The Economist,* December 7, 1991, pp. 97–99. The impact of urban fires in history is discussed in L. E. Frost and E. L. Jones, "The Fire Gap and the Greater Durability of Nineteenth Century Cities," *Planning Perspectives* 4 (1989), pp. 333–347.

For Latin American cities, see John C. Turner, "Barriers and Channels for Housing Development in Modernizing Countries," *Journal of the American Institute of Planners* 33 (1967), pp. 167–180, and "Housing Priorities, Settlement Patterns, and Urban Development in Modernizing Countries," *Journal of the American Institute of Planners* 34 (1968), pp. 354–363; Alejandro Portes and John Walton, *Urban Latin America: The Political Condition from Above and Below* (Austin: University of Texas Press, 1976); Alejandro Portes, "Latin American Urbanization During the Years of Crisis," *Latin American Research Review* 24 (1989), pp. 7–44; and Peter M. Ward, *Mexico City: The Production and Reproduction of an Urban Environment* (London: Belhaven Press, 1990).

The quotations in the chapter are from Peter Hall, *Great Planning Disasters* (London: Weidenfeld and Nicolson, 1980); and Jan Morris, *Among the Cities* (New York: Viking, 1985).

Conclusion

Given the great interest in the topic, the Pacific is surprisingly badly served by the relevant literature. This failing is partly a result of the incoherence of the Pacific as a region. A suitably skeptical discussion orientated largely to current concerns is Gerald Segal, *Rethinking the Pacific* (Oxford: Clarendon Press, 1990). Shorter, more enthusiastic, and stylish is Steffan Linder, *The Pacific Century: Economic and Political Consequences of Asian-Pacific Dynamism* (Stanford: Stanford University Press, 1986).

Two brief introductions written from very different points of view are A. Dirlik, "The Asian-Pacific Idea: Reality and Representation in the Invention of a Regional Structure," *Journal of World History* 3 (1992), pp. 55–79, and P. A. Gourevitch, "The Pacific Rim: Current Debate," *The Annals of the Academy of Political and Social Sciences* 505 (1989), pp. 8–23.

Other contributions worthy of attention are Christopher Coker, "The Myth or Reality of the Pacific Century," *Washington Quarterly* 11 (1988), pp. 5–16; Robert H. Doktor, "The Myth of the Pacific Century," *Futures* (January/February 1990), pp. 78–82; "America, Asia and Europe," *The Economist* (December 24, 1988), pp. 39–47; and "A Flirtation with the Pacific," *The Economist* (September 14, 1991), pp. 35–36.

For a discussion on the origin and use of the term *Pacific,* see O.H.K. Spate, " 'South Sea' to 'Pacific Ocean,' " *The Journal of Pacific History* 12 (1977), pp. 205–211.

Illustrative of the kind of work published on the Pacific today are R. Lloyd George, *The East-West Pendulum* (New York: Woodhead-Faulkner, 1992), and A. Besher (ed.), *The Pacific Rim Almanac* (New York: Harper Perennial, 1992). Both are directed as much to those with a potential business interest in the region as to students of its history or economics.

About the Book and Authors

Analyzing the long-term, historical development of the major economies around the Pacific Rim in language aimed at the general reader, *Coming Full Circle* throws light on the most important relationships in the region today as well as on the prospects for future economic development and political cooperation.

The authors begin with a critique of the popular notion of an integrated "Pacific region," paying particular attention to the influence of geography and environment on population distribution and patterns of regional economic activity. Their study covers the diverse indigenous development of pre-European times, later periods of direct European influence, and the evolution of modern-day urban societies in the region. Finally, they track the rise of the United States and Japan as the dominant regional economic powers and forecast changes we can expect to see in the years ahead, noting in particular the increasing importance of China.

Eric Jones is professor of economics (economic history) at La Trobe University in Melbourne, Australia, and professorial associate of the Graduate School of Management, University of Melbourne. He is author of *The European Miracle: Environment, Economies, and Geopolitics in the History of Europe and Asia*. **Lionel Frost** is lecturer in economic history at La Trobe University and author of *The New Urban Frontier: Urbanisation and City-Building in Australia and the American West*. **Colin White** is senior lecturer in economic history at La Trobe University and author of *Russia and America: The Roots of Economic Divergence*.

Index